D1351793

THE PENGUIN CLASSICS

EDITED BY E. V. RIEU

L32

# THE FOUR
# GOSPELS

A NEW TRANSLATION

FROM THE GREEK

BY E. V. RIEU

PENGUIN BOOKS

Penguin Books Ltd, Harmondsworth, Middlesex
AUSTRALIA: Penguin Books Pty Ltd, 762 Whitehorse Road,
Mitcham, Victoria

—

First published 1952
Reprinted 1953, 1954, 1956, 1958

The designs in this book were engraved on wood
by Reynolds Stone

Made and printed in Great Britain
by William Clowes and Sons Ltd
London and Beccles

# CONTENTS

# INTRODUCTION

THE inclusion of the Gospels in the Penguin Classics series entails no new assessment of their literary, as against their spiritual, importance. For the last hundred years they have stood up to ruthless analysis and have emerged from it supreme in both respects. But there are two implications which I must mention. First, this new translation has behind it no denominational authority. It is a single-handed effort, and the reader is invited to follow one guide only on a voyage of discovery. Secondly, the decision to place the volume side by side with other masterpieces of ancient art brings home to me a truth I did not realize before I undertook my task. The Four Gospels are spiritually supreme largely *because* they are great literature. The two values interlock. Other gospels were written in the first hundred years of the Christian faith, but they failed because in one or both of these respects they showed a weakness. The Church, when it canonized the Four, displayed the excellence of its literary as well as its religious judgement.

If I am right in this conviction it follows that any translation of the Gospels which neglects their artistic qualities is bound to fail. Also that any new translator is bound to ask himself, still more to be asked by others, where, if at all, the time-honoured Authorized Version fails to reproduce the beauty of the great originals. I hope presently to justify the words I have used of these originals, but first I must discuss the Authorized Version and make my own apology.

To judge by some comments which have already reached me, there are still people in this country who believe King James's Bible to be Holy Writ in a sense peculiar to itself. That is the highest praise that a committee of translators could receive, and it is by no means my intention to detract from it. But it does not prove that they did better than the Four Evangelists; and I think we have been far too ready to praise their work at the expense of Mark, Matthew, Luke and John. For instance, Robert Bridges once expressed the view that our Bible 'has not only more beauty than any other vernacular rendering, but is in its vital parts more beautiful and intimate than its originals'. And Dr C. S. Lewis has gone further. He roundly states that 'the New Testament in the original Greek is not a work of literary art'.

I protest against these views, maintaining that no great translation has ever been produced from a poor original. Indeed, the more I hear the Authorized Version praised, the more confidently I argue that the Greek Gospels must needs possess some comparable beauty. But that is not to say that their beauty is the same as that of the Authorized Version; and it has been borne in on me by years of intensive study that they possess a beauty that is all their own.

The difference of spirit is not easy to describe. I find it partly in their greater speed, partly in the sharper definition of the pictures they present and the feelings they evoke. They have a starkness, an urgency and a reality which in our English version are slightly blurred. The Authorized Version, published in 1611, reproduced much of the still older English of Coverdale and Tyndale. Thus it was already old-fashioned when it was written. But I do not attribute the effect I have mentioned to its archaism so much as to another cause. Unlike the Greek, it was not firmly based on the normal speech of its own or any other period. It was too literal a translation and its authors mistook fidelity to the idiom of the Greek for fidelity to its meaning.

I quote a typical passage. Luke reports Jesus as imagining a scene in which a master says to his slave, 'Get something ready for my supper' (17. 8). The Greek, as it should be, is colloquial and the master is not represented as speaking politely – far from it. Yet the Authorized Version puts into his mouth the words, 'Make ready wherewith I may sup'. I contend that no Englishman alive in 1611 or at any other date would have used such an expression; that though the words follow the Greek with some exactitude they do not represent its spirit; and that the point of the parable is blunted by their use.

One may ask why these particular translators should have departed from the standard set by their Elizabethan predecessors who rendered the secular classics in the best and most natural English of their day. I suggest that they did so because they felt the sanctity and importance of the originals so keenly that the use of normal language would have seemed a kind of sacrilege. This sense of awe is natural to anyone who undertakes the translation of these precious documents. It has been with me from first to last. But with a different result. It has made me feel that the meaning, not the idiom, of the originals is sacrosanct.

It is the difference then between the Greek Gospels and the Authorized Version in their over-all effect which, in my opinion, constitutes the best justification for a fresh rendering. It is sometimes urged on behalf of such an undertaking that time has staled the beauty of the Authorized Version and robbed it of its force. I do not think that this is true. It is just as beautiful and intelligible to us as it was to those who first heard it, though it has perhaps become a little too familiar. People also point out that the Authorized Version contains a number of mistakes. But I do not propose to make a list of these and rest my case on them. They amount in all to very little.* Moreover, a learned acquaintance of mine has said to me that he would rather have the Authorized Version with all its mistakes than any other version that could be made. Against such a prejudice there is no arguing, and I hold my peace. But it *is* desirable that something should be said of the handicaps under which the Authorized Version translators were placed by the very date at which they did their work. And foremost among these is the fact that they wrote before the best and most ancient manuscripts had come to hand.

They based their translation on the Greek text first published by Erasmus in 1516. But unfortunately Erasmus had for the most part relied on a single twelfth-century manuscript which is now discredited. In the age that followed the establishment of Christianity at Constantinople the text of the Greek Bible had been standardized and manuscripts differing little from one another were produced in large numbers. We have many such. But if manuscripts are incorrect their multiplication does not enhance their authority; and the authority of these late manuscripts has been upset by the examination, since Erasmus' time, of a handful of far more ancient and valuable manuscripts. The oldest and best of these is the Fourth-Century Codex Sinaiticus, which is now lodged in the British Museum – a unique manuscript which has thrown a great deal of light on the means by

* One curious mistake might be regarded as important. In Mt. 25. 46 the Greek text has 'eternal' punishment and 'eternal' life, but the Authorized Version has 'everlasting' punishment and life 'eternal'.

which our Gospels were preserved and handed down to us through the centuries.*

Two other early manuscripts which have helped us to get back nearer to the Evangelists' own words are the Codex Vaticanus and the Codex Alexandrinus; but both are of somewhat later date, and though Sinaiticus is not always right, I have when in doubt followed its readings, particularly when they are supported by one of the other two. For instance it agrees with Vaticanus, against the vast majority of manuscripts, in giving us the solution to the puzzle presented by *Mark* 6. 20. It is there stated that Herod, when conversing with his prisoner John, 'did many things'. The two Codices show that the word for 'did' must at some date have crept into the other manuscripts in mistake for a word meaning 'was perplexed', which has a somewhat similar sound. And thus they give us a new and vivid picture of the relations that subsisted between the Tetrarch and his other-worldly prisoner.

This is but one instance of the changes introduced by modern scholarship into our texts. Of the other alterations and omissions which readers of the Authorized Version will find in this book, including the passages which, because they are absent from the best manuscripts, I place within square brackets, I can only say that I have been guided by scholars and by my own judgement. And I may here add that I have adopted only one guess. In *John* 20. 17 nobody was able to make satisfactory sense of the words 'Touch me not' till a scholar named Gersdorf pointed out that a slight change in the lettering would give us the meaning 'Do not be alarmed'. This brilliant emendation has convinced me.

Other disadvantages under which the Authorized Version translators laboured may be classed as typographical, but I hope to show that they are by no means unimportant. The ancient manuscripts of the Gospels are innocent of our division into chapters, paragraphs and verses. Not only that, but the words are run together and punctuation is rudimentary. Our present chapter divisions, though attributed by some to Archbishop Stephen Langton, were probably introduced by

* A Codex is a manuscript in *book* form, not like the *scroll* from which Jesus read in the synagogue at Nazareth (Lk. 4). There is an excellent pamphlet on Sinaiticus by H. J. Milne and T. C. Skeat (British Museum: 1951).

Hugo Cardinalis (1200-63), who edited the first concordance that was made. No one can maintain that they are always logical, but for purposes of reference I have kept them. The division of each chapter into verses, as numbered in the Authorized Version, is also useful, but I have abandoned it for two reasons. First, it has no authority behind it. It was the invention, as far as the New Testament is concerned, of a Frenchman, Robert Estienne, who in 1551 printed verse numberings in the fourth edition of his Greek Testament; and in 1557 these numberings made their first appearance here in William Whittingham's translation. Secondly, the division of the text into a number of short verses tends to obscure the sense by obliterating that natural division into paragraphs which all good narrative or ordered argument must possess. The liberty to set out conversations, teaching, stories and all, in the modern style, while adding to the translator's responsibility, affords him many chances of bringing out the logical connections that lurk in an often difficult text. For an instance in narrative, consider *John* 18. 16-18, of which passage Dr Bernard wrote, 'According to the Johannine account Peter's first denial occurred as he was being admitted to the courtyard, whereas the Synoptists put it later, when he was warming himself by the fire.' The artificial separation of verses 17 and 18 seems to bear out this reading of the incident; but there is nothing in the Greek text to warrant it, once we have observed that with v. 16 a paragraph ends, and that vv. 17-18 together make a fresh paragraph, the last part of which gives Peter's position at the time of the denial. When John speaks of the 'damsel that kept the door', he does not imply that she kept it so sedulously as not to take a moment off for a little gossip by the fire.

The absence of quotation marks from the Authorized Version is perhaps an even greater defect. In a passage such as *Luke* 13. 32-33, the reader cannot tell where the message which Jesus asks the Pharisees to deliver to 'that fox' Herod comes to an end, whereas true sense of the whole can be made only by closing the message at the end of v. 32, and regarding v. 33 as an admission which Jesus makes to his audience but does not wish to be conveyed to Herod. Another such problem is presented by the punctuation of *John* 12. 27. But I leave the reader to deal with this himself—he may not agree with me.

Before leaving King James's translators I must refer to one great advantage that they had over us. They wrote at a time when the discussion of spiritual matters in ordinary conversation was far more usual than it is to-day. Consequently they had at their disposal a religious vocabulary which was sure of ready acceptance. Nowadays it is less natural to talk of God; it is embarrassing to mention sin; and no one, when discussing his neighbour, assesses him in terms of righteousness. We have for long been preoccupied with subjects other than religion, and our daily concerns are reflected in our daily speech. It is this fact more than any other that makes it impossible to translate *everything* in the Gospels into the normal idiom of 1952. However, the translator must accept this limitation as a challenge rather than a handicap, blending the old wine with the new in such a manner that the skins hold both.

I pass now to the Greek Gospels themselves, and will first say something of their language. They were written, as we now think, between A.D. 60 and 100, and all in Greek – they were not translations, though it is possible that their authors thought in Aramaic, the Semitic dialect of Jesus' day, and had Greek as a second language. This is not to say that 'the original eye-witnesses' did not begin by preaching Christ in Aramaic at Jerusalem. There is even evidence that in the interval between the Ministry and the publication of our first gospel, informal records of Jesus' deeds and sayings were written in Aramaic as well as in Greek. But directly Christian teaching passed beyond the borders of Syria, if not before, Greek must have taken the place of Aramaic. For Greek, since Alexander's conquest of the Middle East, had become the second language of the peoples in that area; and when the Romans succeeded to a large part of what had been Alexander's dominions, Greek was left as the official language in the eastern half of their Empire.* Not only that but there was such an influx of Greeks into Rome that, in the First Century, Greek might have been heard in the streets of the capital almost as often as Latin; and it was in Greek that the gospel was first preached in Rome.

Jesus talked to his disciples and preached in Aramaic,† but to the Roman centurion it is probable that he spoke in Greek, for the

---

* The nearest modern parallel is the use of English in India during imperial times.

† With a Galilean accent, unless he was more successful than Peter in adapting his speech to that of Jerusalem (Mt. 26. 73).

population of Galilee, his own country, had a large pagan admixture. Pilate, in his capacity as a Roman official in the eastern part of the Empire, would naturally have conversed with him in Greek, not in Aramaic or Latin. Nor is there any reason to suppose that the disciples, mostly Galileans too, did not understand Greek; and I take this opportunity of dispelling the idea that they were recruited solely from the ranks of an illiterate peasant class. John and James, for instance, were the sons of a fishing-smack owner, an employer of hired labour, and John was acquainted with the High Priest, while Matthew the customs-officer could not have conducted his business in 'Galilee of the Gentiles' without some knowledge of Greek as well as of accounts.

This then is the language in which Christianity was given to the world. It had changed much in the thousand years since Homer wrote it, and if one comes from the study of the earlier classics straight to New Testament Greek one experiences the sort of shocks that Dr Johnson or Jane Austen might have received had a copy of a modern novel been put in their hands. Diction, grammar and syntax have all undergone modification and loosening. But the language is still Greek, still beautiful, simpler than that of Plato and Demosthenes, but still charged with untranslatable subtlety. And it did what was asked of it. It enabled four men, undertaking the hardest task that ever faced a writer, to produce the four masterpieces which conquered the world. In the Greek of the Gospels the two streams of our Western heritage unite, and the simple Greek of *Mark* would make an excellent starting-point for any student wishing to acquire the language of the one and the spiritual content of the other.

I have been speaking as though the Evangelists had used the idiom of their day with nothing but personal modifications. But this was not so. Gospel Greek is distinguished by two characteristics, both arising from the fact that its writers were conveying to the world a new system of thought which had its roots in an ancient discipline, a New Testament which was founded on the Old. To do this they impregnated their Greek with Hebrew idiom. It is true that in quoting from the Scriptures they did not for the most part translate direct from the Hebrew but used a Greek translation called the Septuagint which had been made when the Jews were forgetting their ancestral tongue. But the Septuagint was written in highly

Semitic Greek. Such quotations as the Gospel-writers made from it must have struck cosmopolitan readers as quaint and archaic to the same degree as the English of our Old Testament seems old-fashioned to us; and I have therefore used old-fashioned English in translating these quotations. But the Evangelists went further than this in imbuing their language with an Old Testament spirit. Luke, in particular, not only included in his first chapters poems which consist of Greek words yet are Hebrew in form and idiom, but even flavoured his narrative with Hebraistic Greek. And all this was deliberate. The change of style between the long, formal sentence which constitutes his Preface and the Annunciation Narratives that follow is abrupt and complete. I have tried to reproduce it. But it is much easier to present formal Greek in an English dress than to convey in contemporary terms the Hebraistic touches in the rest. If we translate literally we get expressions such as 'With desire I have desired', which are not English. I have compromised by seeking a style which though intelligible and natural does not conform at every point with the English of to-day.

But the task which the Gospel-writers set themselves was not merely to insist on the Jewish origins of Christianity. They had to put Christianity itself, a whole world of new ideas, into a Greek that any-one could understand. And this called for a new terminology. The Gospels are full of ancient Greek words (many of them, like *logos*, as old as Homer) which are used to carry the new ideas that came into the world with Jesus Christ. Good examples are the words for *life*, *spirit* and *truth*, as used in *Mark* 8. 35 and *John* 6. 63 and 3. 21. They are old words with a rich new content, and they present the translator with some of his main difficulties. And the greatest of these is that they do not necessarily mean the same thing every time. For instance, the same word is used of Our Lord's *temptation* by the Devil as is used for the political *test* to which the Pharisees put him when they asked him about the payment of the Roman tax. In the English of 1611, *tempt* covered both meanings. But it does not do so now.

There are also, side by side with these necessary new terms, a few words which I can only describe as clichés or hackneyed expressions that were employed for too many different purposes. One of these, the word from which our *martyr* comes, has for its standard meaning 'to bear witness in court'. But one has only to read the

Authorized Version to realize how its meaning was stretched. An equal variety is found in the uses of the word which is translated *stumbling-block* or *offence*. It continues its long life in our *scandal* and *scandalize*. And this is the meaning it carries in *Mark* 6. 3, where Jesus *shocks* his fellow-townsmen. But it means something very different in *Matthew* 18. 6, where he speaks of *corrupting* 'one of these little ones'. It is certainly one of the many words which it would be wrong to translate in the same way wherever they occur.

One more comment on the Gospel style. Each of the Evangelists uses it in his own way and with his own idiosyncracies. It is partly through a study of these that scholars have decided that Mark did not write the ending to his book which the Authorized Version gives us; also that John did not write the story of the woman caught in adultery, which is in the manner of Luke and is included in his Gospel by some of the manuscripts. But in spite of personal peculiarities the Gospel style is one; and from this uniformity I get the impression that it goes a long way back and was formed before anything was written down – a feeling which strengthens my belief in the authenticity of the Gospel narratives. The manner in which Jesus preached was very close to the manner in which his followers preached him.

This brings me to the much debated question of the formation of the Gospels, and in particular to that enquiry into the sources, priority and relationship of the first three which is known as the Synoptic Problem. I cannot take my readers very far into an enquiry which has proved the most fascinating and the most difficult in the whole history of literature – they would not thank me if I did. But I can at least give them some idea of the points that arise and the conclusions that are reached. Everything hangs, of course, on a minute comparison of the Greek texts, but in order to assist the Greekless reader I have been at pains to bring out in English the more significant differences and similarities in the wording used by Mark, Matthew and Luke when covering the same ground.

The parable of the Sower affords a typical passage for examination (Mk. 4; Mt. 13; Lk. 8). Nobody can doubt that in all three Gospels he is reading one and the same parable. There are editorial differences, but there is also so much identity of wording that we are forced to the conclusion that whichever Evangelist wrote first was copied by one or both of the others. For many reasons (including his Preface) Luke is the most unlikely to have written first, and it becomes a question whether Mark preceded Matthew or Matthew Mark. Most scholars now believe that Mark wrote first; and I concur.* Matthew and Luke have included in their Gospels a great deal of material derived from *Mark*, though with many changes of diction and order.

But it is clear that these two, though both indebted to Mark, filled out their Gospels with a great deal of fresh matter which they did not find in his; and it is contended that both must have derived much of this fresh matter from one and the same source. Consider for instance the lesson of the mote and the beam (Mt. 7; Lk. 6). The difference of wording between the two accounts is so insignificant that we cannot help believing that Matthew and Luke both had at their disposal a source not used by Mark, and also that this source was a written one. It is from cases such as this, and there are many of them, that the idea of a written collection of Our Lord's sayings which was available to Matthew and Luke took shape in the minds of scholars, where it is now firmly established under the title of Q, the initial letter of the German word *Quelle*, source. But even this hypothesis leaves undiscovered the sources of those portions of *Matthew* and *Luke* which, deriving neither from *Mark* nor from Q, must be attributed to the Evangelists' own industry in drawing on yet other written sources, on the oral tradition, or on the memories of individuals. Luke's Preface throws some light on their methods.

However, in the last thirty years or so the attention of many scholars has been directed not so much to the Gospels themselves as to the period of oral teaching that preceded them. They have devoted themselves to the analysis and classification of the stories about Jesus which we find in the Gospels, with a view to deciding by whom, in what community, and with what special purpose each was used before any Gospel-maker wrote it down. It was German scholars who initiated this study, which is known as Form-Criticism. With German thoroughness the various kinds of narrative, the miracles, the parables, the incidents leading up to a pronouncement by Jesus, and the rest, have been arranged in classes and sub-classes like the moths

* But not without noting that in a recent book the Abbot of Downside argues for the priority of *Matthew*.

in a museum; and in certain hands this analysis has taken a destructive turn, inviting us to wonder how many of these stories are authentic and how many were invented by zealous teachers to inculcate some locally needed lesson or for purposes of general edification. But on the whole the study has proved valuable in that it gives us a convincing and vivid picture of what happened in the three decades when Christianity was in its infancy, how Christ was talked about and preached in the growing communities of the faithful, first by the eyewitnesses and then by the 'ministers of the Word', till the stories became stereotyped and were finally put in writing by the Evangelists with the amount of individual editing that I have indicated.

Yet, as a preliminary to the study of the Gospels, too large a dose of Form-Criticism might well reduce one to the condition of a man who stands before a Raphael and keeps on asking where the artist got his paints. I myself avoided this unprofitable state of mind by translating the Gospels first and as far as possible shutting my eyes to all that had been written on the subject.* At a later stage I availed myself of the labours of professional workers in the field in order to correct my mistakes and to check the validity of my first impressions against the findings of modern scholarship. Here is the result.

No one can read the hundredth part of what has been written about the Gospels since they ceased to be regarded as verbally sacrosanct and feel certain that Jesus acted and spoke on each occasion *exactly* as described. On the other hand no one can reasonably doubt that the Gospels are true – the tradition they embody is firmly based on the reports of eye-witnesses. Such a tradition is of course not only selective but liable to interpolations and distortions, as anyone can prove for himself by passing a story round a circle of friends by word of mouth and then comparing the final version with the first. Yet what has impressed me most in the oral tradition as presented to us in the Gospels is its fidelity to detail. Not that we should be surprised at that. Everything that Jesus had said and done was precious both to those who reported him and to their eager audiences. Every word, tone, look and gesture of the Master was carefully reproduced. In fact, when the first Christians spoke about him, I feel that they must

* I may add here that I have neither consulted nor borrowed from any modern translation.

have acted the part, so realistic are the descriptions that have come down to us. And I was happy, on returning to the texts after my excursion into controversial literature, to find that I had received a strong impression of this kind when first translating. I had even felt at some points that the logic of Christ's words could not be brought out unless they were spoken as he spoke them, with the gestures that he made. Also that even the narrative portions cannot always be fully appreciated unless they are read aloud, as the Evangelists intended. For it is becoming increasingly clear that the Gospels were prepared not only to be read in private, but to be read aloud, and to be used in church for liturgical purposes.*

Such is the faith I have acquired in the authenticity of the material which our Gospel-writers undertook, as Luke says, 'to arrange in narrative form'. But it was by no means a foregone conclusion that the stringing together of a number of short narratives and bits of teaching, however true and graphic they might be, would result in an entity that could be called a book, still less a literary masterpiece. It is true that the writers did not feel it their duty, like a modern biographer, to present a balanced view of a whole life, nor to narrate everything in the order of its occurrence – indeed I do not think they always knew it. But they had other difficulties to contend with. They had to arrange their material in suitable sections for liturgical purposes. They had at the same time to create the impression of rapid and relentless forward movement from the divine beginnings to the predestined end. And they had, like the Greek tragic dramatists, to write for an audience who were conscious of that end before the first words of the first line were spoken. That they succeeded as they did constitutes a miracle which is unique in the history of literature and the annals of religion. We can account for it only by remembering that they were inspired by a unique personality. Just as Jesus lived in the oral tradition that preceded the Gospels, so he inspired and unified the writings that eventually summed it up. One might almost say that Jesus wrote the Gospels.

Before discussing the portrait of the Son of Man which emerges from the accounts of the four Evangelists, I must say something of

* See *The Origins of the Gospel according to St Matthew*, G. D. Kilpatrick, 1946; and *The Primitive Christian Calendar*, P. Carrington, 1952.

the men themselves and the manner in which each approached his task. In doing this I shall for the most part follow traditional views, not merely for the sake of brevity, but because I believe that in general the tradition is correct.

St Mark's Gospel is thought to have been written about A.D. 65, and its author is identified with the John Mark who is described in *Acts* 12. 12 as the son of Mary, a lady prominent in Christian circles in the early days at Jerusalem. We have it from Papias, who lived in the first half of the Second Century and is quoted by Eusebius, that Mark was St Peter's 'interpreter' and wrote from his memory of Peter's teaching. It has also been conjectured that Mark's father was the owner of the house where the Last Supper was eaten, Mark being a lad at the time; that Mark got wind of Judas's intentions, rushed off in his night attire to warn Jesus in Gethsemane, and narrowly escaped arrest himself (Mk. 14); and finally that he was the 'young man dressed in a white robe' whom the women found in the tomb (Mk. 16). This is attractive guesswork. What is more to the point is that his Gospel in many ways bears out the statement of Papias. When one reads it one can *hear* Peter saying: 'So, having got rid of the crowd, we carried him off with us, just as he was, in the boat.' (Mk. 4. 36). All Mark had to do was to write 'they' and 'them' for 'we' and 'us', preserving the pronouns 'him' and 'he' which Peter naturally used instead of constantly repeating Jesus's name. 'Peter remembered' is another suggestive phrase (Mk. 11. 21).

However, even if Mark is reproducing Peter's reminiscences it is probable that he had other sources too. And in any case the literary achievement is Mark's not Peter's. He has moulded his disconnected materials into a rapid, consecutive narrative which can best be praised in a very simple way by saying that once one has started reading it one cannot stop, and that however often it is read the spell remains. But it is much easier to feel these effects than to see how Mark secures them. He is certainly a master of detail. But he knows equally well where, for the sake of contrast, to omit it. A single sentence illustrates my meaning: 'Then they crucified him, and parcelled out his clothes, casting lots for them to see what each should have.' Four words for the crucifixion of Christ; fifteen for the men who had nailed him to the cross.

I am not suggesting that Mark was a practised writer. I think his artistry was largely unselfconscious. As a stylist he has faults, even of grammar; but one knows what he means (which cannot always be said of Luke), even when he writes such sentences as 'And first you have the people by the path where it is sown', which I have rendered almost literally. It was therefore not lack of clarity that caused him to be somewhat neglected by the early Church. It was perhaps his brevity that was deplored. He begins abruptly, with no Birth Narrative; and if as is sometimes supposed he finished with the words 'because they feared', he included no account of Christ's appearances after the Resurrection. Nor did he give the long discourses which we call the Sermon on the Mount and the Sermon on the Plain. In fact he reproduces little of Jesus's teaching, and has few parables. Yet in spite of all he misses out there is no fundamental Christian concept that is not to be found, at least in embryo, in Mark. In this book I have abandoned the customary order and put his Gospel first, because he wrote first and should therefore be read first. As a Gospel-maker he not only led the way but he created a pattern which served as a model to the rest. Mark's Gospel is original in every sense of the term.

The author of *Matthew* is identified by various writers from Papias to Jerome with Matthew, or Levi, the customs-officer and disciple, and is stated to have 'written the sayings in Hebrew'. Here we depart from tradition. As we have seen already, *Matthew* closely follows the Greek of *Mark*, incorporating large portions of that Gospel though adding material from other sources. Two conclusions follow. First, the work was not a translation but was written in Greek. Secondly, it was not written by Matthew the apostle. Its author, had he been an eye-witness, would surely not have contented himself with copying, often verbatim, the record of one who was not. At the moment we can affirm nothing, but it is at least a tenable opinion that *Matthew* was written by an unknown author about A.D. 85, for the use of a Jewish-Christian community in one of the cities of the Levant.

None the less, *Matthew* was in ancient times preferred to *Mark*. In manuscripts of the New Testament it usually stands first, and it has been first in the affections of many Christians throughout the centuries. The reason is not far to seek: it lies in the wealth and beauty of the new material that Matthew added to *Mark*: the Bethlehem story; the Lord's Prayer; the Sermon on the Mount; the many fresh parables, in particular those where Jesus struggles in metaphor after metaphor to lodge the Kingdom of Heaven in intelligible terms; and finally in a host of wonderful sayings, such as 'Come in by the narrow gate' and Christ's last words, 'Know too that I am with you every day to the end of time'.

Yet these additions were not made entirely without loss. When Matthew abridges Mark's accounts of Jesus' miracles (Mt. 9. 18–26; Mk. 5. 21–43), one loses, not only vivid detail, but, in spite of the shortening, a sense of pace and movement; the reports take on the character of a catalogue. Nor is Matthew always happy when instead of condensing *Mark* he alters details – in the above passage there was hardly time for the professional mourners to have been called in to Jairus' house before Jesus reached it. And he exaggerates. In *Mark* 6. 8 the disciples are allowed to take a staff for the road; in *Matthew* 10. 10 this is forbidden. In *Matthew* 21 the fig-tree withers 'instantly'; and in 27. 52–3, we are asked to accept the resurrection of 'many sleeping saints' as bodily fact, vouched for by a number of witnesses.

We are presented with a less important discrepancy by Matthew's description of the entry to Jerusalem. Mark tells us how the disciples, on Jesus's instructions, procured a colt and spread their cloaks on its back. Luke and John agree with him. But Matthew, misunderstanding the Hebrew idiom of the prophecy he quotes, states that Jesus had two donkeys brought to him and that the disciples spread their cloaks on both. And he narrowly escapes informing us that Jesus sat on both. This divergence, trivial as it is, does seem to me to throw light on the mentality of Matthew and the lengths to which he was ready to go in his attempts to improve on *Mark*. I was so much interested that I initiated a search among the works of religious artists to find out whether any painter of this scene had followed *Matthew*; and I found out that Fra Angelico had done so. In his picture of the incident, Christ is seated on a magnificent mount, between whose legs one can discern the most diminutive of foals, a charming little animal, too small to support the burden even of a cloak.

Matthew's style is generally judged to be better than Mark's; and in my opinion there is just enough difference to strengthen our conviction that he followed Mark. Had the reverse been true, it is difficult to understand why Mark, with a comparatively good piece of grammar in front of him, should have taken the pains to spoil it. But Matthew by no means always has the best of it in his stylistic changes. Mark's delightful 'Does the lamp come in to be put under the measuring-bowl or the bed?' sounds much more like the way in which Jesus talked than Matthew's more correct 'People do not light a lamp and put it under the measuring-bowl'. Again Mark (10.13) at least allows us to infer that when the people brought their children to Jesus it was the parents, not the children, who were scolded; whereas Matthew's Greek almost compels us to understand that the children themselves were reprimanded (19.13–14). Luke, by making them babies, settles the matter.

But I cannot leave Matthew without putting on record the deep impression which his handling of the Scriptural prophecies makes on my mind. Their wording deserves study.\* An event B does not occur *and so* fulfil a prophecy A; it occurs *in order that* A may be fulfilled. And the prophecies are not uttered *by* but *through* the Prophets. This is a stupendous conception. God makes a Plan, which Jesus volunteers to carry out. His consciousness of having so decided outside the confines of our time and space is emphasized by John; but Matthew dwells on the announcement and the consummation of the Plan as though they were one integrated act. It is illuminating to contrast this noble idea with modern references to Jesus as a 'revolutionary humanitarian'.

I come to *Luke*. Who was the author of what Renan described as the most beautiful book in the world? I am by-passing much controversy when I state it as my opinion that he is 'Luke the beloved physician', who is mentioned in St Paul's *Epistle to the Colossians* and elsewhere in the New Testament; that he was also the author of *Acts* and the companion of Paul; that he was not a pagan but a Jewish convert (I think that no pagan could have so imbued himself with Hebraism); that he wrote his gospel about A.D. 85 for the Greek world at large; and that his own Preface is the best guide to the methods he employed in its composition.

\* I give them where possible as footnotes, not with any idea of detracting from their importance but in order not to break the narrative. And here I may add that all the matter I have given as footnotes to the translation forms part of the original text.

For instance, he certainly borrows wholesale from *Mark*; also apparently from *Matthew*, but in such a way and with so many curious changes (not always happy ones, e.g. in the Lord's Prayer) that we cannot be sure whether he wrote with *Matthew* before him or used parallel sources. But besides suggesting to us that he had access to such written sources, Luke in his Preface obviously claims, as a modern historian might put it, to have examined and sifted the oral tradition; and I think that we may rightly credit to these researches of his that wealth of invaluable new material which we find in his work, from the beautiful Annunciation and Birth Narratives at the beginning to the even more moving Emmaus story at the end. What is interesting is that twice in the glimpses he gives us of Jesus's young mother he draws our attention to her way of quietly taking in events and storing them in her memory, as though he were anticipating a question from the Excellent Theophilus as to the ultimate sources of his information.*

But Luke naturally omits from his Preface the most important fact of all – he is a poet. I do not mean by this that he embroidered his narratives, but rather that he knew how to distil truth from fact. His first two chapters are not so much a record of the Virgin Birth (which is found in them by implication only) as an expression of his deep consciousness of the part which Woman played in bringing the Divine Idea into the light of day. It is by virtue of this poetic insight into reality that Luke's story has not only dominated Christian thought but inspired the major part of Christian art. Matthew's Birth Narrative gave the imagination of later ages the rough material with which was built the lovely edifice that we call Christmas; but Luke's work has never been surpassed by the pictures it inspired.

If I pick out for mention only two of Luke's beautiful stories, that of Jesus's stay with Martha and Mary, and that of the dinner where an uninvited guest anointed the Master's feet, it is because they illustrate Christ's tenderness to women and their devotion to Christ,

---

* See Lk. 2. 19, 51. Luke's portrait of a quiet, thoughtful young woman is one among several considerations that at one time tempted me to attribute the *Magnificat* to Elizabeth rather than Mary (Lk. 1. 46). It is true that the vast majority of manuscripts give us, *And Mary said:* '*My soul, etc.*' But the Greek could equally well mean, *And she* (i.e. Elizabeth) *said:* '*Mary; my soul, etc.*'

and so lead me to another point. Luke is the champion of womankind not only in the first chapters of his Gospel but throughout it. He is the only Evangelist who has dared to inform us that one at any rate of Jesus's tours with his disciples was financed by rich ladies, one of them from Herod's court. I say dared because it went against the grain with the men of the First Century to encourage women to play a leading part in great affairs or even to allow that they had done so. There was a prejudice which we have not yet altogether overcome.

I have spoken all too briefly about our debt to Luke's poetic genius. He had his defects too, the defects of a poet writing prose. He uses a greater variety of words than any of the other Evangelists, and when he tints his Greek with Hebrew colours to write poems on the model of the *Psalms* he does so with consummate skill, but when he introduces similar effects into straightforward narrative the result is less pleasing. This is of course a question of taste. But I have a graver complaint to make. He is curiously vague. In the course of the long Journey to Jerusalem, time and circumstance often disappear entirely and we are left in the air. Also he is impressionistic just where a few added words would have given us a picture sharp, clear and beautiful as any in *Mark* or *John*. For instance he is the only one to tell us that Jesus, when the cock crew at Peter's third denial, gave Peter a look (22. 61). But has anyone ever read this marvellous account without wondering how Jesus, indoors and some way off, could do this to Peter, who is definitely placed by the fire in the courtyard outside? Explanations occur to us, but in doing so they hold us up. Again, half the difficulty of the parable of the Unjust Agent arises from the fact that Luke has not made it clear whether 'the Lord' who approves of the agent's cleverness is the man's employer or Jesus himself. Forced to choose, I have decided on the second alternative as making better sense of what follows. But I could never feel quite sure without asking Luke himself. Indeed, if I could have the privilege of a few moments' talk with the four Evangelists, I must confess it would be Luke whom I would confront with the longest list of questions.

*John* and its authorship remain. I am not much impressed by the theory that John's Gospel was written by another man with the same name. I have delved deep in many books and have ended by pinning my faith to two authorities. The first is Irenaeus (Bishop of Lyons, A.D. 177), who identifies the author with John son of Zebedee, the beloved disciple, saying that he published his Gospel when he was living at Ephesus (A.D. 100?). The second is the Gospel itself, and in particular its last paragraph, which seems to tell us not only what might naturally have happened, but what did happen. The old Apostle, as head of the Christian community at Ephesus, is told by the elders of his church that it is high time that he, an eye-witness, should give them a gospel of his own – 'we know that what he vouches for is true'. So they depute one of their number to serve him as amanuensis. This man correctly describes the beloved disciple as the real author of the book, and having finished his work, which no doubt involved a great deal more than taking down dictation, he adds a note of his own which can either be taken as a piece of pious exaggeration or as a sigh of relief at the completion of a task well done.

Some scholars will, I fear, regard this solution as too simple to be right. But the simplest way can be the best. And the whole book supports this view. If John the apostle wrote in his old age, this is the kind of work we might have expected from him. In the other Gospels he figures as an impulsive and dramatic young man, a great lover and a good hater too, jealous, swift to anger, and intolerant of opposition. He claims the privilege of sitting by the side of Jesus in his glory, and is willing to die for it. He resents the well-meant activities of a rival healer because 'he is not one of us'. He is a 'Son of Thunder' who would have liked 'to call down fire from the sky' in order to destroy the Samaritan villagers who had turned his Master from their doors. And in the Gospel, side by side with a surpassing love and spiritual understanding, we find the same qualities displayed. The author's hatred of the Jews who slew his Lord comes out in every stage of the long controversies he reports, and one is made to feel that he is not only damning them but their successors too, the Pharisaic party of his own day. So also when he exalts John the Baptist only to put him firmly in his place we must remember that long after his execution the Baptist still had followers (see *Acts* 18. 25), whose preference for their own founder might well have incited the protagonist of Christ to jealousy. And John is the only Evangelist whose bitterness induces him to bring a charge of petty larceny against Judas. His reputation for intolerance is supported by a story told about him and one of his antagonists, the heretic Cerinthus. John, as he went into the public baths one day at Ephesus, was told that Cerinthus was in the building, and he promptly changed his mind and left it.

But love and intolerance are not incompatible. John loved and understood his Master better perhaps than any man has done since, and he has passed on to us that love and insight in a book without which Christianity would be a poorer thing. And the book itself might well have had less force, had John appeared in it only as the quiet mystic and not as the fighting champion of Christ with the flaming sword of truth in his hand, like an Angel in his own *Apocalypse*.

Of the depth of his philosophy, which comprehends a world where Time and Space had not yet come to be, I do not here propose to speak; nor of his Christian doctrine, which others have expounded much better than I could, notably the late Archbishop Temple. But in view of what I have said on the interdependence of literary and spiritual values in the Gospels it is not outside my scope to examine the form in which John's genius expressed itself. If Luke is a poet, John is above all things a dramatist. It is not unlikely that he had read Euripides and Plato.* His scenes and dialogues often remind me of the technique of earlier Greek writers, though I admit that I find little or nothing of Greek philosophy in his thought, which is Christian through and through. Even the magnificent Prologue has its dramatic moments – 'Came a man sent forth from God'. And most of the book can be read as a series of scenes, each leading to a climax, such as the dialogue that ends with Jesus's great utterance: 'Before Abraham came to be, I *am*.'

I do not suggest that John set out to write a play, but only that his own intense grip on reality led him to this dramatic form of expression.† Look at his last chapters. None of the other three accounts of

---

* In one respect his dialogue is even more dramatic than Plato's. He never hesitates to put effective speeches and retorts into the mouth of the opposition (e.g. 8. 41).

† Conversely, a perplexing vagueness mars his descriptions when he either did not see or did not understand the incident he is reporting. For instance, what really happened at the wedding-feast in Cana?

the Trial has any moment to compare with that in which Pilate, still examining Jesus inside the Residence, is assailed from without by the menacing roar of the crowd using Caesar's name as a refrain, just when we had almost been brought to think that Jesus after all would be released. And later, at the empty tomb, has any dramatist ever put into the mouth of any character a one-word utterance so charged with emotion as Jesus's 'Mary!'? Finally, if I were trying to convince an unbeliever of the majesty and spiritual stature of the Risen Christ, I would take him straight to the last chapter and ask him to look, through John's eyes, at the Son of Man standing alone on the beach in the light of dawn, with a fire at his feet, on which a fish is cooking for his breakfast.

From such a writer it would be too much to demand that his scenes should be staged in a strictly logical sequence, for dramatic order knows no laws but its own. Yet scholars have often made exactly this demand of John, and have felt so much outraged by his abrupt changes of scene and the frequent lack of a connecting thread that they have invented an accident which somehow caused the manuscript columns to transpose themselves. But however ingeniously they rearrange his matter we are left with many seeming dislocations.

Again, John is often represented as having set himself tacitly to correct the chronology of the Synoptists. But I have my doubts. He certainly fills in some gaps they leave, in particular telling us much about the early visits of Jesus to Jerusalem, which they only hint at (Mt. 23. 37; Lk. 13. 34). But when he places the Cleansing of the Temple at an early date, as against the three Synoptists, is he necessarily right? I think not. If it suited his purpose, which is set forth at the end of Chapter 20, I do not think he would have hesitated to abandon strict chronology. We are applying modern standards when we argue otherwise.

One important question remains. People have often asked whether we can rely on the authenticity of John's reports of the words of Jesus, pointing out that the impression is somewhat different from that which the Synoptists give us. I feel that we can in general rely upon him, but not quite as much as on the verbatim reports that were preserved with such care in the oral tradition. For John seems for the most part to have relied on his own memory, and as a result we often feel that we are hearing Jesus speak through John. In Chapter 3, for example, we have no good reason for not believing that he is reporting the *substance* of Jesus's conversation with Nicodemus. But the wording differs from that of the Synoptic Gospels. In them, Jesus often predicts his crucifixion, but he never speaks of being 'lifted up'. Nor does he call himself 'the Only Son'. Which consideration, among others, induces us to close his speech to Nicodemus at the words 'eternal life', and to regard the rest as comment by John.

And there are still more difficult problems. In the first paragraph of Jesus's prayer (Jn. 17), the most beautiful and profound of all the utterances that have come down to us, are we to suppose that Our Lord really paused to explain the nature of Eternal Life, and in these terms? Or are we right in thinking that John is interposing, as he often does, with an explanation of his own? This is a question that everyone must answer for himself.

In these notes on the Four Evangelists I had hoped to bring out the separate contribution that each has made to the portrayal of Jesus. But I found this impossible; for the particular aspect that each of them stresses is never quite neglected by the rest. For instance, Mark, seeing him through Peter's memory, has more to tell us than the rest about the eyes of Jesus, the angry look with which he quelled the Pharisees, and the loving gaze he turned on the young nobleman who proved to be too rich. But Luke alone tells us how Jesus, with a look and a word, brought Zacchaeus scrambling down from his lofty perch in the sycamore. I will therefore attempt to put into words some impressions of Jesus as a man which the study of all four Evangelists has left on my mind. If these are at all new to my readers, I can only refer back to what I said earlier – the spirit of the Greek is not quite the same as that of the Authorized Version. But I do not propose to quote chapter and verse for every statement; nor, I need hardly say, is this a theological study.

Superimposed on all my previous impressions is one of power, tremendous power, utterly controlled. A strong wind swept through Palestine; but if it rooted up the rotten tree, it did not crush the injured reed. The eyes that carved a way for Jesus through a murderous crowd could also draw a tax-collector to abandon his profession.

It was his eyes that seem to have impressed his followers most deeply. Of the other features of his face they have left no record.

But of his stature we learn this, that he was big and strong. His long stride carried him ahead of his disciples, whom he usually led, and who were sometimes hard put to it to catch him up. It was only when he sat down to teach that he had to raise his eyes to hold his standing listeners.

His voice was powerful. Sitting in an anchored boat he could make it carry across the water to a large crowd standing on the beach. This was his customary teaching voice – the cases where he found it necessary to raise it to a higher pitch are noted. Interruptions must have been frequent when he was arguing with his enemies. When he was preaching to a friendly audience they came in the pauses that he left between his paragraphs. For he did not pile parable on parable with breathless haste.

He was a master of ready speech and witty repartee, but most of the sayings that have come down to us bear every sign of careful preparation. They have the qualities of poetry, and with the aid of paradox, exaggeration, or play on words, were cast in such a shape as would enable them to find their way into the dullest mind and stay there. His way of putting things was as original as the things themselves. He told his disciples to say : 'We are unprofitable servants. We have done our duty.' Who but he would have avoided the less memorable wording, 'We have *only* done our duty'? In fact he chose his wording to make people use their brains, and his biographers have faithfully recorded its peculiarities, seldom venturing to 'correct' him when he looks down on mortal time from the high viewpoint of eternity and uses the present tense for past and future events.

He was a learned man, who knew the ancient Hebrew writ by heart. And though, as far as we know, he wrote nothing for publication, he was a man of letters too, for his parables are *literary* masterpieces. They had to be, or the lessons they conveyed would never have sunk in.

And they are full of quiet humour. The crowds must often have laughed. But did Jesus himself laugh? Later writers say he did; but the Gospels leave us only to read between the lines and yearn for some record of a lighter-hearted moment. I myself venture to find one in Matthew's story of the silver coin that Peter was instructed to discover in a fish's mouth. This has never been explained on a serious level, and I regard it as the confused report of a joke that Jesus made at the expense of Peter or his friends the tax-collectors. He was certainly no glum ascetic, and when he joined these easy-living friends of his to enjoy a glass of wine with them, what was his conversation? Again, we have no reports. Yet it must have had irresistible charm, or they would not afterwards have gathered round 'to hear him speak'.

But there was little relaxation. He had his times of rest and prayer (if prayer was rest), but when in action he was ruthless to himself and well-nigh inexhaustible. Not quite; for the great reservoir of healing power within him was sometimes drained.* Then he evaded the importunate crowds or fell into the sleep of exhaustion. On one occasion he slept through a storm at sea; yet the moment he was wakened he was in command. Sometimes too it seems that the power was not at his disposal. He was of two worlds and always mindful of his great commission; but there were hours of doubt and disappointment. He had his times of exultation, but moments of divine impatience too, when he was homesick for Heaven. He kept his eyes on Satan and he saw him fall like lightning from the sky; but Satan also had his eye on him. The passage from the Jordan to beyond the empty tomb was not an effortless and undisputed progress; and no man can conceive the force that went into the final victory.

I have tried to catch a few glimpses of the Perfect Man through the eyes of his disciples, concentrating on his human attributes because it was as a man that they themselves first learnt to know and love him. Indeed they labour to portray his full humanity and make it clear that it was not till the very end, or after it, that they realized the fact, and understood the purpose, of his descent from Heaven. The significance of his self-revelations was hidden from them for a little while by Providence, to be afterwards made clear; and I have thought it right and natural to follow in the way that Providence laid down for them. For the rest, let the Gospels speak. Of what I have learnt from these documents in the course of my long task, I will say nothing now. Only this, that they bear the seal of the Son of Man and God, they

---

* In my opinion, the fact that Christ passed on to others his powers of healing the bodies and the souls of men shows that his miracles constituted no breach of universal law, and also that he wished us to understand this. The distance at which we lag behind him in our efforts is one measure of the spiritual force he expended.

are the Magna Charta of the human spirit. Were we to devote to their comprehension a little of the selfless enthusiasm that is now expended on the riddle of our physical surroundings, we should cease to say that Christianity is coming to an end – we might even feel that it had only just begun.

E. V. R.

*Highgate, May 1952*

THE GOSPEL AS RECORDED BY

# MARK

THE FIRST WORD OF THE GOOD TIDINGS OF JESUS CHRIST SON OF GOD In accordance with the Scripture in the Prophet Isaiah, *Behold I send my Messenger ahead of thee to prepare thy way; the voice of one crying in the wilderness 'Prepare the way of the Lord: make his paths straight'*, John the Baptizer appeared in the wilderness proclaiming, for the forgiveness of sins, a baptism of repentance. All Judaea went out to him, and all the people of Jerusalem. They openly confessed their sins and were baptized by him in the River Jordan.

John wore clothing made of camel-hair, with a leather belt round his waist, and he ate locusts and wild honey. He preached in these words: 'He is on his way. One greater than I comes after me, whose sandal-straps I am not fit to stoop down and undo. I have baptized you in water; but he will baptize you in the Holy Spirit.'

And now Jesus appeared, coming from Nazareth in Galilee, and was baptized by immersion in the Jordan at the hands of John. He had no sooner come up out of the water than he saw

I

the heavens rent asunder and the Spirit descending like a dove towards him. There was a voice too from the heavens: 'Thou art My son, the Beloved One. In thee I rejoice.'

Immediately after, the Spirit drove him out into the desert. For forty days he stayed there and was tempted by Satan. He was with the wild beasts, and the Angels ministered to his wants.

After John had been arrested, Jesus went into Galilee proclaiming the good news from God. 'The time has come,' he said, 'and the Kingdom of God is near. Repent and put your trust in the Good News.'

As he walked by the Sea of Galilee he saw Simon and his brother Andrew, who were fishermen, casting nets into the sea. Jesus said to them: 'Come, follow me, and I will make you fishers of men.' They left their nets at once and followed him.

Walking a little farther he saw James son of Zebedee and his brother John, also in their boat, putting their nets in order. He called to them at once, and they came away and followed him, leaving their father Zebedee with the paid hands in the boat.

They went into Capernaum and on the first Sabbath he entered the synagogue and taught. His way of teaching filled them with amazement, for he taught them like one with authority and not like the Doctors of the Law.

That very day, in their synagogue, there was a man possessed by an unclean spirit, who cried out: 'What is your business with us, Jesus the Nazarene? Have you come to destroy us? We know who you are, the Holy One of God.'

Jesus rounded on him. 'Hold your tongue,' he said, 'and come out of the man.'

The unclean spirit convulsed the man, gave a loud cry and came out of him. All were amazed. 'What have we here?' they said as they talked the matter over. 'A new doctrine, this! And it has power behind it. He even tells unclean spirits what to do and they obey him.' From that moment his fame spread everywhere, through all the countryside of Galilee.

When he left the synagogue he went straight to the house of Simon and Andrew, with James and John. Now Simon's mother-in-law lay in bed there with fever – they told him about her at once. He went up to her, seized her hand and raised her. The fever left her and she began to wait on them.

Evening came, and when the sun had set they brought to him all that were sick or possessed by demons. The whole town was there, crowding at the door. He cured many that were suffering from this or that disease and cast out many demons, forbidding them to speak, because they knew him.

The next day he rose while it was still dark, and leaving the house, made his way into the open country and prayed there for a while. Simon and his companions went in pursuit, found him, and told him that everyone was looking for him.

He said to them: 'Let us go elsewhere – to the neighbouring country towns – so that I may preach there also; for that is what I came to do.' And he went through the whole of Galilee, entering their synagogues to proclaim his message and casting out demons.

On one occasion he was approached by a leper, who besought him and fell at his feet. 'If you will,' he said, 'you can cleanse me.'

Jesus was filled with compassion. He stretched out his hand, touched him and said: 'I will it. Be cleansed.'

The leprosy left him immediately and he was cleansed. Jesus dismissed him promptly, with a stern injunction. 'Be careful not to say a word to anyone,' he said; 'but go and show yourself to the priest and make the offering for your purification which Moses prescribed so that people might be notified.'

The man went off but at once began to talk freely and blaze the tale abroad, with the result that Jesus was no longer able to enter towns openly. Instead, he stayed outside in places where nobody lived; and people came to him from every quarter.

# 2

WHEN, after some time, he came to Capernaum again, the news went round that he was home, and they flocked to him in such numbers that even the doorway could hold no more. He was telling them of the Word, when he was approached by some people bringing him a paralytic carried by four men. Unable, because of the crowd, to get the man to Jesus, they stripped the roof from over his head and lowered the stretcher, with the paralytic lying on it, through the hole they had made.

Jesus, seeing their faith, said to the paralytic: 'My child, your sins are forgiven.'

Now there were some Doctors of the Law sitting in the room, who thought to themselves: 'How can the man say such a thing? He is blaspheming. Who can forgive sins but God alone?'

Jesus, at once aware, through his spiritual insight, of the nature of their secret thoughts, said to them: 'Why are you entertaining such thoughts? Which is the easier thing, to say to the paralytic "Your sins are forgiven," or to say "Get up, take your stretcher and walk"? However, to teach you that the Son of Man has authority on earth to forgive sins' – and he turned to the paralyzed man – 'I say to you, Get up, take your stretcher and go home.'

The man rose, and picking up his stretcher at once, went out of the house in sight of everyone. They were all filled with awe and praised God. 'We have never seen the like,' they said.

He left the town and walked once more beside the sea. All the people went to him and he taught them.

As he passed along he saw Levi son of Alphaeus sitting by

the custom-house and said to him, 'Follow me'; and he rose and followed him.

So it came about that Jesus sat down to a meal in this man's house and a number of tax-collectors and outcasts joined him and his disciples at table; for there were many of these and they had begun to follow him. But the Doctors of the Pharisaic party, seeing him at table with outcasts and tax-collectors, said to his disciples: 'Why does he eat and drink with tax-collectors and outcasts?'

Jesus, when he heard this, said to them: 'It is not the healthy that need a physician, but the sick. I am here to summon sinners, not the righteous.'

Then, as John's disciples and the Pharisees were fasting, they approached him with another question. 'How is it,' they said, 'that John's disciples and the disciples of the Pharisees are fasting, while yours are not?'

Jesus replied: 'Surely the friends of the bridegroom cannot fast while the bridegroom is with them? So long as they have the bridegroom with them they cannot fast. But a time will come when the bridegroom is taken from them, and that is the time, that is the day, when they will fast.

'Nobody mends an old cloak with a piece of new cloth; or else the new piece drags on the old and the result is a bigger rent. And no one pours new wine into old skins; or the wine will burst the skins, and both wine and skins be lost. Instead, they pour new wine into fresh skins.'

It happened one sabbath day that he was walking through the cornfields and his disciples, as they went, began to pluck the ears of corn. The Pharisees said to him: 'Look! Why are they doing what is forbidden on the Sabbath?'

Jesus replied: 'Have you never read what David did when he and his companions were in need and hungry – how, in the days when Abiathar was High Priest, he went into the House of God and ate the sacrificial loaves, which only the priests have the right to eat, and even gave them to his comrades?'

He also said to them: 'The Sabbath came into being for mankind, not mankind for the Sabbath. Thus the Son of Man is master even of the Sabbath.'

# 3

AGAIN he went to synagogue. There was a man there with a hand that had withered, and they watched Jesus closely to see whether he would heal him on the sabbath day, hoping to have a charge to bring against him.

He said to the man with the withered hand: 'Rise, and stand here in the centre.' And to the others: 'Are we permitted on the Sabbath to choose between doing good and doing evil, saving a life and killing?'

They were silent; and he, after an angry glance round the circle, and grieved at their insensibility, said to the man: 'Hold out your hand.'

The man held it out and it was made sound once more.

But the Pharisees, when they left the synagogue, began at once to plot against him with the partisans of Herod, considering how they might destroy him. And Jesus, accompanied by his disciples, withdrew towards the sea.

He was followed by a great concourse of people, from Galilee, from Judaea, from Jerusalem, from Idumaea and the far side of the Jordan and the neighbourhood of Tyre and Sidon – great crowds, who heard of all he was doing and came to join him.

He told his disciples to have a boat in close attendance on him because of the crowds, to save himself from being crushed. For he healed large numbers, with the result that all who had any affliction threw themselves at him in their eagerness to touch him. Moreover, unclean spirits no sooner saw him than they fell down before him and cried out, 'You are the son of

God.' And in every case he repeatedly forbade them to divulge his nature.

He now went up into the hills and summoned to his side the disciples of his choice. These left their homes and joined him. Then he appointed twelve, whom he called 'apostles', to associate with him and to be sent forth by him as preachers, with authority to cast out demons. Thus he created the Twelve – Simon, to whom he gave the name of Peter; James son of Zebedee and John his brother, whom he nicknamed Boanerges or 'Sons of Thunder'; Andrew; Philip; Bartholomew; Matthew; Thomas; James son of Alphaeus; Thaddaeus; Simon the Zealot; and Judas of Kerioth, the man through whose treachery he was arrested.

They returned to their house, and again such crowds collected as to make it impossible for them even to have a meal. His relatives, when they heard this, set out from home to take him into custody, for people were saying that he was out of his mind.

Meanwhile the Doctors who had come down from Jerusalem were saying, 'He has Beelzebub in him' and 'He casts out demons through their Prince.'

Jesus called them to him and addressed them allegorically. 'How', he asked, 'can Satan cast out Satan? If a kingdom is divided by internal strife that kingdom cannot stand; nor will a household so divided have the strength to stand. If Satan has rebelled against himself and is divided, he cannot stand – his end has come. But one cannot break into the Strong One's house and plunder his goods, unless one begins by tying up the Strong One. After that one will ransack his house.

'Hear the truth. Mankind shall be forgiven everything – their sins and every blasphemy they may utter. But he that blasphemes against the Holy Spirit has no forgiveness ever: he is guilty of a sin that outlasts time.' This was because they said, 'He has an unclean spirit.'

His mother and his brothers now arrived. They stood outside the house and sent him a message asking him to join them.

People were sitting all round Jesus. 'Do you know,' they said, 'that your mother and brothers are outside asking for you?'

Jesus answered them by saying: 'Who are my mother and my brothers?' And with a glance at all those who were sitting round him: 'Behold, my mother and my brothers! Whoever does the will of God is brother and sister and mother to me.'

# 4

ONCE more he began to teach beside the sea. But the crowd that gathered round him was greater than ever; so he got into a boat on the water and sat down there. The people all stood on the shore, facing the sea, and he taught them many things in parables.

In the course of his teaching he said to them: 'Listen to this. Picture the sower going out to sow. It happened, as he sowed, that some of the seed fell by the path and the birds came and ate it up. Other seed fell on a rocky patch where it did not find much soil, and it sprang up at once because the soil was shallow. But when the sun came up, it was scorched, and because it had no roots it withered. Other seed fell among thistles, which grew tall and choked it, so that it yielded nothing. Yet other seeds fell into rich soil, and springing up and growing produced a crop. They yielded up to thirty, sixty, and a hundredfold.'

He concluded by saying: 'He that has ears to hear with, let him hear.' And his followers and the Twelve, when they had him to themselves, asked him about his parables.

'To you,' he said, 'the secrets of the Kingdom of God are revealed. But to those others, who are outside, all is conveyed in parables, so that *they may see with their eyes but not perceive, and hear with their ears but not understand, lest they be converted and forgiven.*'

He resumed: 'You fail to see this parable? How then are you going to understand the rest of them? What the sower sows is the Word. And first you have the people by the path where it is sown. No sooner do they hear it than Satan comes and carries off the Word that was sown in them. In the same way, the next are those who receive the seed on rocky ground. No sooner do they hear the Word than they accept it with joy. But they have no roots in them: they cannot hold out long. As a result, when suffering or persecution comes on account of the Word, they promptly recant. Then there are the others, who receive the seed among thistles. These are people who have listened to the Word, but the cares of this world, the lure of riches, and all the other passions come into play and choke the Word, so that it bears no fruit. The last are those that received the seed on rich soil, the people who hear the Word and embrace it and bear up to thirty, and sixty, and a hundredfold.'

He also said to them: 'Does the lamp come in to be put under the measuring-bowl or the bed? Does it not come in to be put on its stand? For nothing is secret, if not to be revealed; and nothing was ever hidden but to come into the light. If anyone has ears to hear with, let him hear.'

He also said to them: 'Give your minds to what you hear. As you give, so you will receive, measure for measure. Indeed you will receive even more than you give. For more shall be given to the man who has; but from the man who has not, even what he has shall be taken.'

He also said: 'Hear what the Kingdom of God is like. A man casts seed on the earth. Day in, day out, he sleeps and rises, while the seed springs up and grows – he knows not how. Of her own accord earth bears her fruit, first the green blade, then the ear, and then the ripe grain in the ear. But when the crop is ready, he at once sends out the sickle, for the harvest has come.'

He also said: 'To what shall we compare the Kingdom of

9

God? In what parable can we lodge it? It is like a grain of mustard seed which, when sown in the earth, though smaller than any other seed that is there, grows up to be the largest of shrubs and sends out great shoots, so that the birds of the sky are able to roost in its shelter.'

In many such parables as these he talked to them of the Word, in so far as they could understand. Except in parables he used not to address them; but to his own disciples he explained everything when they were alone.

On the same day, when evening came, he said to them: 'Let us cross over to the other shore.' So, having got rid of the crowd, they carried him off with them, just as he was, in the boat. Some other boats accompanied him.

And now there was a great storm. The waves came dashing up into the boat till it was nearly full of water. But he himself was in the stern, with his head on the headrest, fast asleep.

They woke him and said: 'Master, do you not care if we are lost?'

Roused from his sleep, Jesus rebuked the wind and said to the sea: 'Silence! Be still.' And the wind dropped and a great calm ensued.

He said to them: 'Why are you such cowards? Have you no faith yet?'

They were filled with awe and said to one another: 'Who can this be, whom even wind and sea obey?'

# 5

THEY came to the Gerasenes' country on the far side of the Sea, and he had no sooner disembarked than a man with an unclean spirit came out from the tombs and confronted him. This man lived in the sepulchres and had reached a stage when no one could control him even by the use of chains. For he had often been put into fetters and manacles, but had torn the manacles apart and burst the fetters asunder; and no one was strong enough to overpower him. He spent all the time, night and day, in the sepulchres and on the hills, shouting and gashing himself with stones. Now, seeing Jesus from afar, he ran up, fell at his feet and cried in a loud voice: 'What is your business with me, Jesus, son of God the Highest? I adjure you by God not to torment me.' For Jesus had been saying to him: 'Unclean spirit, come out of that man.'

'What is your name?' Jesus asked him.

'My name is Legion,' he replied; 'for there are many of us.' And he begged him earnestly not to expel them from the neighbourhood.

There was a large herd of pigs feeding on the mountain side, and the spirits begged him to send them among the pigs, so that they might enter them.

He gave them leave, and the unclean spirits came out and entered the pigs, with the result that the herd – some two thousand pigs – charged down the cliff into the sea, where they were drowned. Their herdsmen fled and brought the news to the town and countryside; and the people came to see what had really happened. They approached Jesus and saw the demoniac sitting there, dressed and in his right mind – the very man who had had the legion in him. They were terrified, and when those who had witnessed it told them what had happened to the demoniac, and how the pigs had fared, they promptly besought Jesus to leave their neighbourhood.

As he was stepping into the boat, the man who had been possessed begged him to let him stay with him. But Jesus would not allow him. Instead, he said to him: 'Go home now to your own people and tell them what great things the Lord God has done for you, and the mercy he showed you.'

The man left him and proceeded to tell everyone in the Ten Towns the wonderful things that Jesus had done for him; and they all marvelled.

When Jesus had crossed over again in the boat to the other side, he was faced by a great concourse of people, and he stayed by the sea.

And now one of the governors of the synagogue, called Jairus, came up, and seeing him, fell at his feet and began earnestly to beseech him. 'My little daughter,' he said, 'is at the point of death. Will you not come and lay your hands on her so that she may be saved and live?'

Jesus went with him. But he was followed by a large crowd, treading close on his heels. There was a woman too, who for twelve years had suffered from a hemorrhage. She had undergone much at the hands of many physicians and had spent all her resources to no good purpose – in fact she had gone from bad to worse. Now, having heard the stories about Jesus, she came up from behind through the crowd and touched his cloak, for she had been thinking, 'If I can only touch his clothes I shall be saved.'

On the instant, her hemorrhage was staunched and she could feel that she was cured of the affliction. Jesus, conscious at once of power gone out of him, swung round in the throng and said: 'Who touched my clothes?'

'You see how the crowd are jostling you,' said his disciples. 'And yet you ask who touched you?'

He looked all round to discover the woman who had done it. And the woman, who had been frightened and was still trembling (for she knew what had happened to her), came and fell at his feet and told him the whole truth. Whereupon he said: 'Daughter, your faith has saved you. Go now in peace; and be rid of your affliction.'

Before he had finished speaking, people from the synagogue official's house came up and said: 'Your daughter is dead. Why trouble the Master any more?'

Jesus heard them say this but took no notice. 'Do not be afraid,' he said to the governor of the synagogue. 'Only have faith.'

He allowed no one to go with him but Peter and James and James's brother John. When they reached the official's house, he was faced by a disorderly scene – they were weeping and wailing without restraint.

He went in and said to them: 'Why are you wailing and making this commotion? The child is not dead but asleep.'

They laughed at him. But he turned them all out; and taking with him the child's father and mother and his own companions, he went into the room where the child lay, seized her hand and said *Taleitha, koum,* which means, 'Little girl, I bid you get up.'

The little girl rose instantly and began to walk about, for she was twelve. Her people were lost in wonder. But he impressed it upon them that no one must be told; and he also said she should be given something to eat.

# 6

HE left that town and went to his own part of the country, accompanied by his disciples. When the Sabbath came round he began to teach in the synagogue, and most of them when they heard him were confounded. They said: 'Where did the man get this from? What is this wisdom that has been given him, and these miracles that are brought about through him? Is he not the carpenter, the son of Mary, and brother of James and Joses and Judas and Simon? And are not his sisters with us here?' They were shocked by him.

But Jesus said to them: 'A prophet is not without honour except in his own country, his own family and his own house.' And he was unable to do there any miracle of note, though he did lay his hands on a few sick people and cure them. He was amazed at their lack of faith.

He now made a tour of the villages and taught. Then he

summoned the Twelve to him and began to send them out in pairs on missions, giving them authority over unclean spirits. He instructed them to take nothing for the road except a staff – no bread, no knapsack, no money for their purse – but to put sandals on their feet. And he added, 'Do not wear two tunics.'

'When you enter a house anywhere,' he went on, 'stay there till you leave that town.

'If a town does not welcome you, if they will not listen to your words, leave it, and as you do so, shake off the dust from under your feet as a demonstration against them.'

So they set forth and preached, to bring men to repentance, and from time to time cast many demons out and anointed many sick people with oil and cured them.

Rumours came to King Herod's ears, for Jesus' name was on everybody's lips. People were saying: 'John the Baptizer has risen from the dead. That is why the powers are at work in him.' But others said, 'He is Elijah'; and others again, 'He is a prophet, like those of old'. Herod however, when he heard them, said, 'This is John, whom I beheaded, risen from the dead.'

It must be explained that Herod himself had sent and arrested John and thrown him into prison, because of Herodias, his brother Philip's wife, whom he had married, though John had been telling him that it was illegal for him to marry his brother's wife. Herodias thus had a grudge against John and wished to put him to death. But she lacked the power; for Herod was afraid of John, whom he knew to be a just and holy man, and took care to protect him. He let him talk to him and was always left in much perplexity, though he listened to him with pleasure.

Opportunity came when Herod celebrated his birthday by giving a banquet to the nobles of his court, the officers of the army, and the leading men of Galilee. The daughter of Herodias herself came in and danced, to the delight of Herod and his fellow-banqueters. And the king said to the girl: 'Ask what you wish of me and I will give it you.' He even swore to her that he would give her what she asked for up to half his kingdom.

The girl went out and said to her mother: 'What shall I ask for?'

'The head of John the Baptizer,' said her mother.

The girl went in again immediately, hurried up to the king and told him her wish. 'I want you,' she said, 'to give me the head of John the Baptist, forthwith, on a platter.'

The king was sorely grieved, but in view of his oath and the presence of his guests he was not prepared to break faith with her. He despatched an executioner at once with orders to bring him John's head. The man went off, beheaded him in the prison, and bringing the head in on a platter, gave it to the girl, who gave it to her mother. And John's disciples, when they heard the news, came and removed his corpse and laid it in a tomb.

The apostles rejoined Jesus and gave him a full report of their doings and their teaching. He said to them: 'Come away by yourselves to the solitude of the open country, and rest awhile.' This, because people were coming and going continually. They had not even time to eat.

So they went off in their boat to a deserted spot where they could be alone. But their departure was observed; he was recognized by many; and people from all the towns, running round by land, flocked to the place and reached it before them. Thus, when he disembarked, he was faced by a large crowd. He was stirred with compassion for them, since they were like sheep without a shepherd, and he began to speak and taught them much.

By now it was late in the day and his disciples went up to him and said: 'We are in a desolate spot and it is getting late. Dismiss them, so that they may go to the farms and villages round about and buy themselves something to eat.'

'Feed them yourselves,' he replied.

They said: 'Are we to go and spend ten pounds on bread for them to eat?'

'How many loaves have you got?' he asked them. 'Go and see.'

'Five,' they said when they had found out, 'and two fish.'

He then told them all to sit down by companies on the green grass, and they settled down in squares, a hundred or fifty to each. He took the five loaves and the two fish, and looking up to Heaven said a blessing. Then he broke the loaves in pieces, and handed these to the disciples to serve to the people. He also shared out the two fish among them all; and everyone ate and was satisfied. Moreover they picked up enough pieces to fill twelve hampers, including scraps of fish, though five thousand men had fed.

Immediately after, he ordered his disciples to embark and precede him by crossing over to Bethsaida, while he himself dismissed the people. He bade them farewell and then withdrew into the hills to pray.

Night fell; the boat was out at sea; and he was alone on land. He saw them straining at the oars, for the wind was against them, and about the fourth watch of the night he came towards them, walking on the sea, with the intention of passing them. But they, when they saw him walking on the sea, thought it was a ghost and cried aloud; for they all saw him and were terrified.

But he spoke to them at once and said: 'All is well! It is I. Do not be afraid.' Then he climbed on board to join them, and the wind fell. They were utterly dumbfounded, for being dull of comprehension they had drawn no conclusions from the miracle of the loaves.

So they crossed over, made land at Gennesaret and moored. But no sooner had they disembarked than people recognized him and ran about the whole countryside with the news. As a result they went round after him, wherever they heard he was, bringing those who were ill on stretchers. And whenever he came to a village, town, or farm, they laid down the sick in public places and begged him only to let them touch the tassel on his cloak. And all that touched him were saved.

# 7

THE Pharisees, together with some Doctors of the Law from Jerusalem, now bore down on him. Noticing that some of his disciples ate their bread with unpurified, that is unwashed, hands,* these Pharisees and Doctors asked him: 'Why do your disciples not conform to the traditions of our forefathers, but eat their bread with unpurified hands?'

He said: 'How right Isaiah was when he prophesied about you hypocrites! Here is the passage: *These people honour me with their lips, but their heart is far from me. Their worship of me is empty: they make doctrines of the precepts of men.* God's commandments you neglect: man's traditions you observe.'

He also said to them: 'What excellent ways you have of circumventing God's commandments in order to preserve your own tradition! For instance, Moses said, *Honour thy father and thy mother* and *Let him that reviles his father or mother be put to death*. But you have a different ruling. Once a man has said to his father or mother, "I am making Korban (that is a temple-offering) of all the support you might have got from me", you forbid him to do anything more for his father or mother, thus making God's word null and void through

---

* The Pharisees, in fact the whole Jewish community, always wash their hands thoroughly before meals, in strict observance of ancient tradition. When they come in from business they never eat without sprinkling themselves, and there are many other observances they have inherited, such as the rinsing of cups and pots and pans.

the tradition you have inherited. And there are plenty of other things of the same kind that you do.'

Then he called the people to him again and said: 'Listen to me, all of you, and understand. There is nothing external to a man which by entering him can defile him. On the contrary, it is what comes out of a man that defiles him.'

When he had gone indoors, away from the crowd, his disciples questioned him about this parable.

'You too? So dull?' he said to them. 'Do you not see that nothing that enters a man from outside can defile him, since it enters his stomach, not his heart, and passes out in the privy?'*

And he went on: 'It is what comes out of a man that defiles him. It is from within, from men's hearts, that evil thoughts emerge – fornication, thieving, murder, adultery, self-seeking, malice, double-dealing, licentiousness, jealousy, slander, arrogance, and folly. All these evil things come from within and defile a man.'

Leaving that place, he withdrew to the neighbourhood of Tyre, and wishing to remain unrecognized, shut himself up indoors. But he did not succeed in hiding himself. A woman whose daughter had an unclean spirit heard about him at once and came and cast herself at his feet. She was a Greek of Syro-Phoenician descent. She asked him repeatedly to cast the demon out of her daughter.

'First let the children have their fill,' he said to her; 'for it is not right to take the children's bread and throw it to the house-dogs.'

She took this up and said: 'True, Lord; yet the house-dogs under the table *do* feed – on the children's crumbs.'

He said to her: 'Thanks to that saying you may go in peace. The demon has come out of your daughter.' And the woman went home and found her child laid on the bed and the demon gone.

* He thus pronounced every kind of food ceremonially pure.

Leaving the district of Tyre he returned by way of Sidon to the Sea of Galilee across the territory of the Ten Towns. They brought him a deaf man who could hardly speak, and besought him to lay his hand on him. He took the man away from the crowd by himself, thrust his fingers into his ears, spat and touched his tongue. Then, looking up into the heavens, he gave a sigh and said to the man *Ephphatha*, which means 'Be opened.'

The man's ears were opened, the impediment to his speech was removed, and he spoke clearly. Jesus commanded them to tell no one, but the more he did so, the more eagerly they published the news. In fact they were astonished beyond measure. They said: 'How perfectly he has done everything! He not only makes deaf people hear but he makes dumb people talk.'

# 8

DURING these days there was once more a great concourse of people. As they had nothing to eat, he called his disciples to him and said: 'I feel sorry for all these people who for three days now have attached themselves to me and have nothing to eat. If I send them home starving, they will faint on their way – and some of them have come from far.'

His disciples answered: 'Here in the wilderness, where could one find enough bread to satisfy these people?'

'How many loaves have you got?' he asked.

'Seven,' they said.

Then he told the people to settle down on the ground, took the seven loaves, said a blessing, and broke them into pieces. These he gave to his disciples to serve, and they set them before the people. They also had a few small fish. He blessed these and told them to serve them too. And they ate and were satisfied. Moreover seven baskets were filled with the pieces left, though the people were about four thousand.

He dismissed them and immediately embarked with his disciples and came to the neighbourhood of Dalmanutha.

The Pharisees now sallied out and began to dispute with him. To put him to the proof they asked him for a sign from Heaven.

He gave a sigh from the depths of his heart and said: 'Why does this generation ask for a sign? Be assured that no sign whatever shall be vouchsafed to it.'

With that he left them, and once more embarking, set sail for the other shore. But they forgot to provide themselves with bread and had on board with them only a single loaf. So while he was warning them to watch and be on their guard against the yeast of the Pharisees and the yeast of Herod, they were arguing with one another about the bread they had not brought.

Jesus realized this and said: 'Why are you arguing about your lack of bread? Do you not yet perceive nor understand? Are your faculties benumbed? Having eyes, do you not see? And having ears, do you not hear? And do you not remember? How many hampers did you fill with pieces when I divided the five loaves among five thousand people?'

'Twelve,' they said.

'And in the case of the seven among four thousand, how many baskets did you fill with pieces?'

'Seven,' they replied. And he said: 'Do you not understand yet?'

They came to Bethsaida, and the people brought him a blind man and besought him to touch him. He took the blind man by the hand and led him out of the village. Then, after spitting on his eyes and laying his hands on him, he asked: 'Can you distinguish anything?'

The man looked up and said: 'I can distinguish the men, for I see them like trees, walking about.'

He then put his hands once more on his eyes, and the man saw clearly. His sight had been restored and he could now distinguish even distant objects well. Jesus told him to go off to his own house. And he added, 'Do not so much as enter the village.'

Jesus and his disciples travelled thence to the villages round Caesarea, Philip's city; and on the way he asked his disciples a question: 'Who do people say I am?'

'John the Baptist,' they told him; 'others, Elijah; others again, one of the Prophets.'

'But you?' he asked. 'Who do you say I am?'

It was Peter who answered him. 'You are the Christ,' he said. And Jesus admonished them to tell no one about himself.

He now began to teach them that the Son of Man must of necessity suffer much, be repudiated by the Elders and Chief Priests and Doctors of the Law, be put to death, and after three days live again. He dwelt on this pronouncement in the plainest terms.

Peter took him aside and began to remonstrate with him. But Jesus swung round, and facing his disciples, rebuked Peter. 'Get behind me, Satan!' he said. 'For your thoughts are not God's but the world's.'

He gathered the people and his disciples round him and said: 'If anyone wishes to walk in my footsteps, let him renounce self, take up his cross and follow me. For the man who chooses to save his life will lose it; while he that loses his life for my sake and the gospel's shall save it. What advantage is it to a man to gain the whole world and forfeit his life; or what can a man give that is as precious as his life?

'Indeed, if anyone in this perverted, sinful generation is ashamed of me and my words, the Son of Man will be ashamed of him, when he comes in the glory of his Father with the holy Angels.'

HE also said to them: 'In all truth I tell you, some of these standing here shall not taste death before seeing that the Kingdom of God has come in power.'

Six days later Jesus selected Peter, James and John, and took them up, privately and alone, to the top of a high mountain. There he was transformed before them and his clothes began to glisten with a whiteness such as no fuller on earth could achieve. And now Elijah appeared to them, with Moses – they were talking with Jesus. Whereupon Peter said to Jesus: 'Rabbi, it is a good thing that we are here. Let us make three shelters, one for you, one for Moses and one for Elijah.' He did not know what to do or say, for they were overcome with awe. Then came a cloud which enveloped them, and a voice came out of the cloud: 'This is My son, the Beloved One. Listen to him.'

The next moment looking round they saw no one with them but Jesus.

As they came down from the mountain he impressed it on them that they must describe what they had seen to no one till the Son of Man should have risen from the dead. They seized on these words of his and argued with each other as to what he meant when he spoke of 'rising from the dead'.

They put a question to him. 'Why,' they asked, 'do the Doctors of the Law say that first Elijah must come?'

He replied: 'So Elijah comes first and re-establishes everything? What then does the Scripture mean about the Son of Man having to suffer much and be treated with contempt? No; I say to you, not only has Elijah come, but they have wrought their will on him, as was foretold about him in the Scriptures.'

When they rejoined the other disciples they found them in

the centre of a large crowd, and some Doctors of the Law in altercation with them. Astonished at the sight of Jesus, the whole crowd immediately ran up and welcomed him.

'What are you arguing about with my disciples?' he asked them.

A man answered him out of the crowd: 'Master, I brought my son to you with an evil spirit that makes him dumb. Wherever it seizes him it convulses him – he foams at the mouth, he grinds his teeth, and his body stiffens. I asked your disciples to cast it out, but they had not the power.'

Jesus cried out at them: 'O faithless generation! How much longer must I be with you? How much longer must I bear with you? Bring him to me.'

They brought him, and no sooner did he see Jesus than the spirit rent him. He fell to the ground, and writhed there, foaming at the mouth.

Jesus asked his father: 'How long has this been happening to him?'

'It began when he was a child,' said the father. 'And what is more, it has often driven him into the fire and into the water in order to destroy him. But if you can do anything, have pity on us and help us.'

'*If* I can?' said Jesus. 'Everything is possible for one who has faith.'

The father cried out at once: 'I *have* faith. Help me where it fails.'

Then Jesus, seeing that a number of people were running up to them, rebuked the unclean spirit. 'Deaf and dumb spirit,' he said, '*I* command you, come out of him, and never enter him again.'

The spirit gave a cry, and after rending him repeatedly, came out, leaving him like a corpse, so that most of them said, 'He is dead.' But Jesus, taking him by the hand, raised him, and he stood up.

When he had gone indoors and his disciples had him to

themselves, they asked him: 'Why were we unable to drive it out?'

'This kind,' he said, 'can be cast out only with prayer.'

Leaving that place they travelled through Galilee, and he sought to remain unrecognized, as he was teaching his disciples. 'The Son of Man,' he was telling them, 'is delivered into the hands of men, and they will put him to death; and when he has been put to death, after three days he will come back to life.' But they did not understand what he said and were afraid to question him.

They went into Capernaum, and when he was indoors he asked them what they had been quarrelling about on the road.

They held their tongues, for on the way they had had an argument as to which of them was the greatest. He sat down, called the Twelve to him and said: 'If anyone wishes to be the first, he must be the last of all and the servant of all.'

Then he took a little child, set it down in their midst, and putting his arms round it, said to them: 'Whoever in my name welcomes one such little child, welcomes me; and whoever welcomes me, welcomes not me, but Him that sent me.'

'Master,' said John, 'we saw a man using your name to cast out evil spirits, and tried to stop him since he was not one of us.'

'Do not stop him,' said Jesus. 'No one that uses my name to do a miracle can be quick to slander me. For anyone that is not against us is for us.

'Indeed, whoever gives you a cup of water to drink because you are Christ's, that man, believe me, shall not lose his reward. And as for the man who corrupts one of these little ones that have faith, it would be better for him to have been flung into the sea with a large millstone tied round his neck.

'If your hand leads you into evil, cut it off: it is better for you to come into Life maimed than, with both hands, to depart into hell, into the fire that cannot be put out. And if your foot leads you into evil, cut it off: it is better for you to come into Life crippled than, with both feet, to be cast into hell. And if your eye leads you into evil, pluck it out: it is better for you to come into the Kingdom of God with one eye than, with two, to be cast into hell, where *their worm does not die and the fire is never quenched.*

'Indeed, everyone must be salted with fire. Salt is an excellent thing; but if it loses its quality, with what will you season it? Have salt in yourselves – and be at peace with one another.'

# IO

LEAVING that place, he passed into the region of Judaea and the land beyond the Jordan. Crowds once more collected round him, and again he taught them, as his custom was.

He was approached by some Pharisees with a question. 'Is it lawful,' they asked, 'for a man to divorce his wife?' They were putting him to the proof.

By way of answer he asked them: 'What principle did Moses lay down for you?'

They replied: 'Moses laid down the principle of divorce by writ.'

Jesus then said: 'Moses was allowing for the hardness of your hearts when he laid down that principle for you in writing. But from the very beginning of creation God *made mankind male and female. Because of this a man shall leave his father and mother, and the two shall become one flesh.* This means that they are no longer two persons but one. It follows that man must not part what God has united.'

Back in their lodgings, the disciples questioned him about this matter, and he said: 'The man who divorces his wife and marries again is guilty of adultery against her. And if she marries again after divorcing her husband, she commits adultery.'

They brought him some little children to touch; but the disciples scolded them. When Jesus saw this he was indignant and said to them: 'Let the little children come to me. Do not forbid them; for the Kingdom of God belongs to such. Believe me, the man who does not accept the Kingdom of God like a little child shall certainly not enter it.'

Then, after embracing them, he laid his hands on them and called down blessings upon them.

As he left the house to take the road, a man ran up, knelt before him and put a question to him. 'Good Master,' he said, 'what must I do to come into eternal life?'

'Why do you call me good?' said Jesus. 'No one but God is good. You know the commandments – *Thou shalt not murder; Thou shalt not commit adultery; Thou shalt not steal; Thou shalt not perjure thyself; Thou shalt not commit fraud; Honour thy father and thy mother.*'

'Master,' he replied, 'I have kept all these from boyhood.'

Jesus gazed at him and loved him. He said: 'One thing remains for you to do. Go now, sell everything you have, and give to the poor – you will have treasure in Heaven. Then come and follow me.'

He received these words with a sombre look and went away in gloom, for he was a man of property.

Jesus, with a glance around him, said to his disciples: 'How difficult it is for men of wealth to enter the Kingdom of God!'

His disciples were astonished at his words, and Jesus returned to the matter. 'Children,' he said, 'how difficult it is to enter the Kingdom of God! It is an easier thing for a camel to pass through the eye of a needle than for a rich man to enter the Kingdom of God.'

At this their amazement passed all bounds. 'Then who can be saved?' they asked him.

Jesus, with his eyes upon them, said: 'For men it is impossible, but not for God. Anything is possible for God.'

26

Peter began to say to him: 'Did *we* not give up everything and follow you …?'

Jesus said: 'Hear the truth. There is no one that has given up his house, his brothers, his sisters, his mother, his father, his children, or his fields, for my sake and the gospel's, who shall not receive a hundred times as much, now in the present – houses, brothers, sisters, mothers, children, fields, and persecution too – and in the coming age eternal life. But in many cases the first shall be last and the last shall be first.'

Now they were on the road, travelling up to Jerusalem, and Jesus was walking ahead of them. They went in consternation, and their followers too had their fears. He let the Twelve come up with him once more, and began to tell them what would happen to him. 'You see,' he said; 'we are going up to Jerusalem. The Son of Man will be handed over to the Chief Priests and the Doctors of the Law. They will condemn him to death and give him up to the pagans, who will mock him and spit at him and flog him and put him to death. And after three days he will live again.'

James and John, the sons of Zebedee, approached him and said: 'Master, we beg you to grant us a wish, whatever it may be.'

'What do you wish me to do for you?' said Jesus.

They replied: 'Allow us to sit, one on your right hand and one on your left, in your glory.'

Jesus said: 'You do not know what you are asking for yourselves. Can you drink the cup that I drink, or suffer the baptism that I suffer?'

'We can,' they said.

Then Jesus said to them: 'You shall drink the cup that I drink and suffer the baptism I suffer. But as for the seats on my right hand or my left, they are not mine to bestow, but will be given to those for whom they have been prepared.'

When the Ten heard this, they began to grumble about James and John. But Jesus called them to him and said: 'You know that the acknowledged rulers of the pagans exercise despotic powers and their great men have authority over them. It is not so with you. On the contrary, whoever wishes to prove great among you must be your servant, and whoever wishes to be the first of you must be the slave of all. Look at the Son of Man – *he* did not come to be served, but to serve, and to give up his life in redemption for many.'

They reached Jericho; and as he left the town with his disciples and a large following, there was a blind beggar, Bartimaeus son of Timaeus, sitting by the road. Learning that this was Jesus the Nazarene, he began to cry out: 'Son of David, Jesus, have pity on me!'

A number of people told him to hold his tongue, but this only made him cry out all the more: 'Son of David, have pity on me!'

Jesus stopped and said: 'Call him.'

So they called the blind man. 'All is well,' they said to him. 'Get up: he is calling you.'

Bartimaeus threw off his cloak, leapt to his feet and came to Jesus.

Jesus said to him: 'What do you wish me to do for you?'

'To make me see again, Rabbouni,' said the blind man.

'Go now,' said Jesus. 'Your faith has saved you.'

His sight came back at once and he followed him along the road.

# 11

WHEN they had come as near Jerusalem as Bethphage and Bethany, by the Mount of Olives, he sent two of his disciples ahead, saying to them: 'Go to the village you see over there. As you enter it, the first thing you find will be a tethered colt, which nobody has ridden yet. Untie it and bring it. And if anyone asks you why you are doing this, say, "The Lord needs it and will be sending it back to you at once".'

They went off, found the colt tethered by a doorway in the open street, and untied it. Some of the men who were standing about said: 'What are you doing, untying that colt?' They replied as Jesus had told them, and the men let them go. So they brought the colt to Jesus and spread their cloaks on it; and he mounted it.

Many of the people spread their cloaks on the road; others strewed it with greenery they had cut in the fields. And both those that went in front and those that came behind cried: '*Hosanna! Blessed be he that cometh in the name of the Lord!* Blessed be the coming kingdom of our father David! Hosanna in the Heights!'

So he entered Jerusalem and the temple-enclosure. But after looking round at everything there, he left the city, since it was already late in the day, and went to Bethany with the Twelve.

As they came out of Bethany on the following day he felt hungry, and seeing in the distance a fig-tree already in leaf, he went up to it, hoping, because of the leaves, to find something on it. But when he reached it he found nothing but leaves, for figs were not yet in season; and he dealt with the tree by saying to it: 'May no one ever eat any fruit of yours again.' His disciples heard this.

When they reached Jerusalem he went into the Temple and began to drive out all who were buying and selling in the sacred buildings, and he upset the money-changers' tables and the chairs of the people who were selling the doves. He also forbade anyone to carry household goods through the precinct. And he preached. He said to them: 'Do not the Scriptures say *My House shall be called the House of Prayer for all the nations?* But you have turned it into a robbers' den.'

This came to the ears of the Chief Priests and Doctors of the Law, and they sought ways and means of destroying him.

Indeed, they were afraid of him, since the whole populace marvelled at his teaching.

When evening came they used to withdraw from the city. As they passed along in the morning, they saw the fig-tree withered root and branch. Peter remembered, and said to him: 'See, Rabbi! The fig-tree that you cursed is withered.'

For answer, Jesus said to them: 'Have faith in God. I tell you in all truth that if any man orders this mountain to be removed and cast into the sea, and does not waver in his heart, but believes that what he says is done, it will be done for him. Therefore I say to you, whatever you ask for in your prayers, believe it granted and it will be granted. And whenever you stand and pray, forgive others any wrong they have done you, in order that your Father in Heaven may forgive you your own shortcomings.'

Once more they came into Jerusalem, and as he was walking about in the Temple he was approached by the Chief Priests, the Doctors of the Law and the Elders, who said to him: 'By what authority are you acting? And who gave you the right to do these things?'

Jesus replied: 'I will ask *you* for a statement. Answer me, and I will tell you by what authority I am acting. John's baptism – was it sanctioned by Heaven or by man? Answer me.'

They turned this over in their minds, saying to themselves: 'If we say by Heaven, he will ask us "Why then did you not have faith in him?" But suppose we say by man …?'

They were afraid of the people, for everyone was convinced that John was a prophet. In the end they said to Jesus, 'We do not know.' To which Jesus replied: 'Then I too will not tell you by what authority I am acting.'

He began to address them in parables: 'A man planted a vine-yard, fenced it round, dug a pit for the wine-press, built a watch-tower, and then let it to some farmers and went abroad. At vintage-time he sent a servant to the farmers to collect from them his share of the produce of the vineyard. But they seized and thrashed him and sent him off empty-handed. He sent to them again – this time another servant. But they knocked that one on the head, treating him shamefully. He sent them yet another, whom they killed, and many more, of whom they flogged some and slaughtered others. He still had one whom he could send – his own beloved son – and he sent him to them last of all, thinking "They will respect my son". But these farmers said to one another, "This is the heir. Come, let us kill him, and his inheritance will be ours." So they laid hands on him and killed him, and threw him out of the vineyard.

'What will the owner of the vineyard do? He will come and destroy these farmers and give the vineyard to others. Have you not read even this Scripture: *The stone that the builders rejected has become the headstone of the corner. It was the Lord's doing and admirable in our eyes?*'

They now sought to arrest him, knowing well enough that his parable had been aimed at them. But the crowd alarmed them; so they let him be and withdrew.

Next they sent him some of the Pharisees and partisans of Herod to trap him in argument. These people came and said to him: 'Master, we know that you are honest and afraid of no one, having no regard for persons, but teaching the way of God in all sincerity. Are we justified or not in paying the capitation-tax to Caesar? Should we, or should we not, pay?'

But he, detecting their hypocrisy, replied: 'Why are you putting me to this test? Bring me a shilling to look at.'

They brought one and he asked them: 'Whose portrait and inscription are these?'

'Caesar's,' they told him.

Jesus said: 'Pay Caesar what is due to Caesar, and God what is due to God.' And they marvelled at him.

The next to come to him were some of the Sadducees, who do not believe in the resurrection. They put a question to him. 'Master,' they said, 'Moses laid it down for us that if a man with a brother dies, leaving a widow but no issue, his brother should marry his widow and so provide him with descendants. Now there were seven brothers, the first of whom married and left no issue at his death. The second married his widow and died without issue; and the third did the same. In fact all seven died without issue, and last of all the woman herself died. Whose wife will she be in the resurrection, since she was married to all seven of them?'

Jesus replied: 'Are you not at fault – by reason of your ignorance of the Scriptures and the power of God? When people have risen from the dead, they neither marry nor are given in marriage, but are like Angels in Heaven. But in this matter of the dead and their awakening, have you not read in the Book of Moses, in the chapter on the Bush, how God spoke to him and said, *I, the God of Abraham, and the God of Isaac, and the God of Jacob*? He is not the God of the dead, but of the living. You are indeed at fault.'

One of the Doctors of the Law, who had listened to their interrogation and realized how well Jesus had dealt with them, now came up and asked him: 'Which commandment stands first above everything?'

To this Jesus replied: 'The first is this, *Hearken, Israel; the Lord our God is the one Lord, and thou shalt love the Lord thy God with all thy heart, with all thy soul, with all thy thinking and with all thy power*. And this is the second, *Thou shalt love thy neighbour as thyself*. There is no commandment greater than these.'

'Master,' said the Doctor, 'you have well and truly said that He is One and there is no other than He. To love Him with all one's heart, with all one's understanding, and with all one's power, and to love one's neighbour as oneself is a far greater thing than all holocausts and sacrifices.'

Jesus, seeing what good sense his reply had shown, said to him: 'You are not far from the Kingdom of God.' And no one dared to ask him any further questions.

Jesus, preaching in the Temple, took up another point and said: 'How can the Doctors of the Law maintain that the Messiah is a son of David? David himself, writing as a holy prophet, says, *The Lord said to my Lord* "*Sit on my right hand till I lay thy enemies under thy feet.*" David himself calls him Lord. So how can he be David's son?'

The people in general listened to him gladly. In the course of his teaching he said: 'Be on your guard against the Doctors of the Law, who like to walk about in robes and to be saluted in the streets; who like the best seats in the synagogue and the best places at banquets; who devour the livelihood of widows and seek to justify themselves by making lengthy prayers. Their sentence shall be all the more severe.'

He sat down in view of the Treasury and watched the people throwing money into the offertory chests. There were plenty of rich men who put in a great deal. And one poor widow came who threw in a couple of mites, the equivalent of a farthing. Jesus called his disciples to him and said to them: 'Here is a truth for you. This widow, poor as she is, has put more into the chest than all the others. For they have more than they need, and they gave from that; whereas she, who has less than she needs, threw in everything she had, all she has to live on.'

As he was leaving the Temple, one of his disciples said to him: 'Look, Master. What mighty blocks of stone! What marvellous buildings!'

Jesus said to him: 'You see these great buildings? Not a block of stone here shall be left standing on another. All shall be cast down.'

Later, as he sat in view of the Temple, on the Mount of Olives, Peter, James, John and Andrew questioned him privately. 'Tell us,' they said. 'When is this going to happen? And what portent will there be when all these things are about to take place?'

Jesus began to tell them. 'Take care that no one deceives you. Many will appear and use my name, saying "I am he"; and many people will be led astray by them. And when you hear of wars and rumours of war, do not be alarmed. These things must happen; but that is not the end. For nation will rise against nation, and kingdom against kingdom. There will be earthquakes in one land or another; there will be famines. These are only the beginnings of the birthpangs.

'And you must look to yourselves. They will drag you into court and into synagogues. You will be flogged. You will stand before governors and kings on my account, to vouch for me. And before the end, the gospel must be preached to all the nations.

'When they lead you off under arrest do not be anxious beforehand about how to plead, but use the words that will be put into your mouth when the time comes. For it is not you that speak but the Holy Spirit.

'Men will hand over their brothers for execution, and fathers their children; children will rise against their parents and send them to their death; and you are going to be hated by all men because you use my name. But he that endures to the uttermost will be saved.

'But when you see the *abomination of desolation* standing where he should not be,* let those in Judaea take refuge in the hills; let the man on the housetop not come down and go indoors to save any of his household goods; let the man who is out in the fields not turn back to pick up his cloak.

'Alas, in those days, for a woman with a child in her womb or at her breast! Pray that the thing may not happen in winter. For those days will mean such suffering as there has never been since God first made the world, and will not be again; and if the Lord had not shortened the days, no living thing would have escaped. But He did shorten them, for the sake of his own elect.

'If anyone says to you then, "See, here is the Christ", or "He is there", do not believe him. For false Christs and false prophets will arise and produce miracles and portents in order, if possible, to deceive the elect. You, then, must be on your guard. I have forewarned you of everything.

'But in those days, after that time of tribulation, the sun will be darkened and the moon will not give her light; the stars will come falling from the sky, and the mighty ones in heaven will be shaken. *Then* they will see the Son of Man coming in clouds with great power and glory. Then too he will send out the Angels and gather in his elect from the four winds, from the ends of the earth to the ends of heaven.

'Look to the fig-tree for its lesson. When its shoots grow tender and begin to put out leaves, you know that summer is near. In the same way, when you see all these things happening, you must know that *it* is near, nay, at the very door. Indeed I tell you, this generation shall not pass away till all these things have taken place. Heaven and earth shall pass away, but my words shall not.

* Reader, note this well.

'But of that day or hour no one has knowledge – not even the Angels in Heaven, not even the Son, but only the Father.

'See that you keep awake, since you do not know the appointed time – like the doorkeeper who is told to watch when his master goes abroad from home, delegating his authority to his servants and leaving each to his own task. Watch then, for you do not know when the master of the house is coming back – in the evening, at midnight, at cockcrow or at dawn – or else he may suddenly appear and find you sleeping. And what I say to you I say to everyone: Watch.'

# 14

Now the Passover and the Feast of Unleavened Bread were two days off, and the Chief Priests and Doctors of the Law were eager to get him into their power by a stratagem and so put him to death. For they said: 'We must not do this during the Festival, or the people will riot.'

He was at Bethany in the house of Simon the Leper, and was seated at table, when a woman came with an alabaster jar of true and very costly spikenard ointment, which she poured over his head after breaking the jar. Whereupon some of them exchanged indignant comments. 'Why this waste of the ointment?' they asked. 'That ointment might have fetched three hundred shillings or more, and so been given to the poor.'

They reproved her sharply. But Jesus said: 'Let her be. Why are you scolding her? What she has done to me is a beautiful thing. You have the poor among you always and you can be good to them whenever you wish; but me you have not always. She did what she could – by anointing my body she anticipated my burial. And I tell you in all truth that wherever in the whole world the gospel is preached, the thing this woman did will also be spoken of, so that she shall not be forgotten.'

Judas of Kerioth, one of the Twelve, went to the Chief Priests in order to deliver him into their hands. When they heard what he had to say they were delighted. They undertook to give him money, and he sought an opportune moment to betray him.

On the first day of the Festival of Unleavened Bread, when it was the custom to kill the Paschal lamb, his disciples said to him: 'Where do you wish us to go and arrange for you to eat the Passover?'

He despatched two of his disciples with these instructions: 'Go into the city, and you will be met by a man carrying a jug of water. Follow him, and tell the owner of whatever house he enters that the Master wishes to know which is the room where he will be received and can eat the Passover with his disciples. The man will then show you a large upper room furnished with couches. Make ready for us there.'

The disciples, leaving their quarters, went to the city, found everything as he had told them, and made arrangements for the Passover.

Evening came, and he arrived with the Twelve. They were seated at table and were eating, when Jesus said: 'Hear the truth. One of you is going to betray me – one who eats with me.'

Their hearts sank, and one by one they said to him: 'Surely not I?'

He said: 'One of the Twelve, the man who dips his food with me in the bowl. For the Son of Man goes his way, as the Scriptures say of him. But alas for him through whom the Son of Man is betrayed! Better for that man if he had never been born.'

While they were still at table he took a loaf, blessed God, broke it and gave it to them. 'Take this,' he said; 'it is my body.'

Next he took a cup, gave thanks to God, and handed it to them.

They all drank from it, and he said: 'This is my blood, the blood of the Covenant, which is being shed for many. Indeed I tell you, I shall not again enjoy the fruit of the vine till the day when I drink a new kind of wine in the Kingdom of God.'

Then they sang a psalm and went out to the Mount of Olives. And Jesus said to them: 'You will all renounce your faith. Do not the Scriptures say, *I shall strike the shepherd and his sheep will be scattered*? Nevertheless, when I have risen I will precede you into Galilee.'

But Peter said: 'Even if all renounce their faith, I shall never do so.'

'I assure you,' Jesus said to him, 'that to-day, indeed this very night, before the cock crows twice you will disown me thrice.'

But Peter kept protesting, with increasing vehemence: 'Though I have to die with you, I shall never disown you.' And all the rest said the same.

They came to a place called Gethsemane, and he said to his disciples: 'Sit here till I have prayed.' But he took with him Peter, James and John, and in the consternation and the desolation that came upon him now he said to them: 'My heart is heavy to the point of death. Wait here and stay awake.'

Then he went a little farther, threw himself on the ground, and prayed that if possible the hour might pass from him. 'Abba, Father,' he said, 'all things are possible for thee. Take this cup away from me. Yet not what I will, but what thou wilt.'

Coming back, he found them sleeping and said to Peter: 'Simon, are you asleep? Had you not the strength to stay awake for a single hour? Watch and pray that you may not be brought to ordeal. The spirit is eager, but the flesh is weak.'

Leaving them again, he prayed in the same words. Then he

came back and once more found them sleeping, for their eyes were weighed down. And they had nothing to say for themselves.

He returned a third time, and now he said to them: 'Sleep on then and take your rest. But enough. The hour has come – the Son of Man is handed over to sinners. Up now and let us go. See, my betrayer is near.'

And at once, before he had finished speaking, Judas, one of the Twelve, was there, and with him a force armed with swords and sticks, who had been sent by the Chief Priests and the Doctors of the Law and the Elders.

His betrayer had arranged to give them a signal. 'Your man,' he had said, 'is the one I kiss. Arrest him, and take him safely off.' So the moment he arrived he went up to Jesus, said 'Rabbi', and kissed him; and they laid hands on him and arrested him. But one of those who were standing by him drew his sword and struck the High Priest's slave, shearing off his ear.

Then Jesus spoke. He said to them: 'I see you have come out with swords and sticks to capture me as though I were a brigand. Day after day I was among you in the Temple, teaching, and you did not arrest me. But the Scriptures had to be fulfilled.'

And now they all deserted him and fled. But there was one young man, with nothing on him but a linen wrap, who went along with Jesus. They tried to arrest him, but he left the wrap in their hands and fled naked.

They took Jesus off to the High Priest, and all the Chief Priests, Elders and Doctors of the Law assembled. Peter followed him at a distance to a point within the courtyard of the High Priest's palace. There he sat down with the temple-police and warmed himself in front of the fire.

Meanwhile the Chief Priests and the whole Council were casting about for evidence against Jesus on which they could condemn him to death. But they found none. For although many false witnesses came forward against him, their evidence did not tally. At last some men who were prepared to perjure themselves got up and gave evidence against him to the effect that they themselves had heard him say: 'I will pull down this Temple that is made with hands and in three days build another not made with hands.' But even so their statements did not tally.

Then the High Priest rose and going to the centre questioned Jesus. 'Do you make no reply?' he said. 'What of the evidence these men have given against you?'

But he kept silence and made no reply whatever.

Once more the High Priest put a question to him. 'Are you the Christ,' he asked, 'the son of the Blessed One?'

Jesus said: 'I am. Moreover you shall see the Son of Man sitting at the right hand of the Power and coming with the clouds of Heaven.'

The High Priest tore his clothes and said: 'What further need have we of witnesses? You heard this blasphemy. What is your opinion?' And they all declared he had deserved to die.

Some proceeded to spit at him and to cover his face, to strike him with their fists and tell him to prophesy. And the guard, as they took him into custody, belaboured him.

Now as Peter sat down below in the courtyard, one of the High Priest's maidservants came up, and seeing him warming himself there, looked at him closely and said: 'You too were with that Nazarene, Jesus.'

But Peter denied it. He said: 'I don't know him, and I don't know what you are talking about.' Then he went out into the forecourt, and a cock crew.

The maid saw him there and began once more to say to the bystanders: 'This man is one of *them*.' And again he denied it repeatedly.

Once more, after a little while, the bystanders said to Peter: 'You certainly are one of them. For quite apart from other things, you are a Galilaean.'

Peter began to call down curses on himself and swear that he did not know the man they meant. But at that moment the cock crew for the second time, and Peter, remembering how Jesus had said to him, 'Before the cock crows twice you will disown me thrice', cast all restraint away and wept.

## 15

THE first thing in the morning the Chief Priests held a conference with the Elders and Doctors of the Law; and the whole Council, after binding Jesus, took him off and handed him over to Pilate.

Pilate interrogated him. 'Are *you*,' he said, 'the King of the Jews?'

To which he replied: 'The words are yours.'

The Chief Priests then brought a number of charges against him, and Pilate questioned him again. He said: 'Have you no reply whatever to make? See what a number of charges they are bringing against you.'

But Jesus made no further reply, leaving Pilate at a loss.

On a holiday it was his custom to set free for the people any one prisoner whose life they begged of him. Now there was a man called Barabbas who was then in prison, together with the rioters who had been guilty of murder during the recent disturbance. The crowd came up to Pilate and began asking him to do them his customary favour. Whereupon Pilate asked them if they wished him to release for them the King of the Jews; for he had begun to realize that the hierarchy had brought him up for judgement because they were jealous. But the Chief Priests incited the people to ask him to give them Barabbas rather than Jesus.

'In that case,' said Pilate, addressing them once more, 'what am I to do with the man you call King of the Jews?'

'Crucify him!' they shouted back.

'But what crime has he committed?' Pilate asked them – which only made them shout still louder, 'Crucify him'.

Then Pilate, anxious to appease the mob, set Barabbas free for them; and after having Jesus flogged, he handed him over for crucifixion.

The soldiers took him into the palace, that is to say the Residence, and called the whole detachment together. They clothed him in purple, plaited a garland of thorns, put it on him, and then saluted him – 'Hail, King of the Jews!' They beat his head with a cane and spat at him; they knelt down and did him homage. Then, their mockery of him finished, they took the purple off him and dressed him in his own clothes.

And now they took him out to crucify him; and to carry his cross, they impressed a man called Simon, a Cyrenaean, who was passing by on his way in from the country – he was the father of Alexander and Rufus. Thus they brought him to the place called Golgotha, which means the Place of the Skull.

They offered him wine drugged with myrrh, but he refused it. Then they crucified him, and parcelled out his clothes, casting lots for them to see what each should have.

It was the third hour when they crucified him. The charge against him was set forth in writing on a placard, which read *The King of the Jews*. And with him they crucified two robbers, one on his right, the other on his left.

People passing by reviled him. They shook their heads and said: 'Aha! You that pull down the Temple and in three days build it up again, come down now from the cross and save yourself.' So too the Chief Priests, with the Doctors of the Law, exchanged derisive comments. 'He saved others,' they said, 'but he cannot save himself. Let Christ the King of Israel come down now from the cross so that we may see and believe.' Those also who were crucified with him flung taunts at Jesus.

When the sixth hour came there was darkness over the whole country, and it lasted till the ninth. And at the ninth hour Jesus cried out in a loud voice, *Eloi, Eloi, lama sabachthani*, which means, 'My God, my God, why hast thou forsaken me?'

Some of the bystanders, when they heard this, said, 'See; he is calling on Elijah'; and one man ran and soaked a sponge in vinegar, put it on a cane and offered it to him, saying, 'Wait now, and let us see if Elijah comes to take him down.'

But Jesus gave a loud cry and breathed his last; and the curtain of the Temple was torn in two from top to bottom.

The centurion who was standing by in full view of Jesus, seeing his death and the manner of it, said: 'This man was indeed a son of God.'

Watching from afar there were some women too, including Mary Magdalene, Mary the mother of the younger James and Joses, and Salome, who had followed him when he was in Galilee and ministered to his wants; also a number of other women who had travelled up with him to Jerusalem.

It was now late in the day, and as it was the Eve, that is the day before the Sabbath, Joseph of Arimathaea, a Councillor of good standing who was himself in search of the Kingdom of God, went and made his way boldly into Pilate's presence and asked him for the body of Jesus. Pilate wondered whether he could have died so soon. He summoned the centurion and asked him whether he was already dead; and having ascertained the fact from him, he granted Joseph the corpse. Joseph bought some linen, took him down from the cross, wrapped him in the linen and laid him in a tomb that had been cut out of the rock. And he rolled a stone against the entrance of the tomb. Mary Magdalene and Mary the mother of Joses observed the spot where he was laid.

# 16

THE Sabbath passed, and Mary Magdalene, Mary the mother of James, and Salome, bought spices with which they might go and anoint him. Starting very early on the first day of the week they reached the tomb as the sun rose. They had been saying to one another, 'Who will roll the stone away for us from the mouth of the tomb?' Now, they looked up and saw that the stone, which was a very large one, had been rolled back. They entered the tomb, and there, sitting on the right, they saw a young man dressed in a white robe. They were overcome with fear. But he said to them: 'Do not be afraid. Are you looking for Jesus the Nazarene, who was crucified? He has risen: he is not here. See the place where they laid him. But go now and tell his disciples and Peter that he is preceding them to Galilee, where they will see him, as he told them.'

The women came out and fled from the tomb, for trembling and ecstasy had come upon them. They said not a word to anyone, because they feared ...

[Having risen in the morning of the first day of the week, he appeared first to Mary Magdalene, from whom he had cast out seven demons. She went and brought the news to those who had been with him, as they mourned and wept. But they, when they were told that he lived and had been seen by her, did not believe it.

Thereafter he appeared in a different form to two of them as they were walking along on their way into the country; and they went and brought the news to the rest, who did not believe them either.

Later he appeared to the Eleven themselves as they sat at table, and censured their lack of faith and hardness of heart, which had made them disbelieve those who had seen him after he had risen.

And he said to them: 'Go into every part of the world and preach the Gospel to the whole creation. He who has faith and is baptized shall be saved, but he who has no faith shall be condemned. And these are the miracles that will ensue for those that have faith: in my name they will cast out evil spirits; they will speak in strange tongues; they will pick up snakes in their hands; and if they drink poison, it will not hurt them at all. They will lay their hands on the sick and they will be well.'

So then the Lord Jesus, after he had spoken to them, was taken up into Heaven and sat at the right hand of God. They, meanwhile, went forth and preached everywhere, the Lord labouring with them and confirming the Word by the miracles that attested their work.]

# THE GOSPEL AS RECORDED BY
# MATTHEW

THE GENEALOGY OF JESUS CHRIST SON OF DAVID SON OF ABRAHAM · Abraham was the father of Isaac; Isaac of Jacob; and Jacob of Judah and his brothers. Judah was the father of Pharez and Zarah, by Thamar; Pharez of Hezron; Hezron of Aram; Aram of Aminadab; Aminadab of Naashon; Naashon of Salmon; Salmon of Boaz, by Rahab; Boaz of Obed, by Ruth; Obed of Jesse; and Jesse of David the King.

David was the father of Solomon, by Uriah's wife. Solomon was the father of Rehoboam; Rehoboam of Abijah; Abijah of Asa; Asa of Jehoshaphat; Jehoshaphat of Jehoram; Jehoram of Uzziah; Uzziah of Jotham; Jotham of Ahaz; Ahaz of Hezekiah; Hezekiah of Manasseh; Manasseh of Amon; Amon of Josiah; and Josiah of Jeconiah and his brothers – at the time of the Babylonian Captivity.

After the Captivity – Jeconiah was the father of Salathiel; Salathiel of Zerubbabel; Zerubbabel of Abihud; Abihud of Eliakim; Eliakim of Azzur; Azzur of Zadok; Zadok of Achim; Achim of Eliud; Eliud of Eleazar; Eleazar of

47

Matthan; Matthan of Jacob; and Jacob of Joseph, the husband of Mary, who gave birth to Jesus, who is known as Christ.

Thus there were in all fourteen generations from Abraham to David; fourteen from David to the Babylonian Captivity; and fourteen from the Captivity to the Christ.

The birth of Jesus Christ took place in this manner. When his mother Mary had been betrothed to Joseph, it was discovered, before they lived together, that she had conceived to the Holy Spirit. Her husband Joseph, being a man of principle and not wishing to proclaim her guilt, had it in mind to repudiate her privately. He was pondering this step, when a Messenger of the Lord appeared to him in a dream and said: 'Joseph, son of David, do not be afraid to take your wife Mary into your home; for what she has conceived is of the Holy Spirit. She will bear a son and you shall call him Jesus, for it is he who will save his people from their sins. *

Joseph awoke and did as the Angel of the Lord had told him. He took his wife to his home and did not sleep with her till she had borne a son, to whom he gave the name of Jesus.

## 2

AT the time of Jesus's birth, which took place at Bethlehem in Judaea in the reign of Herod the King, there came to Jerusalem some Wise Men from the East. 'Where is the child,' they asked, 'who is born King of the Jews? We saw his star rise and have come to pay him homage.'

* All this took place in order that the words spoken by the Lord through his Prophet might be fulfilled: '*Behold, the maiden shall conceive and bear a son, whom they shall call Emmanuel.*' The meaning of *Emmanuel* is 'God with us.'

When King Herod heard this he was perturbed, and so was all Jerusalem. He gathered together all the Chief Priests and the Doctors of the Law. 'Where,' he asked them, 'is the Christ to be born?' And when they told him that the place was Bethlehem in Judaea,* he called the Wise Men to him secretly, and having ascertained from them the time when the star had appeared, he sent them to Bethlehem with orders to discover the truth in this matter of the child. He said: 'When you have found him, report to me, so that I too may go and pay him homage.'

They set out in obedience to the king, and the star they had seen at its rising led the way for them till it stood over the place where the baby lay. They were overwhelmed with joy at the sight of the star and went into the house, where they found the child with his mother Mary. They prostrated themselves and did homage to him; they opened their caskets and laid before him gifts of gold and frankincense and myrrh. Then they returned to their own country by a different way, having been warned in a dream not to go back to Herod.

After they had left, a Messenger of the Lord appeared to Joseph in a dream and said: 'Awake, and flee into Egypt, taking the child and his mother with you. And stay there till I bring you word; for Herod intends to seek out and destroy the child.' Joseph awoke, took the child and its mother away with him by night and withdrew to Egypt, where he remained until the death of Herod.†

Now Herod was extremely angry when he realized that the Wise Men had played him false. He sent out troops and killed all the children of two or less in Bethlehem and the

---

* Referring him to the Prophet's words: 'And thou, Bethlehem in Juda, art by no means the least among the foremost in Juda, for out of thee shall come a leader who will shepherd my people Israel.'

† So that the words spoken by the Lord through his Prophet, I have called my son from Egypt, might be fulfilled.

whole neighbourhood, reckoning from the date he had ascertained from the Wise Men.*

But after Herod's death an Angel of the Lord appeared in a dream to Joseph in Egypt and said: 'Awake, take the child and his mother with you and go to the land of Israel; for those who wished to take the child's life are dead.' Joseph awoke, took the child and its mother with him and came to the land of Israel. But hearing that Archelaus had succeeded his father Herod as king of Judaea, he was afraid to enter that country. He was warned in a dream, and withdrew into the district of Galilee, where he settled in a town called Nazareth.†

# 3

IT was in those days that John the Baptist began his mission. He preached in the waste lands of Judaea and called on people for a change of heart, saying: 'The Kingdom of Heaven is near, for here is he who was spoken of through the Prophet Isaiah when he said, *The voice of one crying in the wilderness, Prepare the way of the Lord: make his paths straight.*'

John the Baptist wore clothing made of camel-hair, with a leather belt round his waist, and he fed on locusts and wild honey. All Jerusalem and Judaea went out to him, and all the people of the Jordan Valley. They openly confessed their sins and he baptized them in the River Jordan. But observing that

---

* It was then that the words spoken through the Prophet Jeremiah found their fulfilment:

> A voice was heard in Ramah –
> Wailing and loud laments.
> 'Twas Rachel weeping for her children,
> Inconsolably, for they are gone.

† So that the words spoken through the Prophets, *He shall be called a Nazarene*, might be fulfilled.

a number of Pharisees and Sadducees were coming to attend this baptism, he said to them:

'Offspring of vipers, who warned you to fly from the wrath that is on its way? First you must prove your repentance by your deeds. And do not cherish the thought that you have Abraham for father; for I tell you that God could raise children for Abraham from these very stones. But time is short, the axe lies ready at the root of the trees, and in the end every tree that does not bear good fruit is cut down and thrown into the fire.

'I baptize you in water, into repentance. But he that comes after me is greater than I, who am not fit to carry his sandals. He will baptize you in the Holy Spirit and fire. His winnowing-fan is in his hand. He will clear his threshing-floor and gather his grain into the barn; but the chaff he will burn in inextinguishable fire.'

Jesus now came from Galilee to the Jordan and went to John to be baptized by him. But John sought to dissuade him.

'Do you come to *me*?' he said. 'It is I who need to be baptized by you.'

To which Jesus replied: 'Consent now. It behoves us to conform with all right usage.' And John consented.

Jesus was baptized, and he had no sooner come up out of the water than the heavens were laid open and he saw the Spirit of God descending like a dove and coming upon him. There was a voice too from the heavens, which said: 'This is My son, the Beloved One, in whom I rejoice.'

# 4

JESUS was now led by the Spirit up into the desert to be tempted by the Devil. When he had abstained from food for forty days and nights and so was starving, the Tempter approached him and said: 'If you are son of God, order these stones to be turned into loaves.' Jesus replied by citing the Scripture: *Man shall not live on bread alone but on every word that issues from the mouth of God.*

Next, the Devil took Jesus with him to the Holy City, where he made him stand on the cornice of the Temple and said: 'If you are son of God, throw yourself down; for the Scriptures say *He will put his angels in charge of thee and they shall hold thee up on their hands, lest thou dash thy foot against a stone.*' Jesus answered: 'The Scriptures also say *Thou shalt not put the Lord thy God to the proof.*'

Again, the Devil took him to a very high mountain and showed him all the kingdoms of the world and their glory. 'All this,' he said, 'I will give you, if you prostrate yourself and do me homage.' Then Jesus said to him: 'Satan, be gone. For the Scriptures say, *Thou shalt do homage to the Lord thy God and serve him only.*' Thereupon the Devil let him be, and Angels came and ministered to his wants.

When he heard that John had been arrested he withdrew into Galilee. Leaving Nazareth he went and settled in Capernaum, which is by the sea, in the territory of Zabulon and Naphthali.* And now Jesus began to preach and call on people for a change of heart. 'For the Kingdom of Heaven,' he said, 'is near.'

As he was walking by the Sea of Galilee, he saw two brothers, Simon, who was called Peter, and his brother Andrew. They were fishermen and were casting a net into the sea. 'Come, follow me,' he said to them, 'and I will make you fishers of men.' They left their nets at once and followed him.

Walking on, he saw another pair of brothers, James son of Zebedee and his brother John, in the boat with Zebedee their

---

* So that the words spoken through the Prophet Isaiah might be fulfilled: *Land of Zabulon and land of Naphthali, over by the sea, beyond the Jordan, Galilee of the Gentiles – the people that sat in darkness saw a great light; and a light rose on them that sat in the shadowy region of death.*

father, putting their nets in order. He called them, and they immediately left the boat and their father, and followed him.

He went round the whole of Galilee teaching in their synagogues, proclaiming the good tidings of the Kingdom, and curing every sort of illness and infirmity among the people. His fame spread through the whole of Syria. They brought him all that were sick and suffering from this or that disorder and affliction, the demoniacs, the lunatics, the paralytics – and he cured them. He was followed by large crowds from Galilee and the Ten Towns, from Jerusalem and Judaea, and from beyond the Jordan.

# 5

SEEING the crowds, he went up into the hills. There he sat down and his disciples gathered round him. Then he began to speak and taught them in these words:

'Happy the poor in the spirit; for theirs is the Kingdom of Heaven.

'Happy those that mourn; for they shall be comforted.

'Happy the gentle; for they shall inherit the earth.

'Happy those that hunger and thirst for righteousness; for they shall be satisfied.

'Happy those that show mercy; for mercy shall be shown to them.

'Happy the pure in heart; for they shall see God.

'Happy the peace-makers; for they shall be called sons of God.

'Happy those that have been persecuted for righteousness; for theirs is the Kingdom of Heaven.

'Count yourselves happy when the time comes for people to revile you and maltreat you and utter every kind of calumny against you on account of me. Rejoice and glory in these things, since your reward is great in Heaven. Was it not thus that they persecuted the Prophets before you?

'You are the salt of the earth. But if the salt loses its quality, what can make it salt again? It is good for nothing after that but to be thrown away and trampled underfoot.

'You are the light of the world. A city built on a hill-top cannot be concealed.

'Again, people do not light a lamp and put it under the measuring-bowl, but on its stand, where it gives light to everyone in the house. Let your light so shine upon the world that it may see the beauty of your life and give glory to your Father in Heaven.

'Do not imagine that I came to abolish the Law or the Prophets. I came, not to annul them, but to bring them to perfection. For I tell you in all truth, while heaven and earth remain, the Law shall not be docked of one letter or one comma till its purpose is achieved. Therefore the man who abolishes one of these little rules and teaches people to forget it shall count for little in the Kingdom of Heaven; whereas the man who acts and teaches in accordance with them shall count for much in the Kingdom of Heaven. Believe me, if you do no better than the Doctors and Pharisees in your observance of the Law, you shall certainly not enter the Kingdom of Heaven.

'You have been told that our forefathers were given the commandment, *Thou shalt not murder*, and that all murderers are answerable to the law. I go further and I say to you that anyone who is angry with his brother is answerable too; that anyone who reviles his brother is liable to find himself in court; that anyone who calls him fool is liable to find himself condemned to hell.

'If then you bring your offering to the altar and there remember that your brother has a grudge against you, leave your offering there before the altar, go and make friends with your brother first, and then come back and offer your gift.

'Come to terms with your accuser quickly, while you are on your way with him to court; or he may hand you over to the judge, and the judge hand you over to the warder, and you be thrown into prison. Indeed I tell you, you shall not come out of it till you have paid the last farthing.

'You have heard the commandment, *Thou shalt not commit adultery*. But I say to you that any man who looks at a woman with desire has already in his heart committed adultery with her.

'If your right eye leads you into evil, pluck it out and throw it away. It is better for you that one part of you should be lost than that your whole body should be cast into hell. And if your right hand leads you into evil, cut it off and throw it away. It is better for you that one of your limbs should be lost than that your whole body should descend to hell.

'It has been laid down that when a man divorces his wife he shall give her a writ to that effect. But I say to you that when a man divorces his wife for anything but fornication he causes her to commit adultery; and the man who marries a divorced woman commits adultery.

'Again, you know that our forefathers were told, *Thou shalt not swear falsely, but shalt fulfil thine oaths to the Lord*. But I tell you not to swear at all, neither by Heaven, because it is the throne of God; nor by the earth, because it is his footstool; nor by Jerusalem, because it is the Great King's city. Nor should you swear by your own head, since you have not the power to make a single hair white or black. It is enough for you to say "Yes, yes," "No, no." Anything beyond this is rooted in evil.

'You have heard of the principle, *An eye for an eye and a tooth for a tooth*. But I say to you, Do not resist evil. If anyone strikes you on the right cheek, turn the left towards him also. If anyone sees fit to sue you for your tunic, let him have your cloak as well. If anyone impresses you to go a mile, go along with him for two. Give to the man that asks you;

and from one who wants to borrow from you do not turn away.

'You have heard it said, *Thou shalt love thy neighbour and hate thine enemy.* But I say to you, Love your enemies and pray for those that persecute you, so that you may become children of your Father in Heaven, who causes his sun to rise on the wicked and the good, and rains on the just and the unjust alike.

'For if you love the people who love you, what reward do you get? Do not even tax-collectors do as much? And if you are gracious to your brothers only, what special goodness have you shown? Do not even pagans show as much?

'You then must be perfect, as your Father in Heaven is perfect.

# 6

'BE careful not to exercise your virtues in public with a view to being seen, or you will get no reward from your Father in Heaven. When you give alms, do not do it with a flourish of trumpets, as the hypocrites do in the synagogues and streets, so that people may think well of them. Believe me, they have had their reward. But when you practise charity, do not let your left hand know what your right hand is doing, so that your charity may be in secret; and your Father who sees in secret will render you your due.

'Again, when you pray, do not behave like the hypocrites, who like to stand and pray in the synagogues and at the street corners, so that people may see them. Believe me, they have had their reward. But when you wish to pray, enter your private room and when you have shut your door pray to your Father who dwells in secret; and your Father who sees in secret will render you your due.

'In your prayers, do not rely on empty repetition, as the

pagans do, thinking that their many words will ensure them hearing. Do not copy them, for God your Father knows your wants before you ask him. This then is how *you* should pray:

> Our Father in Heaven,
> Thy Name be hallowed;
> Thy Kingdom come;
> Thy will be done;
> As in Heaven, so on earth;
> Give us the bread of life to-day;
> And forgive us our debts,
> As we have forgiven our debtors;*
> And do not bring us to ordeal;
> But save us from evil.
> [For Thine is the kingdom, the power and the glory,
> Into the ages. Amen.]

'When you fast, do not look gloomy like the hypocrites, who disfigure their faces so that people may see that they are fasting – and believe me, they have had their reward. But when you fast, put oil on your head and wash your face, so that you may not appear to others to be fasting, but only to your Father who dwells in secret; and your Father who sees in secret will render you your due.

'Do not amass for yourselves treasure on earth, where moth and rust destroy, and thieves break in and steal. But amass for yourselves treasure in Heaven, where neither moth nor rust destroys, and thieves do not break in and steal. For where your treasure is, there your heart will be also.

'The lamp of the body is the eye. So, if your eye is sound, your whole body will be bright. But if your eye is evil, your whole body will be dark. And if the light in you is darkness, how great the dark will be!

* Jesus added in explanation, 'If you forgive other people their shortcomings, your Heavenly Father will forgive you yours; but if you do not forgive other people their shortcomings, your Father will not forgive yours either.'

'No one can be the slave of two masters. Either he will hate the one and love the other, or he will cling to one and despise the other. You cannot be a slave to God and Mammon too.

'I bid you therefore not to fret about your lives, and what to eat and drink; nor about your bodies, and what to put on them. Is not life more than food, and the body more than clothing? Look at the birds of the sky. They neither sow nor reap, nor bring the harvest into barns; and yet your Heavenly Father feeds them. Are you not of greater consequence than they?

'Can any one of you by fretting add a moment to his years? Then why be troubled about clothes? Learn from the lilies of the fields and how they grow. They do no work, they do not spin. But I tell you that not even Solomon in all his glory was robed like one of these. And if God so clothes the grass of the fields, which is there to-day and thrown into the oven to-morrow, will he not all the more clothe you, slow though you are to trust him?

'Then do not fret and say, "What are we going to eat or drink?" or "What will there be for us to wear?" - things that the pagan world pursues - for your Heavenly Father knows that all these things are your necessities. No; pursue the Kingdom and God's goodness first, and these things too will all be yours.

'Do not then be anxious about to-morrow, for to-morrow will look after itself. To-day's trouble is enough for to-day.

# 7

'Do not judge, lest you be judged. For you will be judged by the standards you yourselves apply; and as you give, so you will receive, measure for measure.

'Why do you note the little splinter in your brother's eye,

and take no notice of the beam in yours? How can you say to your brother, "Let me remove the splinter from your eye," while all the time you have that beam in yours? Hypocrite, begin by removing the beam from your own eye, and then you will see clearly enough to pull the splinter out of your brother's.

'Do not give holy things to dogs, nor scatter your pearls in front of swine, or they may trample them underfoot, and turn and tear you to pieces.

'Ask and you shall receive. Seek and you shall find. Knock and the door shall be opened to you. For everyone that asks receives; every seeker finds; and to everyone that knocks the door is opened. After all, would any man among you hand his son a stone when he asks for a loaf of bread; or a snake when he asks for a fish? Well then, if you that are evil know how to give your children what is good, how much more will your Father in Heaven give good things to those that ask him.

'In all respects then, treat your fellowmen as you would wish them to treat you. The Law and the Prophets are summed up in this.

'Come in by the narrow gate, for the way to destruction is a broad and open road which is trodden by many; whereas the way to life is by a narrow gate and a difficult road, and few are those that find it.

'Beware of false prophets, who come to you in sheep's clothing but underneath are ravening wolves. You will know them by their fruits; for people surely do not go to thorns for grapes, or to thistles for figs? Every good tree bears fine fruit, and a rotten tree bears bad fruit. A good tree *cannot* bear bad fruit, nor can a rotten tree bear fine fruit. Every tree that does not bear fine fruit is cut down and thrown on the fire. You see then that you will know them by their fruits.

'Not everyone that says Lord, Lord, to me shall come into the Kingdom of Heaven, but only he that does the will of my Father in Heaven. Many will say to me, when the Day comes,

"Lord, Lord, did we not prophesy in your name, cast out demons in your name, and in your name do many miracles?" Then I shall let them hear the truth: "At no time did I recognize you. *Depart from me, ye workers of iniquity.*"

'Anyone then who listens to these sayings of mine and acts accordingly may be compared to the prudent man who built his house on rock. The rain fell, the rivers rose, the winds blew. They beat upon the house; but the house did not fall, for it was founded on rock. And anyone who listens to these sayings of mine and does not act accordingly will be like the foolish man who built his house on sand. The rain fell, the rivers rose, the winds blew. They stormed against the house; it fell; and what a fall it had!'

When Jesus came to the end of this discourse, the people were filled with amazement at his teaching; for he taught them like one with authority and not like the Doctors who usually taught them.

# 8

WHEN he came down from the hills, he was followed by large crowds. And there suddenly appeared a leper, who approached him and did obeisance, saying, 'Lord, if you will, you can cleanse me.'

Jesus stretched out his hand, touched him and said: 'I will it. Be cleansed.' And his leprosy was cleansed immediately.

Jesus said to him: 'See that you tell no one, but go and show yourself to the priest and make the offering which Moses prescribed so that people might be notified.'

As he came into Capernaum he was approached by a centurion begging him for help. 'Lord,' he said, 'my boy at home has been struck down – by paralysis – he is in agony.'

Jesus said: 'Am *I* to come and heal him?'

'Lord,' replied the centurion, 'I am not worthy to receive you under my roof. But you have only to say the word and my boy will be cured. For I too am a man who derives his powers from above, with soldiers under me; and I say to this one, Go, and he goes; to another, Come, and he comes; and to my slave, Do this, and he does it.'

When he heard this, Jesus was amazed and said to those that followed him: 'I can say in all truth that nowhere in Israel have I found such faith. And I tell you that many will come from the rising and the setting sun and sit down to banquet with Abraham, Isaac and Jacob in the Kingdom of Heaven; while the heirs of the Kingdom shall be cast into the outer darkness, where there will be weeping and gnashing of teeth.'

To the centurion, Jesus said: 'Go now; and your reward shall be equal to your faith.' And in that very hour his boy was cured.

Coming into Peter's house, Jesus found Peter's mother-in-law prostrated by fever. He took her hand, the fever left her, and she rose and began to wait on him.

Evening came, and they brought him a number of people possessed by evil spirits. He cast out the spirits with a word, and he healed all those who were sick.★

When Jesus saw what crowds surrounded him, he gave the order to cross over to the other shore. But now one of the Doctors of the Law came forward and said to him: 'Master, I will follow you wherever you are going.'

Jesus replied: 'Foxes have holes, and the birds of the sky have nests, but the Son of Man has nowhere to lay his head.'

Another of his pupils said to him: 'Lord, give me leave to go and bury my father first.'

'Follow me,' Jesus answered; 'and let the dead bury their dead.'

Jesus embarked and his disciples followed him on board.

★ So that the words spoken through the Prophet Isaiah might be fulfilled: *He took our infirmities on himself and bore our diseases.*

Out at sea there was a great storm: the ship was hidden by the waves. But Jesus slept.

They went and woke him. 'Lord,' they said, 'save us! We are lost.'

Jesus said: 'Why are you such cowards? How little faith you have!' Then he stood up and rebuked the wind and the sea; and a great calm ensued.

The men were amazed. They said: 'What kind of man is this whom even winds and sea obey?'

He reached the farther shore, and had landed in the country of the Gadarenes, when he was confronted by two men who were possessed by demons. They came out of the tombs and were so savage that nobody could pass that way. Now they cried out at him: 'Son of God, what is your business with us? Have you come here, before the time, to torment us?'

A large herd of pigs was feeding some way off, and the demons begged him, if he cast them out, to despatch them into the herd.

'Be gone!' he said to them. And they came out and went off into the pigs, with the result that the whole herd charged down the cliff into the sea and perished in the water. The herdsmen took to their heels and fled to the town, where they told the people everything, including what had happened to the demoniacs. The whole town turned out to meet Jesus, and when they found him they besought him to remove himself from their neighbourhood.

# 9

HE embarked, crossed over and came to his own town. And now they brought him a paralytic laid out on a bed. Seeing their faith, Jesus said to the paralytic: 'Take heart, my child: your sins have been forgiven.'

Whereupon some of the Doctors of the Law said to themselves, 'The man is blaspheming.' But Jesus, who knew their thoughts, said: 'Why are you thinking evil? Which is the easier thing, to say "Your sins have been forgiven", or to say "Get up and walk"? However, to teach you that the Son of Man has authority on earth to forgive sins' – and he turned to the paralytic – 'Get up, take your bed and go home.'

The man got up and went home; and the people seeing this were filled with awe, and praised God for giving such authority to men.

Passing on, Jesus saw a man called Matthew sitting by the custom-house and said to him: 'Follow me.' And he rose and followed him.

So it came about that Jesus sat down to a meal in this man's house, and a number of tax-collectors and outcasts came and joined him and his disciples at table. The Pharisees saw this and said to his disciples: 'Why does your master eat and drink with tax-collectors and outcasts?'

When he heard this, he said: 'It is not the healthy who need a physician, but the sick. Go and learn the meaning of the words *I set my heart on mercy, not on sacrifice.* I am here to summon sinners, not the righteous.'

John's disciples now came to him and said: 'How is it that we and the Pharisees fast a great deal, whereas your disciples do not fast?'

Jesus replied: 'Surely the friends of the bridegroom cannot mourn as long as the bridegroom is with them? But a time will come when the bridegroom is taken from them. Then they will fast.

'Nobody mends an old cloak with a piece of new cloth, for the new piece would drag on it, and the result be a bigger rent. Nor do people pour new wine into old skins; or the skins burst, the wine runs out, and the skins are lost. Instead, they pour new wine into fresh skins, and both are saved.'

He was speaking to them of these matters when one of the

Elders came up, did obeisance to him and said: 'My daughter has just died; but come and lay your hand on her and she will live.'

Jesus rose and went with him, followed by his disciples. But now a woman who had suffered from a hemorrhage for twelve years came up behind him and touched the tassel on his cloak, saying to herself, 'If I can only touch his cloak, I shall be saved.'

Jesus swung round, saw her, and said: 'Take heart, my daughter. Your faith has saved you.' And from that moment she was saved.

Coming to the Elder's house Jesus found the flute-players and a number of other people making a din. 'Away with you!' he said. 'The little girl is not dead but asleep.'

They laughed at him. But when the people had been sent away, he went in and seized her hand. The little girl returned to life; and before long everyone in all the country round had heard the tale.

When Jesus left the place he was pursued by two blind men crying, 'Son of David, have pity on us!'

They came up to him when he reached his house, and he said to them: 'Have you faith in my power to cure you?'

'Yes, Lord,' they answered.

Then he touched their eyes and said: 'Your reward shall be equal to your faith.' And their eyes were opened.

Jesus sternly forbade them to let anyone know. But they left the town and sang his praises to everybody in the country-side.

These two were no sooner out of the house than a dumb man with a demon in him was brought to Jesus. The demon was cast out and the dumb man spoke. This so amazed the people that they said, 'Never have such things been seen in Israel.' But the Pharisees began to say, 'It is through their Prince that he casts demons out.'

Jesus made a tour of all the towns and villages, teaching in their synagogues, announcing the good news of the Kingdom, and curing every kind of illness and infirmity. He was moved to compassion for them when he saw the people distraught and foundering, like sheep without a shepherd; and he said to his disciples; 'The harvest is plentiful, but the labourers are few. Ask the Lord of the Harvest to send out labourers to reap it for him.'

# IO

HE summoned his twelve disciples and gave them authority to cast out unclean spirits and to cure every kind of illness and infirmity.

Here are the names of the twelve apostles – first, Simon who was known as Peter, and his brother Andrew; James son of Zebedee, and his brother John; Philip and Bartholomew; Thomas and Matthew the customs-officer; James son of Alphaeus, and Thaddaeus; Simon the Zealot, and Judas of Kerioth, the man through whose treachery he was arrested.

These are the twelve men whom Jesus sent out on a mission; and these are the instructions he gave them:

'Do not stray into the pagan lands; and go into no Samaritan city. Go rather to the lost sheep of the House of Israel. And wherever you go, let it be known that the Kingdom of Heaven is near.

'Cure the sick, bring back the dead to life, cleanse lepers, cast demons out.

'You did not pay for what you were given: take no pay for what you give.

'Provide yourselves with no gold, no silver, no copper for your purse; no knapsack for the road; no second tunic; no sandals; no staff. The workman earns his keep.

'When you come to a town or village, find out which of

its folk is worthy, and stay with him till you leave the place. As you enter the house, greet it. If the house is worthy, let your blessing be upon it. If not, let it come back and be with you.

'If anyone does not welcome you or will not listen to your words, leave his house or town, and as you do so shake the dust from your feet. Believe me, the land of Sodom and Gomorrha will have less to suffer on the day of judgement than that town.

'Know that I am sending you out like sheep among wolves. So be cunning as snakes, and innocent as doves.

'Be on your guard against mankind. They will drag you into court, and scourge you in their synagogues. You will even be haled before governors and kings on my account, to vouch for me to them and to the pagans. But when they bring you up for trial, do not give anxious thought to the manner and wording of your defence. When the moment comes, the words will be put into your mouth. For it is not you that speak, but the Spirit of your Father that speaks in you.

'Men will hand over their brothers for execution, and fathers their sons; children will rise against their parents and send them to their death; and you are going to be hated by all men because you use my name. But he that endures to the uttermost will be saved.

'When they persecute you in one city, take refuge in the next; for I tell you in all truth that you will not have passed through all the cities of Israel before the coming of the Son of Man.

'A pupil does not rise above his teacher, nor a slave above his master; it is enough for the pupil to be like his teacher and the slave like his master. If people called the master of the house Beelzebub, will they not vilify his household even more?

'Then do not be afraid of them. Nothing is hidden that

shall not be disclosed; nothing secret that shall not be known. Utter in daylight what I tell you in the dark; and proclaim on the housetops what you have heard in whispers.

'Do not be frightened by people who kill the body but cannot kill the soul. Fear rather Him that can destroy both soul and body in hell.

'Is it not true that two sparrows are sold for a penny and one of them shall not fall dead without your Father? But every single hair upon *your* heads is numbered. Cease then to fear: you are more valuable than many sparrows.

'Therefore I say, Let anybody tell the world that he is mine, and I will tell my Heavenly Father I am his. But the man who disowns me to the world I will disown before my Heavenly Father.

'Do not imagine that I have come to bring peace on earth. I have not come to bring peace but a sword. Indeed I have come to sow discord between a man and his father, between a daughter and her mother, and between a daughter-in-law and her mother-in-law. His own household will be a man's enemies.

'The man who loves father or mother more than me is not worthy of me; he that loves son or daughter more than me is not worthy of me; and he that does not take his cross and follow in my steps is not worthy of me.

'He that wins his life will lose it, and he that loses his life for my sake shall win it.

'He that welcomes you welcomes me, and he that welcomes me welcomes Him that sent me forth.

'The man who welcomes a prophet because he *is* a prophet shall have a prophet's reward; the man who welcomes a good man because he *is* a good man shall have a good man's reward; and the man who gives so much as a cup of cold water to one of these little ones because he *is* a disciple, that man, believe me, shall not lose his reward.'

# 11

WHEN Jesus had finished instructing his twelve disciples, he left the place where he had been and went to teach and preach in their cities.

Now when John in his prison heard of the wonderful things that the Christ had been doing, he sent him a message by his own disciples.

'Are you,' he asked him, 'he that was coming, or are we to expect another?'

'Go and tell John what you hear and see,' said Jesus in reply. 'The blind see once more; the lame walk; lepers are cleansed; the deaf hear; dead men are brought back to life, and beggars are proclaiming the Good News. Happy the man who finds no fault in me.'

They left him, and Jesus began to talk to the people about John. He said: 'What did you go out into the desert to see? A reed swaying in the wind? No. Then what did you go out to see? A man in fine clothing? But it is in the palaces of kings that people in fine clothes are found. Then why did you go out? To see a prophet. Yes, indeed, someone even greater than a prophet. For he is the man to whom the Scripture points: *Behold I send my Messenger ahead of thee to prepare thy way before thee.*

'Believe me, among men born of woman none greater than John the Baptist has appeared, though even the lesser ones in the Kingdom of Heaven are greater than he. And ever since John the Baptist's days, the Kingdom of Heaven has been assaulted, and strong men have been taking it by storm. For all the Prophets and the Law pointed to John; and if you are ready to believe it, he is the Elijah who was due to come. He that has ears to hear with, let him hear.

'But to whom can I compare this generation? I am reminded of children sitting in the market-place and calling to their friends, "We piped to you, but you did not dance; we sang you dirges, but you did not beat your breasts." For John came, eating nothing, drinking nothing – and they say he is possessed. Then came the Son of Man, who eats and drinks – and they say, "Look at that glutton and drunkard, a friend of tax-collectors and outcasts." And yet God's ways were proved to have been wise by their results.'

Then he began to denounce the cities in which most of his miracles had been done, because they did not repent: 'Alas for you, Chorazin! Alas for you, Bethsaida! For if the miracles that were done in you had been done in Tyre and Sidon, they would long since have repented in sackcloth and ashes. But mark my words; on the day of judgement Tyre and Sidon will have less to suffer than you. And you, Capernaum! Shall you be raised to Heaven? No; thrust down to Hades. For if the miracles that were done in you had been done in Sodom, Sodom would still be there. But mark my words; on the day of judgement the land of Sodom will have less to suffer than you.'

It was now that Jesus said: 'Father, I thank thee, Lord of Heaven and earth, for hiding these things from wise and clever men and revealing them to simple folk. Indeed I thank thee, Father, for having chosen this way.

'All was entrusted to me by my Father. No one but the Father comprehends the Son. Nor does anyone comprehend the Father but the Son and those to whom the Son is willing to reveal him.

'Come to me, all you that toil and are heavy-laden, and I will give you rest.

'Put on my yoke and learn from me, who am gentle and humble in heart – and you will find rest for your souls. For my yoke is easy and my burden light.'

# 12

ON a sabbath day at about this time Jesus was walking through the cornfields. His disciples were hungry and began to pluck ears of corn and eat them. The Pharisees noticed this and said to him: 'Look! Your disciples are doing something forbidden on the Sabbath.'

He replied: 'Have you not read what David did when he and his companions were hungry, how he went into the House of God, and they ate the sacrificial loaves, which neither he nor his companions but only the priests had the right to eat? Or have you not read in the Law that on sabbath days the priests in the Temple break the Sabbath yet incur no blame?

'However, I say to you that something greater than the Temple is here. And if you had known the meaning of the words *I have set my heart on mercy not on sacrifice*, you would not have condemned the innocent. For the Son of Man is master of the Sabbath.'

He went on from there and entered their synagogue. As he did so, a man with a withered hand appeared. So they questioned Jesus, hoping to have a charge to bring against him. 'Is one permitted to heal on the Sabbath?' they asked.

Jesus said to them: 'What man is there among you with a sheep, who will not get hold of it and lift it out on the Sabbath if it falls into a pit? But surely a man is of greater consequence than a sheep? It follows that it is lawful to do good on the sabbath day.'

Then he said to the man: 'Hold out your hand.' He held it out, and it was made sound once more, like the other.

But the Pharisees, when they left the synagogue, plotted against him with a view to his destruction. Jesus knew this and went elsewhere. He was followed by many and he cured them all, sternly forbidding them to draw attention to himself.*

They now brought him a man whom a demon had made blind and dumb. He cured him, and the dumb man spoke and saw. All the people were astounded. 'Can this be David's son?' they asked. But when the Pharisees heard, they said: 'If the man casts demons out, it is only through Beelzebub their Prince.'

But Jesus, who knew what they were thinking, said to them: 'Kingdoms are brought to ruin by internal strife. No town, no house, can fight against itself and stand. If Satan casts out Satan, he is fighting himself, and how can his kingdom stand? Again, if I cast out demons through Beelzebub, through whom do your own people cast them out? You stand condemned by *them*. On the other hand, if I cast out demons through the Spirit of God, it would seem that the Kingdom of God confronts you. How can anyone break into the Strong One's house and plunder his goods unless he begins by tying up the Strong One? After that he will ransack his house.

'He that is not with me is against me; and he that does not gather with me casts away. Which leads me to say this. Man shall be forgiven every kind of sin and blasphemy; but blasphemy of the Spirit shall not be forgiven. Whoever speaks against the Son of Man shall be forgiven; but he that speaks against the Holy Spirit shall not be forgiven either in this age or in the age to come. Either pronounce the tree a good one and its fruit good, or pronounce it rotten and its fruit rotten. For by its fruit the tree is known.

* So that the words spoken through the Prophet Isaiah might be fulfilled: *Behold my servant whom I have chosen, my beloved, with whom my soul is content. I will put my spirit in him, and he shall proclaim Judgement to the pagans. He will not wrangle or cry out, nor will anyone hear his voice in the streets. He will crush no injured reed nor quench a smoking wick, till he has carried Judgement to victory. And his name will bring hope to the pagans.*

'Children of vipers, how can anything you say be good when you yourselves are evil? For it is what fills the heart that comes out at the lips. The good man, from the good that fills his heart, produces good; and the bad man evil from his evil store. And I would have you know that on the Judgement Day men shall be called to account for every idle word they utter. Out of your own mouth you shall be acquitted, and out of your own mouth condemned.'

Presently some of the Doctors and Pharisees arguing with Jesus said: 'Master, we should like to see a sign from you.'

He replied: 'It is a wicked and unfaithful generation that asks for a sign, and the Prophet Jonah's is the only sign it shall be given. For just as Jonah spent three days and nights in the belly of the whale, the Son of Man will spend three days and nights in the heart of the earth. Men of Nineveh when they rise on the Judgement Day with this generation will condemn it; for they repented when Jonah preached to them, whereas to-day something greater than Jonah is here. When the Queen of the South is raised at the Judgement with this generation, she will condemn it; for she came from the ends of the earth to hear Solomon's wisdom, whereas to-day something greater than Solomon is here.

'When the unclean spirit has gone out of a man, it wanders through waterless places, seeking repose, which it does not find. Then it says, "I will go back to the home I left." And if, on reaching the house, it finds it untenanted, swept and in good order, it goes and brings along with it seven other spirits worse than itself, and they all go in and settle there, with the result that the man's condition in the end is worse than it was in the beginning. That is what will happen to this wicked generation.'

While Jesus was still talking to the people, his mother and brothers arrived and stood outside, wishing to speak to him. Someone told him, and he replied: 'Who is my mother, and who are my brothers?' And with his hand held out to his disciples: 'Behold, my mother and my brothers! For whoever does the will of my Father in Heaven is brother and sister and mother to me.'

## 13

JESUS went out of doors that day and sat by the sea. But the crowd gathered round him in such numbers that he got into a boat and sat down there. The people all stood on the beach, and he taught them many things in parables.

He said: 'Picture the sower going out to sow. As he sowed, some of his seeds fell by the path, and the birds came and ate them up. Others fell on rocky patches where they did not find much soil, and sprang up at once because the soil was shallow. But when the sun came up they were scorched, and because they had no roots they withered. Others fell among thistles, which grew tall and smothered them. Others again fell on rich soil and produced a crop, some a hundredfold, some sixty, some thirty. He that has ears, let him hear.'

At this point the disciples came forward and said to him: 'Why do you talk to them in parables?'

'To you,' replied Jesus, 'the secrets of the Kingdom of Heaven are revealed; but not to them. For more shall be given to the man who has – he shall be enriched; but from the man who has not, even what he has shall be taken. I talk to these people in parables because they have eyes but do not see; they have ears but do not hear or understand. It is in them that Isaiah's prophecy is finding its fulfilment: *You shall hear with your ears, but you shall not understand; you shall see with your eyes, but you shall not perceive. For this people has become coarse within; they have ears that are hard of hearing, and they have shut their eyes, lest one day they see with their eyes, hear with their ears, understand in their hearts and be converted, and I heal them.* But your eyes are privileged because they see, and your ears because they hear. Indeed I tell you, many prophets and upright men have longed to see what you see, and have not seen it; and to hear what you hear, and have not heard it.

'To you then I will explain the parable of the sower. When anyone hears the Word of the Kingdom and does not understand it, the Evil One comes and flies away with what was sown in his heart. There you have the man who received his seed by the path.

'The man who received it on rocky ground is one that hears the Word and accepts it at once with joy. But he has no roots in him, he cannot hold out long; and when suffering or persecution comes on account of the Word, he promptly recants.

'The man who received it among thistles is also one who hears the Word; but the cares of this world and the lure of riches choke the Word, and he becomes unfruitful.

'Finally, the man who received the seed on rich soil is one who hears the Word and understands it. He indeed bears fruit, producing in some cases a hundredfold, in others sixty, in others thirty.'

He put another parable before them: 'The Kingdom of Heaven might be compared to a man who sowed good seed in his field. But when everybody was asleep his enemy came, sowed darnel in among the corn and escaped, with the result that as the green corn came up and ripened, the weeds appeared as well.

'The farmer's men went up to him and said: "Sir, did you not sow good seed in your field? If so, where do the weeds come from?"

'He said: "An enemy has done this."

'"Then would you like us to go and collect the weeds?" said his men.

'"No," he replied, "or else, as you collect the weeds, you may root up the corn along with them. Let them grow up together till the harvest; and at harvest-time I shall say to the reapers, First collect the weeds and tie them up in bundles to be burnt; then reap the corn and bring it into my barn."'

Another parable he put to them was this: 'The Kingdom of Heaven is like a grain of mustard seed that a man takes and sows on his land. It is the smallest of all seeds, but when it has grown it is bigger than any shrub and becomes a tree, so that the birds of the sky come and roost among its branches.'

He told them another parable: 'The Kingdom of Heaven is like the yeast that a woman takes and conceals in three pounds of wheat-meal till the whole is leavened.'

Throughout this discourse Jesus spoke to the crowd in parables. Indeed, except in parables he used not to address them.* Now, he dismissed the people and went to his house, where his disciples approached him and said: 'Expound to us the parable about the weeds in the field.'

Jesus said: 'The sower of the good seed is the Son of Man. The field is the world, and the good seed stands for the children of the Kingdom. The weeds are the children of evil, and the enemy that sowed them is the Devil. The harvest is the end of time, and the reapers are Angels. Just as the weeds are gathered and burnt in the fire, so shall it be when this age comes to an end. The Son of Man will send out his Angels, who will gather from his Kingdom all that corrupts and all those that live in iniquity, and cast them into the fiery furnace, where there will be weeping and gnashing of teeth. Then the righteous will shine out like the sun in the Kingdom of their Father. He that has ears, let him hear.

'The Kingdom of Heaven is like treasure buried in a field. When a man finds it he covers it up and is so filled with joy that he goes and sells all he has and buys the field.

'Again, the Kingdom of Heaven is like a merchant looking out for beautiful pearls. He finds one of great value, and goes and sells all he has and buys it.

'Again, the Kingdom of Heaven is like a seine cast into the

* So that the words spoken through the Prophet might be fulfilled: *I will open my mouth in parables. I will utter what has been kept secret ever since the creation.*

sea and catching fish of every kind. When it is full, they drag it up onto the beach, sit down, and collect the good fish in baskets, but throw away the bad. It will be the same at the end of this age. The Angels will go out, pick the wicked from among the good and cast them into the fiery furnace, where there will be weeping and gnashing of teeth.

'Have you understood all this?'

'Yes,' they told him.

'It follows that a Doctor of the Law has only to be schooled in the Kingdom of Heaven to be like a householder with a store of treasures new and old at his disposal.'

When Jesus had finished these parables, he left the neighbourhood and moved to his own part of the country. There he taught the people in their synagogue. They were filled with amazement and asked each other: 'Where did the man get this wisdom and these powers? Is he not the carpenter's son? Is not his mother called Mary, and his brothers James and Joses and Simon and Judas? And are not all his sisters with us? Where then did the man get all this?' They were shocked by him.

But Jesus said to them: 'A prophet is not without honour except in his own country and his own house.' And because of their lack of faith he did not do many miracles there.

# 14

HEROD the Tetrarch now heard of Jesus's fame, and said to his attendants: 'This man is John the Baptist. He has risen from the dead. That is why the powers are at work in him.'

It must be explained that Herod had arrested John, bound him and put him in prison, because of Herodias, his brother Philip's wife, whom John had been telling him he could not marry. Herod wished to put him to death but was afraid of popular feeling, for John was looked up to as a prophet.

However, at Herod's birthday celebrations Herodias' daughter danced before the company and Herod was delighted with her, so much so that he swore he would give her anything she asked of him. The girl, who had been prompted by her mother, said: 'Give me John the Baptist's head, here, on a platter.' The king was distressed, but in view of his oath and the presence of his guests, he gave orders that she should have it, and sent and beheaded John in the prison. The head was brought in on a platter and given to the girl, who took it to her mother. John's disciples came and removed his corpse and buried it. Then they went and told Jesus, who, when he heard the news, withdrew by ship to a deserted spot where he could be alone.

But the people, when they heard of this, came out of their towns and went after him on foot. So Jesus disembarking was faced by a large crowd. He was stirred with compassion for them and he cured those among them who were ill.

Evening came, and his disciples went up to him and said: 'We are in a desolate spot and supper-time has passed already. Dismiss the people so that they can go to the villages and buy themselves provisions.'

But Jesus said: 'There is no need for them to go. Feed them yourselves.'

'All we have with us,' said his disciples, 'is five loaves and two fish.'

'Bring them here to me,' said Jesus, and told the people to sit down on the grass.

He took the five loaves and the two fish and looking up to Heaven said a blessing. Then he broke the loaves and handed them to his disciples, who gave them to the people; and everyone ate and was satisfied. Moreover, they picked up enough pieces left to fill twelve hampers, though apart from women and children some five thousand men had fed.

Immediately after, he ordered the disciples to embark and precede him by crossing over, while he himself dismissed the people. When he had seen the people off, he went up into the hills by himself to pray. Night fell, and he was there alone.

Meanwhile the boat, by now well out from land, was struggling with a choppy sea, for the wind was against her. But in the fourth watch of the night Jesus made his way to them, walking over the sea. When the disciples saw him walking on the sea they were terrified. They thought it was a ghost and cried out in their fear.

But Jesus spoke to them at once and said: 'All is well! It is I. Do not be afraid.'

Peter answered him: 'Lord, if it is you, bid me come to you across the water.'

'Come,' he said.

Peter got out of the boat and started to walk across the water to Jesus. But when he saw what a gale was blowing, he was frightened. He began to sink and cried: 'Lord, save me!'

Jesus quickly reached out, took hold of him and said: 'Where is your faith? Why did you hesitate?' And no sooner had they got into the boat than the wind fell.

Then the men on board did obeisance to Jesus. 'You are indeed a son of God,' they said.

So they crossed over and made land at Gennesaret. The people of the place, recognizing Jesus, sent out all round the countryside and fetched in to him all that were sick. These begged him only to let them touch the tassel on his cloak. And all that did so were saved.

# 15

SOME Doctors of the Law and Pharisees from Jerusalem now came to Jesus and said: 'Why do your disciples violate the traditions of our forefathers? They do not wash their hands before their meals.'

'And why do you,' retorted Jesus, 'violate the commandment of God in favour of your own tradition? Did not God say, *Honour thy father and thy mother* and *Let him that reviles his father or mother be put to death.* But *you* lay it down that a man who says to his father or mother, "I am making a temple-offering of all the support you might have got from me," shall no longer be bound by filial duty. Thus for the sake of your own tradition you have made God's word null and void. You hypocrites! How right Isaiah was when he prophesied about you: *These people honour me with their lips, but their heart is far from me. Their worship of me is empty: they make doctrines of the precepts of men.*'

Then he called the people to him and said: 'Listen and understand. It is not what goes into a man's mouth that defiles him, but what comes out of it.'

The disciples now went up to him and said: 'Do you realize that the Pharisees took offence at what you said?'

But Jesus replied: 'Any plant not planted by my Heavenly Father shall be torn up by the roots. Leave them alone: they are blind leaders. And when one blind man leads another, both will fall into a pit.'

Peter returned to the parable and asked him to explain it. Jesus said: 'You too? Still so dull? Do you not see that what goes in at the mouth passes into the stomach and is discharged in the privy; whereas what comes out of it arises from the heart, and this is what defiles a man? For out of the heart come evil thoughts, murder, adultery, fornication, thieving, perjury, slander. These are the things that defile a man. As for eating with unwashed hands, that defiles no one.'

Jesus left this part of the country and moved to the neighbourhood of Tyre and Sidon. And now a Canaanite woman who came from the borderlands approached him. She kept calling out: 'Have pity on me, Lord, son of David. My daughter is tormented by a demon.' But he gave her not a word in reply.

His disciples went and asked him to dismiss her, because she was shouting after them. And now he said: 'My mission was to no one but the lost sheep of the House of Israel.'

But the woman came up and did obeisance to him. 'Lord, help me,' she said.

He replied: 'It is not right to take the children's bread and throw it to the house-dogs.'

'True, Lord,' she said, 'for even the house-dogs are fed – on the crumbs that fall from their masters' table.'

'Lady,' said Jesus now, 'your faith is great indeed. Have your wish.' And from that moment her daughter was well.

Leaving the district, Jesus skirted the Sea of Galilee and went up into the hills. There he sat down and was approached by a large crowd, who brought with them the lame, the blind, the deaf, the maimed and many others, and cast them down at his feet. He cured them, to the amazement of the crowd, who, when they saw the dumb speaking, the lame walking, and the blind seeing, gave glory to the God of Israel.

But Jesus called his disciples to him and said: 'I feel sorry for all these people who for three days now have attached themselves to me and have nothing to eat. I should not like to send them away starving, or they may faint on their way home.'

The disciples said: 'In this wilderness, where could we find enough bread to satisfy so large a crowd?'

'How many loaves have you got?' he asked them.

'Seven,' they said, 'and a few small fish.'

Then he told the people to settle down on the ground. He took the seven loaves and the fish, said a blessing, and broke them into pieces, which he handed to his disciples. The disciples gave them to the people, and they all ate and were satisfied. Moreover seven baskets were filled with the pieces left, though apart from women and children four thousand men had fed.

He now dismissed the crowd, embarked, and came to the district of Magadan.

# 16

THE Pharisees and Sadducees approached him and by way of putting him to the proof asked him to show them a sign from Heaven.

This was his answer: 'In the evening you say, "It is going to be fine: the sky is red"; and in the morning, "A stormy day: the sky is red and angry." You hypocrites, who can tell the weather by looking at the sky, but cannot read the signs of the times. It is a wicked and unfaithful generation that craves for signs; and Jonah's is the only sign it shall be given.' With that he left them.

When they crossed to the other shore the disciples forgot to provide themselves with bread. Jesus said to them: 'Watch, and be on your guard against the yeast of the Pharisees and Sadducees.'

Discussing this with one another they decided that he must have been referring to their lack of bread. But Jesus knew what they were thinking and rebuked them for their want of faith. 'Why are you arguing about your lack of bread?' he asked. 'Do you not see yet, nor remember the five loaves and the five thousand, and the number of hampers you filled; nor the seven loaves and the four thousand, and the number of baskets you filled? How can you fail to see that when I told you to beware of the yeast of the Pharisees and Sadducees I was not talking about bread?' Then they realized that the yeast of which he had been warning them was not the yeast we use for bread but the doctrine of the Pharisees and Sadducees.

When Jesus reached the neighbourhood of Caesarea, Philip's city, he put a question to his disciples: 'Who do people say the Son of Man is?'

'Some,' they replied, 'say John the Baptist; others, Elijah; others again, Jeremiah or one of the Prophets.'

'But you?' said he. 'Who do you say I am?'

It was Simon Peter who answered. 'You are the Christ,' he said, 'the son of the living God.'

'You are privileged, Simon son of Jonah,' replied Jesus; 'for it was not flesh and blood that revealed this to you, but my Father in Heaven. And in my turn I say to you, You are Peter, and on this rock I will build my church – the Gates of Hell will not be stronger. I will give you the keys of the Kingdom of Heaven. Whatever you forbid on earth, Heaven shall forbid; and whatever you allow on earth, Heaven shall allow.' At the same time he admonished the disciples to tell no one that he was the Christ.

It was then that Jesus Christ began to make it clear to his disciples that he must of necessity go to Jerusalem, suffer much at the hands of the Elders and Chief Priests and Doctors of the Law, be put to death, and on the third day be restored to life. Peter drew Jesus to himself and began to remonstrate with him. He said, 'Heaven save you, Lord! This *shall* not be your fate.'

But Jesus turned his back on him and said: 'Get behind me, Satan. You are a snare in my path, for your thoughts are not God's but the world's.'

Jesus then said to his disciples: 'If anyone wishes to walk in my footsteps let him renounce self, take up his cross and follow me. For the man who chooses to save his life will lose it; while he that loses his life for my sake shall find it. How will a man have profited by winning the whole world and forfeiting his life? Or what can a man give that is as precious as his life? For it is ordained that the Son of Man shall come in his Father's glory with his Angels, and shall then requite each man according to his deeds. In all truth I tell you, some of these standing here shall not taste death before they see the Son of Man come in his Kingdom.'

## 17

Six days later, Jesus selected Peter, James, and his brother John, and took them up alone to the top of a high mountain. There he was transformed before them. His face shone like the sun and his clothes were white as light itself. And now there appeared to them Moses and Elijah, talking with Jesus. Whereupon Peter said to him: 'Lord, it is a good thing that we are here. If you are willing, I will make three shelters, one for you, one for Moses, and one for Elijah.'

He was still speaking when a bright cloud enveloped them. And out of the cloud came a voice that said: 'This is My son, the Beloved One, in whom I rejoice. Listen to him.'

When the disciples heard this they prostrated themselves and were overcome with awe. But Jesus came up and touched them. 'Rise,' he said, 'and do not be afraid.' Then they looked up and saw no one there but Jesus himself.

As they came down from the mountain Jesus impressed it on them that they must tell no one of the vision till the Son of Man should have risen from the dead.

The disciples put a question to him: 'Now why do the Doctors of the Law say that first Elijah must come?'

He replied: 'So Elijah is coming and will re-establish everything? No; I say to you that Elijah has come already, and they did not recognize him but wrought their will on him. So too the Son of Man is going to suffer at their hands.' The disciples understood then that he had been speaking to them about John the Baptist.

When they rejoined the people a man came to him, knelt down before him and said: 'Lord, have pity on my son, who suffers severely from epilepsy, often falling into the fire and as often into water. I took him to your disciples, but they were unable to cure him.'

'O faithless and perverse generation!' Jesus exclaimed.

'How much longer must I be with you? How much longer must I bear with you? Bring him here to me.' He then rebuked the lad; the demon came out of him; and from that moment he was well.

But the disciples approached Jesus privately and asked: 'Why were we unable to drive it out?'

'Because of your lack of faith,' said Jesus. 'The truth is that if you have faith like a grain of mustard seed you will say to that mountain "Move over there," and it will move; and you will find nothing impossible.'

At the time when they were gathering their forces in Galilee, Jesus said to them: 'The Son of Man is going to be delivered into the hands of men. They will put him to death and on the third day he will come back to life.' And they were filled with sorrow.

They reached Capernaum, and the collectors of the temple-tax, accosting Peter, said: 'What of your master? Does he not pay his tax?'

Peter said, 'He does.'

Then he joined the rest indoors and was about to say something when Jesus spoke. 'What do you think, Simon? On whom do the kings of the world levy their import or capitation taxes? On their citizens or on foreigners?'

Peter said, 'On foreigners.'

'So citizens are exempt,' said Jesus. 'However, to avoid offending these people, go to the sea, throw in a hook and take the first fish that comes up. When you open its mouth you will find a silver coin. Take that and give it them on my account and yours.'

# 18

AT this time the disciples came to Jesus with a question. 'Who is greatest,' they asked, 'in the Kingdom of Heaven?'

He called a little child to him, set it down in their midst and said: 'Hear the truth. Unless your hearts are changed and you become like little children, you will not enter the Kingdom of Heaven at all. He then, the man who makes himself humble as this little child, is the greatest in the Kingdom of Heaven; and the man who in my name welcomes one such little child welcomes me. But as for the man who corrupts one of these little ones that have faith in me, his best course would be to have a large millstone tied round his neck and to be sunk in the depths of the sea. Alas for the world and its corruption! Corruption there must be; but alas for the man who causes it!

'If your hand or your foot leads you into evil, cut it off and throw it away: it is better for you to come into life crippled or maimed than, with both your hands and feet, to be cast into the fire of eternity. And if your eye leads you into evil, pluck it out and throw it away: it is better for you to come into life with one eye than, with two, to be cast into hell fire.

'See that you do not look down on any of these little ones; for I would have you know that their Ambassadors in Heaven see the face of my Heavenly Father for ever.

'What do you think? If a man has a hundred sheep and one of them has strayed, does he not leave the ninety-nine on the hills and go and look for the one that strayed? And if he has the good fortune to find it, does it not make him happier than the ninety-nine that did not wander? Indeed it does. And the same is true of your Father in Heaven: it is not his will that a single one of these little ones should be lost.

'If your brother does wrong, go and have it out with him in private. If he listens to you, you will be the richer by a brother. But if he refuses to listen, call in one or two other people so that all that is said may be vouched for by two or three witnesses. If he pays no attention to these, report the matter to the church. And if he pays no attention even to the church, you may treat him as a pagan or a tax-collector.

'I tell you in all truth that whatever you forbid on earth shall be forbidden by Heaven, and whatever you allow on earth shall be allowed by Heaven.

'Another truth. If any two of you on earth agree in making any prayer, it shall be granted by my Father in Heaven; for where two or three are gathered together in my name, there am I in the midst of them.'

Peter went up to him and said: 'Lord, how many times must I let my brother do me wrong, and forgive him? Seven times?'

Jesus replied: 'Not seven, I should say, but seventy times seven, as you may learn from this parable of the Kingdom or Heaven.

'There was a king who decided to settle accounts with his retainers. The first they brought to him was one who owed him a hundred thousand pounds. But as he had no means of paying, his master ordered him to be sold, with his wife and his children and all his possessions, and payment to be made from the proceeds. The servant fell at his feet and besought him. He said: "Be patient with me, and I will pay you all."

'The man's master was sorry for him. He let him go free, and he cancelled the loan. But as the man went off he met one of his fellow-servants who owed him five pounds, and he seized him by the throat and cried: "You owe me something. Pay up!"

'The other threw himself on the ground and pleaded with him. "Be patient with me," he said, "and I will pay you." But the man refused. He went instead and had him imprisoned till he should pay his debt.

'Now when his fellow-servants saw what had happened they were much distressed and went and told the whole story to their master, who then summoned the man and denounced him as a wicked servant. "I cancelled all that debt of yours," he said, "because you pleaded with me. Ought you not to have been merciful to your fellow-servant, as I was to you?" Indeed, his master was so angry with him that he handed him over to the jailers till he should pay back all he owed.

'That is what my Heavenly Father will do to you if you do not each forgive your brother from your heart.'

# 19

WHEN he had brought this part of his teaching to an end Jesus left Galilee and moved into that district of Judaea which is on the far side of the Jordan. He was followed by large crowds and he healed them there.

Wishing to test him, some Pharisees approached him with a question. 'Is it lawful,' they asked, 'to divorce one's wife on any grounds one may allege?'

He answered: 'Have you not read that the Creator *made human beings male and female* in the beginning?' And he quoted further, *'Because of this a man shall leave his father and mother and cling to his wife, and the two shall become one flesh.* This means that they are no longer two persons but one. It follows that man must not part what God has united.'

'Why then,' they said, 'did Moses lay down the principle of divorce by writ?'

He replied: 'Moses was allowing for the hardness of your hearts when he permitted you to divorce your wives. But things were not so in the beginning. And what I say to you is that the man who divorces his wife for anything but fornication and marries again is committing adultery.'

The disciples said to him: 'If that is the case between man and wife, it is better not to marry.'

He replied: 'It is not everyone that can accept that ruling, but only those that hear the call. Some people were born eunuchs; others were made so by men; and there are people who have chosen that condition for the sake of the Kingdom of Heaven. Let him that can, obey the call.'

Some little children were brought to him in order that he might lay his hands on them and pray. The disciples scolded them. But Jesus said: 'Let the children be. Do not forbid them to come to me; for the Kingdom of Heaven belongs to such.' And he laid his hands on them.

He was already on his way elsewhere when a man came up to him and said: 'Master, what good deed can I do to win eternal life?'

He replied: 'Why do you ask me for a definition of *good*? There is One only who is good. However, if you wish to enter Life, keep the commandments.'

'Which do you mean?' asked the man.

Jesus said: '*Thou shalt not murder; Thou shalt not commit adultery; Thou shalt not steal; Thou shalt not perjure thyself; Honour thy father and mother;* and *Thou shalt love thy neighbour as thyself.*'

'All these I have kept,' said the young man. 'What more must I do?'

Jesus said to him: 'If you wish to be perfect, go and sell your possessions and give to the poor – you will have treasure in Heaven. Then come and follow me.'

But the young man when he heard these words went away in gloom, for he was a man of property. And Jesus said to his disciples: 'Indeed how difficult it is for a rich man to enter the Kingdom of Heaven. I say it again. It is an easier thing for a camel to pass through the eye of a needle than for a rich man to enter the Kingdom of God.'

The disciples were astounded when they heard this. 'If that is so, who can be saved?' they said.

Jesus, with his eyes upon them, said: 'For men it is impossible; but anything is possible for God.'

Peter spoke up and said to Jesus: 'Did *we* not give up everything and follow you? What shall we get by that?'

And Jesus said to them: 'Hear the truth. When the world is born anew and the Son of Man takes the throne of his glory, you that have followed me will also be seated, on twelve thrones, governing the twelve tribes of Israel. And everyone that has given up houses, brothers, sisters, father, mother, children, or fields, for the sake of my name, shall be many times repaid and come into eternal life. But in many cases the last shall be first and the first shall be last.

## 20

'FOR the Kingdom of Heaven is like a landowner who went out the first thing in the morning to hire labour for his vineyard. He agreed with the hands for a shilling a day and sent them into his vineyard. Going out again at the third hour he saw some others standing idle in the market-place and said to them, "Go into the vineyard too, and I will pay you what is right." So they went; and going out again at the sixth hour and at the ninth he did the same.

'But when he went out at the eleventh hour he found more of them standing about and said, "Why do you stand idle like this all day long?" They said, "Because nobody has hired us." So he told them also to go into his vineyard.

'When evening came the owner of the vineyard said to his bailiff, "Call in the hands and pay them their wages. Begin with the last and finish with the first." So those that were hired at the eleventh hour came up, and they were given a shilling each.

'But when the first to be hired came up, expecting to be given more, they too were paid a shilling each. They took the money but grumbled at their employer. They said, "These men that came last have only done an hour, yet you put them on a level with us that have worked all day in this heat."

'He dealt with this by saying to one of them: "My friend, I am doing you no wrong. Did you not agree with me for a shilling? Take your due and go. It is my pleasure to pay this man who came last the same as you. May I not do what I like with my own people? Or are you jealous because I am good?"

'Thus the last shall be first and the first last.'

Jesus decided to go up to Jerusalem. On the road he took the twelve disciples aside and said to them: 'You see; we are going up to Jerusalem. The Son of Man will be handed over to the Chief Priests and Doctors of the Law. They will condemn him to death and give him up to the pagans to be mocked and scourged and crucified; and on the third day he will come back to life.'

The mother of Zebedee's sons went up to him now with her sons, did obeisance, and made him a petition. 'What is it that you wish?' he asked.

She said: 'Ordain that these two sons of mine shall sit, one on your right hand and one on your left, in your Kingdom.'

Jesus replied: 'You do not know what you are asking for yourselves. Can you drink the cup that I am going to drink?'

'We can,' they said.

Then Jesus said: 'You shall certainly drink my cup. But as for the seats on my right hand and my left, they are not mine to bestow, but will be given to those for whom they have been prepared by my Father.'

When the Ten heard this they grumbled about the two brothers. But Jesus called them to him and said: 'You know that the rulers of the pagans exercise despotic powers and their great men have authority over them. It is not so with you. On the contrary, whoever wishes to be great among you must be your servant, and whoever wishes to be first among you must be your slave. So with the Son of Man – *he* did not come to be served, but to serve, and to give up his life in redemption for many.'

As they left Jericho a large crowd followed him. And there were two blind men sitting by the road, who when they heard that Jesus was passing cried out: 'Lord, have pity on us, Son of David!'

People told them to hold their tongues, but this only made them cry out all the louder: 'Lord, have pity on us, Son of David!'

Jesus stopped, called them to him and said: 'What do you wish me to do for you?'

'Lord,' they said, 'we want our eyes to be opened.'

Jesus was moved to compassion and touched their eyes. Their sight came back at once and they followed him.

# 21

THEY had approached Jerusalem and reached Bethphage, by the Mount of Olives, when Jesus sent two of the disciples ahead, saying: 'Go to the village you see over there. The first thing you find will be a tethered donkey, and a colt with her. Untie them and bring them to me. And if anyone says something to you, tell him that the Lord needs them but will send them back at once.'*

The disciples went and did as Jesus told them. They brought the donkey and the colt, and on them spread their cloaks. Jesus sat on these.

Most of the people spread their cloaks on the road, while others were cutting branches from the trees and strewing them there. And both those that went in front of him and

* This took place so that the words spoken through the Prophet might be fulfilled: *Say to the Daughter of Sion, 'Behold thy King is coming to thee, humble and mounted on an ass and on a colt, the foal of an ass.'*

those that came behind cried: 'Hosanna to the Son of David! *Blessed be he that cometh in the name of the Lord!* Hosanna in the Heights!'

When he entered Jerusalem the whole city was stirred. 'Who is this?' it asked. And the crowds said: 'This is the Prophet Jesus, from Nazareth in Galilee.'

Jesus went into the Temple, drove out all who were buying and selling in the sacred buildings, and upset the money-changers' tables and the chairs of the people who were selling the doves. He said to them: 'The Scriptures say, *My House shall be called the House of Prayer.* But you turn it into a robbers' den.'

Blind and lame people came to him in the Temple and he cured them. But the Chief Priests and the Doctors of the Law were indignant when they saw the wonderful things he did, and the children who were shouting in the Temple, 'Hosanna to the Son of David!' They said to him: 'Do you hear what they are saying?'

'Yes,' said Jesus. 'Have you never read the Scripture, *Thou hast ordained thy praises to be sung by little children and babes at the breast*? Then he left them and went out of the city to Bethany, where he spent the night.

In the morning on his way back to the city he felt hungry, and seeing a fig-tree by the road went up to it. But finding nothing on the tree but leaves he said to it, 'May you be barren for ever.' And the fig-tree withered instantly.

The disciples when they saw this were amazed and said: 'How did the tree come to wither so suddenly?'

For answer Jesus said: 'I tell you in all truth that if you have faith and do not waver you will not only do what I did to the fig-tree, but if you order this mountain to be removed and cast into the sea, it will be done. And whatever you ask for in your prayers, with faith, you will receive.'

When he had gone into the Temple, the Chief Priests and Elders of the people went up to him as he was teaching and said: 'By what authority are you acting? And who gave you that authority?'

Jesus replied: 'I will ask *you* for a statement. Make it, and in my turn I will tell you by what authority I am acting. John's baptism – was it sanctioned by Heaven or by man?'

They turned this over in their minds, saying to themselves: 'If we say by Heaven, he will ask us, "Why then did you not have faith in him?" Whereas, if we say by man, we have reason to fear the people, who all take John for a prophet.'

In the end they said to Jesus: 'We do not know.' And his answer was like theirs: 'I too will not tell you by what authority I am acting.

'But what do you say to this? A man with two sons went to one of them and said, "Son, go and work in the vineyard to-day." He replied, "I will, sir," but he did not go. The man then went to his other son and gave him a similar order. He refused to go; but he was sorry later and he went. Which of the two carried out his father's wishes?'

'The one who went later,' they replied.

'Most solemnly I warn you,' Jesus said, 'that the tax-collectors and harlots have the lead of *you* on the road to the Kingdom of God. For John showed you the way to righteousness and you had no faith in him. The tax-collectors and the harlots had faith in him. But you, even after seeing that, did not repent and have faith in him.

'Listen to another parable, about a landowner who planted a vineyard. He fenced it round, dug a wine-press in it, built a watch-tower, and then leased it to some farmers and went abroad. When vintage-time drew near he sent his servants to the farmers for his share of the produce. But the farmers seized them, thrashed one, killed another and stoned a third. He then sent servants again, this time in greater numbers. But they treated them in the same way. Finally he sent them his son, thinking, "They will respect my son." But when the farmers saw the son they said to one another, "This is the heir. Come, let us kill him and seize his inheritance." So they laid hands on him, threw him out of the vineyard and killed him. Well now, when the owner of the vineyard comes, what will he do to those farmers?'

They said: 'He will see to it that a bad set come to a bad end, and will lease the vineyard to other farmers, who will let him have his fruit in due season.'

Then Jesus said: 'Have you never read in the Scriptures, *The stone that the builders rejected has become the headstone of the corner. It was the Lord's doing and admirable in our eyes?* On that authority I tell you that the Kingdom of God shall be taken from you and given to a people who produce that Kingdom's fruits. Moreover, the man who falls upon that stone will be shattered, but the man on whom it falls will be reduced to dust.'

When they heard these parables of his the Chief Priests and Pharisees realized that he was speaking of them. They sought to arrest him but were afraid of the people, because they looked on him as a prophet.

# 22

ADDRESSING them later Jesus spoke once more in allegory. 'The Kingdom of Heaven,' he said, 'is like a king who was celebrating his son's marriage. He sent out his servants to remind the people who had been invited to the wedding; but they refused to come. He did the same again, sending further servants to whom he said: "Tell the guests that I have prepared my wedding-breakfast; my bulls and fatted cattle have been killed and all is ready. Come to the wedding."

'But they took no notice and went off, one to the farm he owned, another to his shop, while the rest, seizing the king's servants, abused and killed them. The king was furious. He sent his army out, destroyed the murderers and burnt their town. Then he said to his servants: "The wedding-feast is ready, but the guests have proved unworthy. Go then where the roads lead out of town, and call anyone you see to the wedding." So they went out into the roads and collected everyone they saw, good and bad alike, with the result that the full number sat down to the wedding-feast.

'But when the King came in to look at his guests he found a man there who was not dressed for a wedding. "My friend," he said, "how did you get in here without wedding clothes?" The man had nothing to say for himself; and the King said to the stewards: "Bind him hand and foot and cast him into the outer darkness, where there shall be weeping and gnashing of teeth."

'Thus you see that many are called, but few are chosen.'

The Pharisees now went and cast about for some means of tripping him up in argument. In the end they sent him their disciples and some of Herod's partisans with instructions to say: 'Master, we know that you are honest and teach the way of God in all sincerity; also that you are afraid of no one, having no regard for persons. So tell us what you think. Are we justified or not in paying the capitation-tax to Caesar?'

Jesus, who knew their evil ways, replied: 'You hypocrites! Why are you putting me to this test? Show me the coin with which we pay the tax.' And when they had brought him a shilling he asked them: 'Whose portrait and inscription are these?'

'Caesar's,' they told him.

'Very well,' said Jesus. 'Pay Caesar what is due to Caesar, and God what is due to God.' This left them marvelling. They let him be, and went.

On the same day he was approached by some Sadducees, who expressed their disbelief in the resurrection and set him a problem. 'Master,' they said, 'Moses laid it down that if a man died childless, his brother should marry his widow and so provide him with descendants. Now we know of a case where there were seven brothers, the first of whom married and died, and being without issue left his wife to his brother. This brother did the same, and so did the third, and so on to the seventh. Last of all the woman died. Now since she was married to all seven, whose wife will she be in the resurrection?'

Jesus answered: 'You are at fault through your ignorance of the Scriptures and the power of God. In the resurrection there is no marrying or giving in marriage; people are like Angels in Heaven. But in this matter of the resurrection of the dead, have you not read God's words to you, *I am the God of Abraham and the God of Isaac and the God of Jacob?* He is not the God of the dead, but of the living.'

The people, when they heard this, were filled with admiration for his teaching. But when the Pharisees heard that he had reduced the Sadducees to silence they put their heads together; and one of them who was a Lawyer approached him with a searching question. 'Master,' he asked, 'which is the most important commandment in the Law?'

Jesus said: '*Thou shalt love the Lord thy God with all thy heart, with all thy soul, and with all thy thinking.* This is the greatest and first commandment. The second and comparable commandment is this: *Thou shalt love thy neighbour as thyself.* All the Law and the Prophets hang on these two commandments.'

The Pharisees by now had gathered round, and Jesus questioned them. 'What,' he asked, 'do you think about the Messiah? Whose son is he?'

'David's,' they replied.

'Then how,' said Jesus, 'can David, writing as a prophet, call him *Lord* and say, *The Lord said to my Lord "Sit on my right hand till I lay thy enemies under thy feet"*? If David calls him *Lord,* how can he be his son?'

Not a man could answer him a word. Nor from that day did anyone dare to ask him any further questions.

## 23

JESUS now addressed the people and his own disciples: 'The Doctors and the Pharisees have taken Moses' seat. You therefore must faithfully observe all the rules they lay down for you. But do not imitate their deeds; for they talk but do not act. They make up heavy burdens and lay them on men's shoulders – burdens they will not lift a finger to remove. Everything they do is done for show. They broaden their phylacteries and lengthen the tassels on their cloaks; they love the best places at banquets and the best seats in the synagogue; they like people to salute them in the street and call them Rabbi.

'Do not let people call you Rabbi. You have one Master only, and you are all brothers.

'Call no one your Father on earth. You have one Father only, and he is in Heaven.

'And do not be called Leaders. You have one Leader only, and he is the Christ.

'The greatest among you will be your servant. The man who exalts himself shall be humbled, and the man who humbles himself shall be exalted.

'But alas for you, Doctors and Pharisees, hypocrites who shut the gates of the Kingdom of Heaven on mankind; who do not enter it yourselves, but stop the people that are coming in.

'Alas for you, Doctors and Pharisees, hypocrites that cross sea and land to make one convert, and when you have succeeded, leave him twice the child of Hell you are yourselves.

'Alas for you, blind leaders, who say that when a man swears by the Temple he is not committed; but when he swears by the gold of the Temple he has bound himself. Blind fools! Which of the two is greater, the gold or the Temple that has made it holy?

'Again, you say that when a man swears by the altar he is not committed; but when he swears by the offering that lies upon it he has bound himself. Blind fools! Which of the two is greater, the offering or the altar that makes it holy? In swearing by the altar is a man not swearing also by all that lies upon it? In swearing by the Temple is he not swearing also by Him that dwells in the Temple? And in swearing by Heaven is he not swearing by the throne of God and by Him that sits upon it?

'Alas for you, Doctors and Pharisees, hypocrites that pay your tithes of mint, anise and cummin, but disregard the weightier obligations of the Law – justice, mercy, and good faith. These are the duties that you should have carried out, while not neglecting those. Blind leaders! You filter your wine to get rid of a gnat, and you swallow a camel.

'Alas for you, Doctors and Pharisees, hypocrites that clean the outside of the cup and bowl, whose contents are the fruit of rapine and unbridled greed. Blind Pharisee, clean first the inside of the cup and bowl, in order that the outside may be clean as well.

'Alas for you, Doctors and Pharisees, hypocrites that are like whitewashed tombs, which make a fine show from without, but are full inside of dead men's bones and every kind of filth. Thus, you are law-abiding men to outside view; yet there is nothing but hypocrisy and wickedness within you.

'Alas for you, Doctors and Pharisees, hypocrites that build the Prophets' tombs and adorn the monuments of righteous men, and as you do this say, "Had we lived in our fathers' time we should not have joined with them in the shedding of the Prophets' blood." You thus admit that you are the sons of those that killed the Prophets. Then do as they did, and complete your fathers' work! Serpents, offspring of vipers, how can you save yourselves from being sent to hell?

'Know now why I am sending you prophets and wise and learned men, some to be killed and crucified by you, some to be scourged in your synagogues and chased from town to town. It is to bring upon your hands the blood of every righteous man that has been killed on earth, from Abel the Good to Zachariah son of Barachiah, whom you slew between the Altar and the Shrine. Indeed I tell you, the guilt of all that blood will fall upon this generation.

'Jerusalem, Jerusalem, you that slay the prophets and stone those that are sent you, how often have I longed to gather your children to me as a hen gathers her chickens under her wings, and they would not come. And now, *you have your city to yourselves*. For I tell you, from this day you shall not see me till you say, *Blessed be he that cometh in the name of the Lord!*'

# 24

JESUS was on his way out of the Temple when his disciples came forward and asked him to admire its architecture. He said to them: 'You see all this? I prophesy to you that not a block of stone here will be left standing on another. All shall be cast down.'

Later, as he sat on the Mount of Olives, he was approached by the disciples privately. 'Tell us,' they said, 'when is this going to happen? And what portent will there be of your advent and the end of the age?'

For answer Jesus said: 'Take care that no one deceives you. For many will appear and use my name, saying "I am the Christ"; and many people will be led astray by them. You are going to hear of wars and rumours of war. Beware of panic. These things must happen; but that is not the end. For nation will rise against nation, and kingdom against kingdom. There will be famines and earthquakes in one land or another. But all these things are only the beginnings of the birthpangs.

'Those are the days when they will have you put to torture

and to death. You will be hated by the pagan world because you use my name. Then too many will recant; they will betray one another, they will hate one another. Many false prophets will arise and lead many astray; and since iniquity will be at large, love will grow cold in the hearts of most. But he that endures to the uttermost will be saved. Moreover, these good tidings of the Kingdom must be proclaimed throughout the peopled world to let the pagan nations know.

'And then the end will come.

'When therefore you see *the abomination of desolation*, which the Prophet Daniel spoke of, standing *in a holy place*,* let those in Judaea take refuge in the hills; let the man on the housetop not come down to save his household goods; let the man in the fields not turn back to pick up his cloak.

'Alas, in those days, for the woman with a child in her womb or at her breast! Pray that you may not have to flee in winter or on the sabbath day. For there will be such suffering then as there has never been since the world began, and will not be again. If those days had not been shortened no living thing would have escaped. But they shall be shortened, for the sake of the elect.

'If anyone says to you then "See, here is the Christ!" or "He is there!" do not believe him. False Christs and false prophets will arise and produce great miracles and portents in order, if possible, to lead even the elect astray. But I have forewarned you. And therefore if they say to you "See, he is in the desert!" do not go out, or "He is hiding in our midst," do not believe them; for as the lightning leaps across the sky from east to west, so will be the advent of the Son of Man.

'Where the corpse is, there the vultures will foregather. And directly after those days of tribulation the sun will be darkened and the moon will not give her light, the stars will fall down from the sky and the mighty ones of heaven will be

* Reader, note this well.

shaken. *Then* the sign of the Son of Man will appear in the sky. Then too all the peoples of the earth will beat their breasts; and they will see the Son of Man coming on the clouds of Heaven with great power and glory. He will send out his Angels with a great trumpet, and they will gather in his elect from the four winds, from one horizon to the other.

'Look to the fig-tree for its lesson. When its shoots grow tender and begin to put out leaves, you know that summer is near. In the same way when you see all this you must know that *it* is near, nay, at the very door. Indeed I tell you, this generation shall not pass away till all these things have taken place. Heaven and earth shall pass away, but my words shall not.

'But of that day and hour no one has knowledge – not even the Angels of Heaven, not even the Son, but only the Father.

'For the advent of the Son of Man will be like the time of Noah. In the days before the Flood people were eating and drinking, marrying and giving in marriage, up to the very day when Noah entered the ark; and they knew nothing till the Flood came and swept them all away. Such will be the advent of the Son of Man. There will be two men in the fields – one is taken and the other left; two women grinding at the mill – one is taken and the other left.

'Watch therefore, since you do not know the day when your Lord is coming. You may be sure that if the owner of the house had known at what time of night the burglar was coming he would have stayed awake and not allowed his house to be broken into. Be vigilant yourselves, because the Son of Man is coming when you least expect him.

'And who proves himself the wise and faithful servant when his master has left him to direct his household and give out their daily food? That servant, happy man, whom his master when he comes finds in the faithful discharge of these duties. That surely is the man whom he will make director of his whole estate. But if that wicked servant says to himself, "My master is long in coming," and takes to bullying his fellow-servants, to gluttony and drinking with the tipplers, his Lord will come on a day when he did not expect him, at a time he did not know. And he will tear him to pieces and consign him to the hypocrites' lot. There will be weeping there and gnashing of teeth.

# 25

'HEAR what the Kingdom of Heaven will resemble *then*.

'Ten maidens had to meet the bridegroom; so when they left their homes they took their lanterns with them. Now five of them were wise. But five were foolish, for they took their lanterns but they brought no oil; whereas the wise ones took some oil in flasks as well as in their lanterns.

'The bridegroom was late; so they all nodded and slept. But in the middle of the night somebody cried, "The bridegroom! Go and meet him." This woke up all the girls, and they trimmed their lanterns. The foolish said to the wise, "Give us some of your oil: our lanterns are going out." To which the wise replied, "But there may not be enough for you and us. You had better go to an oilshop and buy some for yourselves." So they went off to buy some.

'Meanwhile the bridegroom came. The girls who had been ready went in with him to the wedding, and the door was shut. But presently the other girls returned. "Lord, Lord," they said, "open the door for us." And he replied, "Indeed I do not know you."

'Watch therefore, since you do not know the day or time.

'And hear another parable. There was a man who called his servants to him before going abroad and entrusted them with his riches. He let one have five talents; another, two;

another, one – adjusting the amount in each case to the man's ability. Then he started on his journey.

'The man who got five talents went at once and traded with them; he made another five. So did the man with two; he made another two. But the man with one went and dug in the ground and hid his master's money.

'Time went by, but at length their master returned. When he called them to account, the man who got five talents came forward with his extra five. "Sir," he said, "you let me have five talents. Here are five more that I have made." His master replied: "Well done, my good and faithful servant! You have been trustworthy with a little: I will entrust you with much. Share your master's joy." In the same way the man with two talents came forward and said, "Sir, you let me have two talents. Here are two more that I have made." And his master said: "Well done, my good and faithful servant! You have been trustworthy with a little: I will entrust you with much. Share your master's joy."

'The man who had one talent also came up. "Sir," he said, "I knew you for a hard man, who harvests where he has not sown, and gathers where he has not winnowed. So I was afraid and I went and hid your talent in the ground. Here then you have what is yours."

'His master replied: "Wicked and lazy servant! You knew that I harvest where I have not sown, and gather where I have not winnowed. Accordingly you should have put my money in the bank, and on my return I would have recovered it with interest. Take the talent from him, and give it to the man with ten. For in every case more shall be given to the man who has – he shall be enriched; but from the man who has not, even what he has shall be taken. Cast the unprofitable servant into the outer darkness, where there shall be weeping and gnashing of teeth."

'When the Son of Man comes in his glory, and all the Angels with him, he will sit down on the throne of his glory.

All the nations will be gathered before him, and he will sort out the people like a shepherd sorting out his sheep and goats. The sheep he will put on his right hand and the goats on his left. Then the King will say to those on his right: "Come, you blessed ones that belong to my Father; inherit the Kingdom prepared for you from the foundation of the world. For I was hungry and you gave me food; I was thirsty and you gave me drink; I was homeless and you brought me in; naked and you clothed me; I was sick and you visited me; I was in prison and you came to my side."

'To this the righteous will reply: "When, Lord, did we see you hungry and feed you; or thirsty and give you drink? When did we see you homeless and bring you in; or naked and clothe you? And when did we see you sick or in prison and come to your side?"

'And the King will answer: "I tell you in all truth that in so far as you did these things to one of these my brothers, these little ones, you did them to me."

'Then he will turn to those on his left and say: "Depart from me, accursed people, into the eternal fire prepared for the Devil and his angels. For I was hungry and you did not feed me; I was thirsty and you did not give me drink; I was homeless and you did not bring me in; naked and you did not clothe me; sick and in prison and you did not visit me."

'They too will answer him and say: "Lord, when did we see you hungry or thirsty or homeless or naked or sick or in prison, and fail to look after you?"

'"Hear the truth," the King will say to them. "In so far as you did not do these things to one of these little ones, you did not do them to me." And they will depart into eternal punishment, but the righteous into eternal life.'

## 26

IT was after speaking to them thus on all these matters that Jesus said to his disciples: 'You know that two days hence there comes the Passover, and that the Son of Man is handed over to be crucified.'

Meanwhile the Chief Priests and the Elders of the people assembled in the court of the High Priest, whose name was Caiaphas. They plotted to get Jesus into their power by a stratagem and put him to death. But they said: 'We must not do this during the Festival, or the people may riot.'

While Jesus was staying at Bethany in the house of Simon the Leper he was approached by a woman with an alabaster jar of very precious ointment, which she poured on his head as he sat at table. The disciples when they saw this were indignant. 'Why this waste?' they asked. 'That might have fetched a good price, and so been given to the poor.'

Jesus overheard and said to them: 'Why are you scolding the woman? What she has done for me is a beautiful thing. You have the poor among you always; but me you have not always. In pouring this ointment on my body she was preparing for my burial. I tell you in all truth that wherever in the whole world this gospel is preached, the thing this woman did will also be spoken of, so that she shall not be forgotten.'

One of the Twelve, the man called Judas of Kerioth, now went to the Chief Priests and said: 'What are you willing to give me if I deliver him to you myself?' They paid him thirty silver pieces, and from that time Judas sought an opportune moment to betray him.

On the first day of the Festival of Unleavened Bread the disciples came to Jesus and said: 'Where do you wish us to arrange for you to eat the Passover?'

He said: 'Go to so-and-so in the town and tell him that the Master says, "My time is near. I and my disciples are keeping the Passover in your house."' The disciples did as Jesus told them and made arrangements for the Passover.

Evening came, and he took his place at table with the twelve disciples. While they were eating he said: 'Hear the truth. One of you is going to betray me.'

Sick at heart they began to say to him one after the other: 'Lord, surely it is not I?'

He replied: 'One that has dipped his hand in the bowl with me will be my betrayer. The Son of Man goes his way, as the Scriptures say of him. But alas for him through whom the Son of Man is betrayed! Better for that man if he had never been born.'

Judas, his betrayer, took this up and said: 'Rabbi, surely it is not I?' And Jesus answered: 'It is you that have said it.'

While they were still at table Jesus took a loaf, blessed God, broke it and gave it to the disciples. 'Take and eat this,' he said; 'it is my body.'

Next he took a cup, gave thanks to God, and handed it to them, saying: 'Drink all of you from this. For here is my blood, the blood of the Covenant, which is being shed for many, for the forgiveness of sins. Moreover I tell you that I shall not again enjoy this fruit of the vine till the day when I drink a new kind of wine with you in the Kingdom of my Father.'

Then they sang a psalm and went out to the Mount of Olives.

Jesus now said to them: 'This very night you will all renounce your faith in me. Do not the Scriptures say, *I shall strike the shepherd and the sheep of his flock will be scattered*? Nevertheless, when I have risen I will go before you into Galilee.'

But Peter said: 'Though all renounce their faith in you, I shall never do so.'

'I assure you,' Jesus answered, 'that this very night before the cock crows you will disown me thrice.'

Peter said: 'Even if I have to die with you, I shall never disown you.' And all the other disciples said the same.

Jesus now came with them to a place called Gethsemane and said to the disciples: 'Sit here while I go over there and pray' But he took with him Peter and the two sons of Zebedee; and in the anguish and the desolation that came upon him now, he said to them: 'My heart is heavy to the point of death. Wait here and stay awake with me.'

Then he went a little farther and prostrated himself in prayer. 'My Father,' he said, 'if it is possible, let this cup pass from me. Nevertheless, not as I will, but as thou wilt.'

Coming back to the disciples, he found them sleeping and said to Peter: 'So you had not the strength to stay awake with me for a single hour? Watch and pray that you may not be brought to ordeal. The spirit is eager, but the flesh is weak.'

For the second time he went away and prayed. 'My Father,' he said, 'if it cannot be that this cup should pass without my drinking it, let thy will be done.'

And once more coming back he found them asleep, for their eyes were heavy.

Leaving them, he withdrew again and prayed for the third time in the same words as before. And now he came back to the disciples and said: 'Sleep on then and take your rest. And yet the hour is near when the Son of Man is handed over to sinners. Up now and let us go. See, my betrayer is near.'

Before he had finished speaking, Judas, one of the Twelve, appeared, and with him a large force armed with swords and sticks, who had been sent by the Chief Priests and Elders of the people. His betrayer had arranged a signal with them. 'Your man,' he had said, 'is the one I kiss. Arrest him.' So he went straight up to Jesus, said 'Greetings, Rabbi' and kissed him.

Jesus said: 'My friend, do what you have come for.' And they came forward, laid hands on Jesus and arrested him.

Whereupon one of those with Jesus put his hand to his sword, drew it, and struck the High Priest's slave, shearing off his ear.

Jesus said to him: 'Put your sword back in its place; for all that draw the sword shall perish by the sword. Or do you suppose that I could not call upon my Father and that he would not in a moment have a greater force than fifty thousand Angels at my side? But then, how could the Scriptures be fulfilled which say, It shall be thus?'

It was now that Jesus said to the crowd: 'I see you have come out with swords and sticks to capture me as though I were a brigand. Day after day I sat in the Temple, teaching, and you did not arrest me. But all this has happened so that what the Prophets wrote may be fulfilled.'

All the disciples now deserted him and fled. But the men who had arrested Jesus took him off to the palace of the High Priest, Caiaphas, where the Doctors and the Elders then assembled. Peter followed him at a distance as far as the courtyard of the High Priest. There he went in and sat down with the guard. He wished to see the end.

Meanwhile the Chief Priests and the whole Council were casting about for evidence against Jesus, on which, though false, they could condemn him to death. But they found none, though many false witnesses appeared. At last two men came forward and said: 'This man claimed that he could pull down the Temple of God and in three days build it up again.'

The High Priest rose and said to him: 'You make no reply? What of the evidence these men have given against you?'

But Jesus kept silence. And now the High Priest said: 'I put you under oath by the living God to tell us, if you are indeed the Christ, the son of God.'

Jesus replied: 'The words are yours. This much I add to them, The time has come when you will see the Son of Man sitting at the right hand of the Power and coming on the clouds of Heaven.'

At this the High Priest tore his clothes and said: 'He has blasphemed. What further need have we of witnesses? You heard this blasphemy just now. What is your opinion?' And they all declared he had deserved to die.

Then they spat in his face and struck him with their fists. Others, belabouring him, said: 'Prophesy to us, Messiah. Which of us struck you?'

Meanwhile as Peter sat outside in the courtyard a maid-servant came up to him and said: 'You too were with Jesus of Galilee.'

Peter denied it in front of everyone. 'I don't know him,' he said. 'What are you talking about?'

He went out to the gatehouse, where another maid saw him and said to the people there: 'This fellow was with Jesus of Nazareth.'

And again he denied it, with an oath. 'I do not know the man,' he said.

A little later the bystanders went up to Peter and said: 'You too are certainly one of them. For quite apart from other things, your accent betrays you.'

Peter began to call down curses on himself and swear that he did not know the man. But at that moment the cock crew, and Peter, remembering how Jesus had said to him, 'Before the cock crows you will disown me thrice,' went out and wept bitterly.

# 27

MORNING came, and the Chief Priests and Elders of the people met in full council to decide on measures against Jesus that would ensure his execution. After binding him they led him off and handed him over to Pilate, the Procurator.

But Judas, his betrayer, when he saw that he had been condemned, repented and brought back the thirty silver pieces to the Chief Priests and Elders. He said: 'I have done wrong. I have brought an innocent man to his death.'

'That is your business,' they said. 'Why should we care?' Whereupon Judas left the money as an offering in the Temple and withdrew. Then he went and hanged himself.

But the Chief Priests took the money out, arguing that it was not lawful to put it in the Treasury since it was the price of blood. After discussing the matter they spent it on the purchase of the Potter's Field where foreigners could be buried. Hence the field was called the Field of Blood.* And it bears that name to-day.

Jesus stood before the Procurator, who interrogated him. 'Are *you*,' he asked, 'the King of the Jews?'

'The words are yours,' said Jesus. And to all the charges of the Chief Priests and Elders he made no reply.

Pilate then said to him: 'Do you not hear what a case they are building up against you?' But Jesus made the Procurator no reply on any point whatever, leaving him completely at a loss.

On a holiday it was the Procurator's custom to set one prisoner free for the people, leaving the choice to them. On this occasion they had a man in prison called Barabbas, who was a popular hero. So Pilate, when he was faced by the crowd, said: 'Whom do you wish me to set free – Jesus Barabbas or Jesus who is called Christ?' For he was well aware that they had brought him up for judgement because they were jealous.

At this point, Pilate, as he sat in his official chair, received a message from his wife. 'Do nothing to that innocent man,' she said. 'I dreamt about him in the night and was much distressed on his account.'

* Here was fulfilment for the words spoken through the Prophet Jeremiah: *They took the thirty silver pieces, the price of the Precious One on whom some Israelites had set a price, and spent them on the Potter's Field. Thus the Lord instructed me.*

Meanwhile the Chief Priests and the Elders had persuaded the crowd to ask for Barabbas and let Jesus be destroyed. So when the Procurator returned to the matter and asked them which of the two they wished him to set free, they said Barabbas.

'In that case,' said Pilate, 'what am I to do with Jesus who is called Christ?'

They all shouted: 'Let him be crucified!'

'But what crime has he committed?' said the Procurator – which only made them shout still louder, 'Let him be crucified!'

When Pilate saw that he was doing no good, but that on the contrary a riot was impending, he took some water, washed his hands before the crowd and said: 'I am innocent of this man's blood. It is your affair.' And with one accord the people answered: 'Let his blood be on our heads and the heads of our children.'

Then he set Barabbas free for them, and after having Jesus flogged, he handed him over for crucifixion.

The Procurator's bodyguard took Jesus with them to the Residence, where they gathered the whole detachment round him. They stripped him and dressed him in a scarlet cloak. They plaited a garland of thorns, placed it on his head, and put a cane in his right hand. They knelt before him and in mockery saluted him – 'Hail, King of the Jews.' They spat at him, and taking the cane they beat him on the head with it. Then, their mockery of him finished, they took off the cloak, dressed him in his own clothes, and led him away to be crucified. And as they left the town, they fell in with a Cyrenaean called Simon, and impressed the man to carry his cross.

They came to a place called Golgotha, which is known as the Place of the Skull, and there they gave him wine to drink, mixed with gall. He tasted this but would not drink it. Then they crucified him, and parcelled out his clothing, casting lots. And they sat down there to guard him.

They had fixed above his head a placard on which the charge against him was set forth in writing – *This is Jesus the King of the Jews.* Two robbers were crucified with him, one on the right and one on the left.

People passing by reviled him. They shook their heads and said: 'You that pull down the Temple and in three days build it up again, save yourself. If you are a son of God, come down from the cross.'

So too the Chief Priests with the Doctors and the Elders made derisive comments. They said: 'He saved others, but he cannot save himself. He is the King of Israel; let him come down now from the cross, and we shall believe in him. He put his trust in God: let God save him now, if he wants him. Did he not say, I am the son of God?' Even the robbers who were crucified with him flung the same taunts at Jesus.

From the sixth to the ninth hour the whole country was darkened. At about the ninth hour, Jesus cried out in a loud voice, *Eloi, Eloi, lema sabachthani,* which means, 'My God, my God, why hast thou forsaken me?'

Some of the men standing there, when they heard this, said: 'It is Elijah he is calling on.' And one of them ran quickly and fetched a sponge, which he filled with vinegar, put on a cane and offered to Jesus. But the rest said: 'Leave him alone and let us see if Elijah comes to the rescue.'

But Jesus cried out again in a loud voice and yielded up his life. And now the curtain of the Temple was torn in two from top to bottom. There was an earthquake and the rocks were split; tombs were thrown open and the bodies of many sleeping saints arose, and when he himself had risen, came out of their tombs and entered the Holy City, where many people saw them.

When the centurion and the men who were guarding Jesus with him saw the earthquake and the prodigies, they were filled with awe and said: 'This was indeed a son of God.'

Watching from afar there were also a number of women

who had followed Jesus from Galilee, ministering to his wants. Among them were Mary Magdalene, Mary the mother of James and Joseph, and the mother of Zebedee's sons. And later in the day there came a man called Joseph, a wealthy Arimathaean, who had himself been a pupil of Jesus. This man had approached Pilate with a request for the body of Jesus, and Pilate had given orders that it should be handed over to him. So Joseph took the body, wrapped it in clean linen and laid it in his own new tomb which he had cut in the rock. And before he went away he rolled a large stone against the entrance of the tomb. Mary Magdalene and the other Mary were there; they sat where they could see the grave.

On the next day, the day that follows the Eve, the Chief Priests and Pharisees approached Pilate in a body. 'Your Excellency,' they said, 'it has occurred to us that while he was still alive that impostor said, "After three days I come back to life." We ask you therefore to have the grave protected for three days. We are afraid that the disciples may come and steal him away and say to the people, "He has risen from the dead." If they do, the final imposture will be worse than the first.'

'You can have your guard,' said Pilate. 'Go and make the grave secure as best you can.' So they went and did so. They not only mounted watchmen but they sealed the stone.

# 28

AFTER the Sabbath, towards dawn on the first day of the week, Mary Magdalene and the other Mary came to look at the grave. And behold, the earth began to shake – an Angel of the Lord came down from Heaven, approached, and having rolled the stone away sat down on it. He was like lightning to the eye and his clothes were white as snow. The watchmen quaked for fear of him and lay like dead men. And now the Angel spoke and said to the women: 'No need for you to fear. I know you are looking for Jesus, who was crucified. He is not here; for he has come back to life, as he said he would. Approach and see the place where he lay. Then go quickly and tell his disciples that he has risen from the dead and is preceding them to Galilee, where they will see him. I have spoken.'

Leaving the tomb at once, in awe and great joy, they ran to tell his disciples. And now Jesus himself met them.

'Greetings,' he said. And they came forward, seized his feet and worshipped him.

Then Jesus said: 'Do not be afraid. Go and tell my brothers to set out for Galilee. They will see me there.'

While the women were on their way, some of the guard went into the city and reported to the Chief Priests all that had happened. These held a meeting with the Elders, and after debating the matter gave the soldiers a large bribe and said: 'Your story must be that his disciples came by night and stole him away while you were asleep. If this comes to the Procurator's ears we will put things right with him and see that you have nothing to fear.' The soldiers took the money and carried out their instructions, with the result that this story has been current in Jewish circles ever since.

Meanwhile the eleven disciples made their way to Galilee, to the mountain where Jesus had arranged to meet them. When they saw him they worshipped him. But some were unconvinced.

Jesus came forward and spoke to them. He said: 'I have been given full authority in Heaven and on earth. Set forth and make all peoples your disciples, baptizing them into the Name of the Father and the Son and the Holy Spirit, and teaching them to keep all the commandments I gave you.

'Know too that I am with you every day to the end of time.'

# THE GOSPEL AS RECORDED BY
# LUKE

*Seeing that many have undertaken to arrange in narrative form such accounts of the momentous happenings in our midst as have been handed down to us by the original eye-witnesses and ministers of the Word, I too have thought fit, having kept in close touch with the whole course of these events, to write a history, which I dedicate to you, Theophilus, in the hope of bringing home to Your Excellency the truth of what you have already learnt.*

IN the reign of Herod, King of Judaea, there was a priest called Zacharias, of the Order of Abijah. His wife was one of Aaron's daughters, and her name was Elizabeth. Both were righteous in the sight of God, living a blameless life in full observance of the commandments and precepts of the Lord. They had no children as Elizabeth was barren; and both were well advanced in years.

One day, when he was acting as priest in his Order's week of Temple service and the priesthood cast lots as usual, it fell to him to go into the Shrine of the Lord and burn the incense. While this was being done the whole congregation stayed outside and prayed. But to him a Messenger of the Lord appeared, standing on the right of the altar of incense. Zacharias was overwhelmed at the sight, and terror seized him. But the Angel said: 'Have no fears, Zacharias, for your prayer was heard; and your wife Elizabeth will bear you a son, and you shall call him John. To you he will be a joy and a delight, and many others will rejoice at his birth; for he will be great in the sight of the Lord. He shall drink no wine and no strong liquor, and from the moment of his birth he will be filled with the Holy Spirit. He will turn many of Israel's sons to the Lord their God, in whose sight he will walk forward in the spirit and power of Elijah, to turn the hearts of fathers to their children, to cause the disobedient to embrace the wisdom of the righteous, and so make ready for the Lord a people well prepared.'

Zacharias said to the Angel: 'How can I tell that this is true? I am an old man and my wife is well advanced in years.'

'I am Gabriel,' the Angel answered him. 'My place is at the side of God, and I was sent to speak to you and give you these good tidings. Learn then that you shall be silent and bereft of speech until the day when these things come to be, because you did not trust my words – words that in their due time shall be fulfilled.'

Meanwhile the congregation waited for Zacharias and wondered why he lingered in the Shrine. When he did come out he could say nothing to them, and they understood that he had had a vision in the Shrine. He could only nod to them, and his dumbness did not pass away.

When his term of duty in the Temple was over he went home. And his wife Elizabeth in due course conceived. Then for five months she withdrew herself from view, saying that this was what the Lord had planned for her at the time when he deigned to bring her humiliation to an end.

In the sixth month the Angel Gabriel was sent by God to a town in Galilee called Nazareth, to a maiden betrothed to a man named Joseph, of the house of David. The maiden's name was Mary. Gabriel went in to her and said: 'Greetings, lady of grace! The Lord is with you.'

She was cast into confusion by his words and asked herself what this salutation might portend.

'Have no fears, Mary,' said the Angel; 'for you have found grace with God. Know that you will conceive and bear a son, whom you shall call Jesus. He will be great and shall be known as the son of the Most High. The Lord God will give him the throne of his father David. He shall reign over the House of Jacob into the ages, and of his Kingdom there shall be no end.'

But Mary said to the Angel: 'How will this be brought about, seeing that I have not lain with any man?'

The Angel replied: 'The Holy Spirit will come upon you and the Power of the Most High will draw its shadow over you. Wherefore the Child too is holy, and shall be called the son of God. Learn also that Elizabeth herself, your kinswoman, has conceived a son in her old age – for six months she has been with child, though people called her barren. But nothing is impossible for God.'

Mary said: 'I am the bondswoman of the Lord. Let me be dealt with as you say.' And the Angel left her.

Mary then set out and made her way with haste into the hill-country, to a town in Judaea, where she went into Zacharias' house and greeted Elizabeth. When Elizabeth heard Mary's greeting, the baby leapt in her womb and she was filled with the Holy Spirit. She uttered a loud cry and said:

'Blessed are you among women,
    And blessed is the fruit of your womb!
But how have I deserved
    That the mother of my Lord should come to me?
For no sooner did your greeting reach my ears
    Than the baby in my womb leapt in his delight.

I too was happy in the trust I felt,
> For the words that reached me from the Lord are
> coming to fulfilment.'

And Mary said:
'My soul magnifies the Lord,
> And my spirit has exulted in my saviour God;

For he looked upon his servant's lowliness –
> And all generations from to-day will call me happy.

For the Mighty One has done great things for me,
> And his Name is holy.

His mercy for those that fear him
> Stretches from generation to generation.

He has wrought a victory with his arm:
> He has scattered the proud in the conceit of their
> hearts;

He has dragged dynasts from their thrones and exalted
> the humble,
> Filled the hungry with good things and sent away the
> rich man empty;

He has embraced his servant Israel,
> So that, as he told our fathers,

His mercy may be kept in mind
> By Abraham and by his sons for ever.'

Mary stayed with her for about three months. Then she returned to her own house.

And now Elizabeth's time came and she bore a son. Her neighbours and kinsmen, when they heard that she had been granted this signal mercy by the Lord, joined in her gladness. On the eighth day they came to circumcise the child, and had begun to call him Zacharias after his father, when his mother intervened. 'No,' she said; 'he shall be called John.'

'But in your family,' they said, 'nobody bears that name.' And in the language of signs they asked his father what he wished him to be called.

Zacharias sent for a tablet, and on this he wrote: 'His name is John.' They were amazed. And suddenly his lips and tongue were freed, and he spoke and praised God.

Their neighbours were all filled with awe. Throughout the hill-country of Judaea the tale in all its details passed from mouth to mouth, and all who heard it took it to their hearts and pondered on the future of this little child. As well they might; for the hand of God was on him.

His father Zacharias was filled with the Holy Spirit and broke into prophecy:

'Blessed be the Lord, the God of Israel,
  For he has visited and brought redemption to his people,
Forging a weapon of salvation for us
  In the House of his servant David,
As promised through his ever holy prophets,
    Salvation from our foes and from the hands of all that
      hate us;
Extending his mercy to our forefathers,
  And pointing to the holy covenant he made
When he swore to our father Abraham
    That we, released from fear and from our enemies'
      hands,
Should serve him in holiness and righteousness,
  Abiding in his presence all our days.
And you, little one, shall be Prophet of the Most High,
  For you will go before the Lord to prepare his ways,
To give his people knowledge of salvation
  In the forgiveness of their sins,
Through the compassion of our God,
  By which the Day will dawn on us from Heaven
To give light to those that sit in darkness and the shadow
    of death,
  And to guide our feet into the way of peace.'

The child grew up and gathered spiritual strength. And he lived in the waste lands till the day when he announced himself to Israel.

AT this time Caesar Augustus issued a decree that a census of the whole world should be made.* Accordingly all the people went to be registered, each to his own town. Among them, Joseph travelled up for this purpose from the town of Nazareth in Galilee to David's town of Bethlehem in Judaea, belonging as he did to the House and Line of David; and he took with him Mary his wife, who was with child. While they were there her time came and she bore her son, her firstborn, whom she wrapped in swaddling-clothes and laid in a manger, because there was no room for them at the inn.

In the neighbourhood there were some shepherds living in the fields and taking it in turns to watch their flock by night. To them an Angel of the Lord appeared. The glory of the Lord shone round them and they were overcome with awe. But the Angel said: 'Have no fears; for I bring you good tidings, news of a great joy which the whole people will share. To-day, in David's town, there has been born for you a saviour, who is Christ the Lord. Know by this token – you will find a babe in swaddling-clothes lying in a manger.'

And with the Angel there suddenly appeared a multitude of others from the Heavenly Host, praising God and singing: 'Glory in the Heights to God, and on earth peace in men of good will.'

When the Angels left them and withdrew into Heaven, the shepherds said to one another: 'Let us go over now to Bethlehem and see this marvel of which the Lord has given us news.'

They came with eager haste and found them all, Mary and Joseph, and the baby lying in the manger. Once they had seen, they made it known how word had come to them about

* This was the first census – when Quirinius was Governor of Syria.

the child; and all who heard their story were amazed at what the shepherds told them. But Mary took note of all these things and turned them over in her heart. Meanwhile the shepherds went back to their flock, glorifying and praising God for the news they had heard and the sight that had confirmed it.

When the eighth day came round and the child could be circumcised, he was given the name of Jesus, which the Angel had given him before he was conceived. And when they had completed the term of their purification as prescribed by Moses, they took him up to Jerusalem to present him to the Lord in accordance with his law, *Every male that opens the womb shall be dedicated to the Lord;* and to offer a sacrifice as laid down in the Law of the Lord, *A pair of turtle-doves or two little pigeons.*

Now there was in Jerusalem a man called Symeon, who was righteous and devout and lived in the belief that Israel would one day be comforted. To him there came the spirit of prophecy and it was revealed to him by the Holy Spirit that he should not see death before setting eyes on the Lord's Anointed. Impelled by the Spirit, he went into the Temple; and when Jesus' parents had brought in the child to submit him to the customary rites, Symeon took him into his arms and blessed God in these words:

'Now lettest thou thy bondsman go, my Sovran Lord,
    According to thy word, in peace;
For my eyes have seen the salvation
    Thou hast prepared for all nations to behold,
A light of revelation to the pagans,
    And a glory for thy people Israel.'

The child's father and mother were lost in wonder at all that was said about him. Symeon blessed them and said to Mary his mother: 'This child is destined to set many in Israel on the downward or the upward path, and to serve as a revelation, which will be disputed – indeed the sword will pierce you also to the heart. Thus the inmost thoughts of many shall be brought into the light of day.'

And there was Hannah, a prophetess, the daughter of Phanuel of the tribe of Asher. She was very old, having lived with her husband for seven years after marriage, and by herself as a widow for as much as eighty-four years. She was never far from the Temple, where she worshipped night and day with fasts and prayers. And there at that very moment she appeared and rendered thanks to God, talking afterwards about the child to everyone who hoped to see Jerusalem redeemed.

Meanwhile, after observing every detail of the sacred Law, they went back into Galilee, to their own town of Nazareth. And the child grew big and strong. He was filled with wisdom and the grace of God was with him.

Every year his parents used to go to Jerusalem for the Passover Festival. When he was twelve they went up for the Festival as usual, and remained there for the days prescribed. But when they set out for home, the boy Jesus stayed behind in Jerusalem. His parents did not know, and they went a day's journey under the impression that he was in the caravan. Then they began to look for him among their relatives and friends, and finding that he was not there, returned to Jerusalem in search of him. So it was not till the third day that they found him. He was in the Temple, sitting in among the Doctors and putting questions to them as well as listening to what they said. Everyone who heard him was amazed at the understanding he showed in his replies. His parents were astounded when they saw him, and his mother said: 'My child, why did you treat us like this? Your father and I have been looking for you in the greatest distress.'

'Why need you look for me?' he said. 'Did you not know that I *must* be in my Father's House?' But they failed to understand what he was telling them.

He travelled down with them, came to Nazareth, and lived

under their direction, while his mother stored up in her memory all that had occurred. And Jesus increased in wisdom and stature, and in favour with God and man.

## 3

IN the fifteenth year of Tiberius Caesar's reign, when Pontius Pilate was procurator of Judaea, Herod tetrarch of Galilee, his brother Philip tetrarch of the lands of Ituraea and Trachonitis, and Lysanias tetrarch of Abilene; when Annas and Caiaphas were High Priest; word from God came to John son of Zacharias in the wilderness, and he went through the whole Jordan valley proclaiming, for the forgiveness of sins, a baptism of repentance – all in accordance with the Scripture in the book of the sayings of Isaiah the Prophet:

The voice of one crying in the wilderness:
'Prepare the way of the Lord;
Make his paths straight.
Every valley shall be filled,
And every mount and hillock shall be humbled.
There shall be straight roads instead of crooked ways,
Smooth roads instead of rough,
And every living thing shall see
The saving hand of God.'

John, therefore, used to say to the multitudes who came out to be baptized by him: 'Offspring of vipers, who warned you to fly from the wrath that is on its way? First you must prove your repentance by your deeds. And do not think of saying to yourselves that you have Abraham for father; for I tell you that God could raise children for Abraham from these very stones. But time is short, the axe lies ready at the root of the trees, and in the end every tree that does not bear good fruit is cut down and thrown into the fire.'

'Then what are we to do?' the people asked him.

He replied: 'Let the man who has two tunics share with another who has none; and let the man who has some food do likewise.'

Tax-collectors too came to be baptized. 'Master,' they said, 'what are we to do?'

'Exact no more than your scale allows,' said John.

Even soldiers consulted him. 'What of us?' they said. 'What are we to do?'

'Bully no one, blackmail no one, and be content with your pay.'

Now the people were expecting something. Everyone was wondering whether John might be the Christ. Therefore John used to say to them all: 'I baptize you with water. But *he* is on his way, one greater than I, who am not fit to undo his sandal-straps. He will baptize you in the Holy Spirit and fire. His winnowing-fan is in his hand, to clear his threshing-floor and gather the grain into his barn. But the chaff he will burn in inextinguishable fire.'

With many another and varied exhortation he gave his good tidings to the people. But Herod the Tetrarch, denounced as he was by him in the matter of Herodias his brother's wife, and all his other crimes, added one more to them by throwing John into prison.

Meanwhile, when all the people had been baptized and Jesus after his own baptism was praying, heaven was laid open and the Holy Spirit descended on him in bodily shape like a dove. And there was a voice from heaven: 'Thou art My son, the Beloved One. In thee I rejoice.'

Jesus himself when he began his mission was about thirty years of age, being the son, as was supposed, of Joseph, whose line went back, through Eli, Matthat, Levi, Melchiah, Janna, Joseph, Mattathiah, Amos, Nahum, Esli, Nagge, Maath, Mattathiah, Shimei, Josech, Judah, Jehonan, Rhesa, Zerubbabel, Salathiel, Neriah, Melchiah, Addi, Cosam, Almodad,

Er, Jesus, Eleazar, Jorim, Matthat, Levi, Symeon, Judah, Joseph, Jonam, Eliakim, Melea, Menna, Mattatha, Nathan, David, Jesse, Obed, Boaz, Salmon, Naashon, Aminadab, Aram, Hezron, Pharez, Judah, Jacob, Isaac, Abraham, Terah, Nachor, Serug, Reu, Peleg, Heber, Salah, Cainam, Arphaxad, Shem, Noah, Lamech, Methuselah, Enoch, Jared, Mahalaleel, Cainam, Enos, Seth, to Adam son of God.

# 4

FILLED with the Holy Spirit, Jesus left the Jordan and for forty days was guided by the Spirit in the wilderness and tempted by the Devil. He ate nothing during this time, and when it came to an end he was starving. The Devil said to him: 'If you are son of God, order this stone to turn into a loaf.' Jesus answered him by citing the Scripture, *Man shall not live on bread alone.*

The Devil also led him to a height, and showing him all the kingdoms of the peopled world in a moment of time, said: 'All this power and the glory of these kingdoms I will give to you, since it is vested in me and I give it to whomever I choose. Thus, if you do me homage, it shall all be yours.' Jesus answered him by citing the Scripture, *Thou shalt do homage to the Lord thy God and serve him only.*

He also took him to Jerusalem, where he made him stand on the cornice of the Temple and said: 'If you are son of God, throw yourself down from here; for the Scriptures say, *He shall put his Angels in charge of thee to keep thee from harm* and *They shall hold thee up on their hands; lest thou dash thy foot against a stone.*' Jesus answered him: 'It is laid down that *Thou shalt not put the Lord thy God to the proof.*'

When the Devil after tempting him in every way had done, he withdrew from him till a fresh occasion should present itself.

In the power of the Spirit, Jesus returned to Galilee. His fame spread through the whole countryside. He taught in their synagogues and everybody praised him.

He came to Nazareth, where he had been brought up, and went into the synagogue on the sabbath day, as he had always done. He stood up to read, and when they handed him the Book of the Prophet Isaiah, he unrolled the book and found this text:

'The Spirit of the Lord is on me,
    For He anointed me to bring good tidings to the poor.
He has sent me to proclaim deliverance to captives,
    And new eyes for the blind,
Setting the shattered free,
    And heralding an age acceptable to God.'

Jesus rolled up the book, gave it back to the minister and sat down. The eyes of the whole congregation were riveted upon him. And he began. 'To-day,' he told them, 'in your very hearing, this text is finding its fulfilment.'

They soon began to recognize his power, and astonished as they all were at his eloquence, they asked themselves, 'Is not this Joseph's son?'

Jesus now said: 'I have no doubt that you will quote me the proverb "Physician, heal yourself," and tell me to do here also, in my own country, all you have heard of as happening to Capernaum.' And he went on: 'The fact is that no prophet is accepted in his own country. I will remind you of a truth. In Elijah's day there were many widows in Israel when no rain fell for three and a half years and there was famine everywhere; and yet Elijah was not sent to help a single one of them, but he *was* sent to a widow at Zarephath, a city of Sidon. Again, in the Prophet Elisha's time there were many lepers in Israel, none of whom were cured; but Naaman, a Syrian, *was* cured.'

When they heard this the whole congregation was filled with wrath. They broke up the gathering, hurried him

out of their town and took him to the brow of the hill
on which it was built, intending to throw him down the
cliff. But he passed through the midst of them and went his
way.

He came down to Capernaum, which is a town in Galilee,
and taught them on the sabbath days. His way of teaching
filled them with amazement, for his words had the ring of
authority.

In the synagogue there was a man with an unclean spirit,
who cried out in a loud voice: 'Ha! What is your business
with us, Jesus the Nazarene? Have you come to destroy us?
I know who you are, the Holy One of God.'

Jesus rounded on him. 'Hold your tongue,' he said, 'and
come out of the man.'

The demon flung him into their midst, and without having
done him any harm came out of him. They were all filled
with awe. 'What is this teaching?' they said as they discussed
the matter. 'He gives his orders to unclean spirits with authority and power, and they come out.' There was no place in the
countryside that did not hear about him.

On leaving the synagogue, he went into Simon's house.
Now Simon's mother-in-law was suffering from high fever
and they consulted him about her. Jesus, standing over her,
rebuked the fever and it left her. She got up immediately and
began to wait on them.

As the sun set, all those with friends who were suffering
from this or that disease brought them to him; and he cured
them, laying his hands on every one. Not only that, but
demons came out of many others, crying aloud, 'You are
the Son of God.' These he sternly forbade to speak, because
they knew that he was the Christ.

When daylight came he left the house and made his way
into the open country. The crowd set out in search of him,
and when they came upon him they did their best to make
him stay with them. But he said to them: 'It is my duty to

proclaim the Kingdom of God to the other cities also. I was sent forth for that.' And he carried his message to the synagogues of Judaea.

# 5

HE was standing one day by the Lake of Gennesaret with the crowds pressing hard upon him as they listened to the Word of God, when he saw two boats drawn up by the water, while the fishermen who had come out of them washed their nets. He got into one of them, which belonged to Simon, and asked him to stand off a little from the shore. Then he sat down and taught the people from the boat.

When he had finished speaking he said to Simon: 'Take her out into deep water and lower your nets for a catch.'

'Master,' replied Peter, 'we toiled away all night and caught nothing. However, I will take your word for it and lower the nets.'

They did so, and netted an enormous catch of fish. Their nets were at breaking-point and they signalled to their mates in the other boat to come and help them. When these had come, they filled both boats till they threatened to founder.

Seeing this, Simon Peter fell at Jesus' knees and said: 'Leave me, for I am a sinful man, Lord.' Indeed, he and all his crew were filled with awe at the number of fish they had caught; and so were James and John, the sons of Zebedee, who were partners of Simon's.

'Do not be afraid,' Jesus said to Simon. 'From now on you will be catching men.' And they brought their boats back to land, left everything, and followed him.

During his stay in one of the cities, there suddenly appeared a man who was covered with leprosy. When he saw Jesus he prostrated himself in supplication. 'Lord,' he said, 'if you will, you can cleanse me.'

Jesus stretched out his hand, touched him and said: 'I will it. Be cleansed.' And the leprosy left him immediately.

Jesus ordered him to tell no one. 'But go and show yourself to the priest,' he said, 'and make the offering for your purification which Moses prescribed so that people might be notified.'

Yet Jesus' fame was more than ever blazed abroad, and large crowds gathered to hear him and to be cured of their infirmities, though he often retired into the solitudes to pray.

One day, surrounded by Pharisees and Lawyers from Jerusalem and every town in Galilee and Judaea, he was teaching and in full possession of the healing power of God, when some men arrived, carrying on a couch a paralytic whom they wanted to bring in and lay down before him. But the house was so packed with people that they could not see a way to get him in. So they went up on the roof, and through the tiles let him down into the middle of the gathering, couch and all, at Jesus' feet.

Seeing their faith, Jesus said: 'Man, your sins have been forgiven you.'

The Doctors of the Law and the Pharisees began to turn this over in their minds. 'Who is this blaspheming?' they said. 'Who can forgive sins but God alone?'

Jesus, aware of their thoughts, said: 'What are you thinking to yourselves? Which is the easier thing, to say "Your sins have been forgiven you," or to say "Get up and walk"? However, to teach you that the Son of Man has authority on earth to forgive sins' – and he turned to the paralyzed man – 'I say to you, Get up, take your couch, and walk home.'

The man rose immediately in view of the people, picked up the couch he had been lying on, and went home praising God. They were all dumbfounded and praised God in their awe. 'We never thought,' they said, 'to see what we have seen to-day.'

After this he left the town and observed a tax-collector

called Levi sitting by the custom-house. 'Follow me,' he said. And abandoning everything he rose and followed him.

In honour of Jesus, Levi gave a great reception in his house, and a large company of tax-collectors and others sat down with them at table. The Pharisees and the Doctors of their party made this a bone of contention with his disciples. 'Why,' they asked, 'do you eat and drink with tax-collectors and outcasts?'

Jesus said to them: 'It is not people in good health that need a physician, but those who are ill. I am here to call sinners, not the righteous, to a change of heart.'

They said: 'John's disciples fast regularly and say their prayers, as do those of the Pharisees, whereas yours eat and drink.'

Jesus replied: 'Surely you cannot make the friends of the bridegroom fast as long as the bridegroom is with them? But a time will come. And when the bridegroom is taken from them, that is the time, those are the days, when they will fast.'

He also gave them a parable: 'Nobody tears a piece from a new cloak to mend an old one; otherwise, not only will he make a hole in the new one, but the piece that came from it will fail to match the old. And no one pours new wine into old skins; or the new wine will burst the skins and run out, and the skins will be lost. No; we must pour new wine into fresh skins.

'Again, no drinker of old wine cares for new. "The old suits me," he says.'

# 6

ONE sabbath day he was walking through the cornfields and his disciples, plucking ears of corn, began to rub them in their hands and eat them.

Some of the Pharisees said: 'Why are you doing what is forbidden on the Sabbath?'

Jesus answered them by saying: 'Have you not read even this, what David did when he and his companions were hungry, how he went into the House of God, and taking the sacrificial loaves which only the priests have the right to eat, ate them and shared them with his comrades?' And he also said to them: 'The Son of Man is master of the Sabbath.'

On another sabbath day when he went to the synagogue and taught, there was a man there whose right hand was withered, and the Doctors and Pharisees watched him closely to see whether he would heal on the Sabbath, hoping to have a charge to bring against him. But he knew their thoughts and said to the man with the withered hand: 'Rise, and stand here in the centre.'

The man rose and stood there, and Jesus said to them: 'I put a question to you. Are we permitted on the Sabbath to choose between doing good and doing evil, saving a life and destroying?'

Then, after looking at each of them in turn, he said to the man: 'Hold out your hand.' He did so, and his hand was made sound once more.

But they were infuriated and began to ask each other what they should do to Jesus.

One day at about this time he went out into the hills to pray. He spent the night in prayer to God, and when morning came he summoned his disciples and selected from among them twelve, whom he called 'apostles' – Simon, whom he also called Peter, and his brother Andrew; James and John; Philip; Bartholomew; Matthew; Thomas; James son of Alphaeus; Simon, who was called the Zealot; Judas son of James; and Judas of Kerioth, who became a traitor.

He brought them down and took his stand on a level piece of ground with a large gathering of his own followers and a multitude of other folk from all over Judaea, from Jerusalem, and from the coastal regions of Tyre and Sidon, who had come to listen to him and to be cured of their diseases. People plagued by unclean spirits were restored to health; and everybody in the crowd struggled to touch him, for power was coming out of him and healing all.

Then, raising his eyes to rest on his disciples, Jesus said:

'Happy, you that are poor; for yours is the Kingdom of God.

'Happy, you that hunger now; for you shall be satisfied.

'Happy, you that weep now; for you shall laugh.

'Count yourselves happy when, on the Son of Man's account, people detest you, cast you out, revile you, and brand the name you bear. Rejoice when that time comes, and leap for joy, since your reward is great in Heaven. Did not their fathers treat the prophets so?

'But alas for you that are rich; for you have had your consolation.

'Alas for you that are filled now; for you shall hunger.

'Alas for you that laugh now; for you shall mourn and weep.

'Alas for you when all mankind applaud you. Did not their fathers do the same for the false prophets?

'But to you whose ear I have, Love your enemies, I say; be good to those that hate you; call blessings down on those that curse you; and pray for those that show you malice. To him that strikes you on the cheek, present the other; and do not grudge your tunic to the man who takes your cloak. Give to everyone that asks you; and from the man who takes your goods demand no restitution. Treat your fellowmen as you wish them to treat you.

'If you love those that love you, what thanks have you deserved? Even sinners love the people who love them. And if you do good to those that do good to you, what thanks have you deserved? Even sinners do as much. And if you lend where you expect returns, what thanks have you deserved?

Even sinners lend to sinners in the hope of full repayment. No; love your enemies, be good to them and lend, despairing of no one – and your reward will be great and you will be sons of the Most High. For He is kind himself to thankless and to evil men.

'Be compassionate, like your Father. Do not judge, and you shall not be judged; do not condemn, and you shall not be condemned; forgive, and you shall be forgiven. Give, and you shall receive – there will be poured into your lap good measure, pressed down, shaken together and running over. For as you give, so you shall receive, measure for measure.'

He also gave them a parable: 'Can one blind man lead another? Will they not both fall into a pit? Pupils are no better than their teacher – training only leaves them like him.

'Why do you note the little splinter in your brother's eye and take no notice of the beam in yours? How can you say to him, "Brother, let me remove the splinter from your eye," while failing to observe the beam in yours? Hypocrite, begin by removing the beam from your own eye, and then you will see clearly enough to pull the splinter out of your brother's.

'Good trees do not bear rotten fruit; rotten trees do not bear good fruit. We know our trees by the fruit that each produces. We do not go to thorn-trees for our figs, nor gather grapes from brambles. The good man, from the good that fills his heart, produces good; and the bad man evil from his evil store. In either case, it is what fills the heart that comes out at the lips.

'Why do you call me Lord, Lord, and not do what I say? Anyone who comes to me, listens to my words, and acts accordingly – shall I give you an idea of what he is like? He is like a man who, in building his house, dug and went deep and laid his foundations on the rock; so that when the river rose in flood and beat against the house, it was not strong enough to shake it, for it was well built. But anyone who

hears and does not act is like a man who built his house on
soil, with no foundations, so that when the river beat against
it, it collapsed at once. And what a fall it had!'

# 7

WHEN Jesus had imparted to the listening people all he wished
to say, he went into Capernaum.

A centurion there had a slave who was sick – indeed, he
was at death's door. His master set great store by him and so,
having heard about Jesus, he sent him a deputation of Jewish
Elders begging him to come and save his servant. These presented themselves to Jesus and earnestly besought him. They
said: 'The man is one who has deserved this kindness at your
hands, for he loves our people and he built us our synagogue
himself.'

Jesus went with them and had nearly reached the house
when the centurion sent him a message by some friends.
'Lord,' he said, 'do not put yourself out. I am not worthy to
receive you under my roof. Nor, for that reason, did I pre-
sume to come to you myself. But you have only to say the
word and my boy will be cured. For I too am a man who
derives his powers from above, with soldiers under me; and
I say to this one, Go, and he goes; to another, Come, and he
comes; and to my slave, Do this, and he does it.'

When he heard this Jesus was amazed at the man; and turning to the crowd that followed him, he said: 'I tell you, not
even in Israel have I found such faith.' And the messengers,
when they got back to the house, found the slave in perfect
health.

Some time after this he went to a city called Nain, with his
disciples and a large following. And it so happened that as he
came up to the city gate a man who had died was being car-

ried out for burial. He was the only son of his mother and she was a widow – many people from the town were with her. When he saw her the Lord was filled with compassion and said to her, 'Weep no more.' Then he went up and touched the bier. The bearers stopped, and he said, 'Young man, I say to you, arise.' And the dead man sat up and began to talk.

Jesus gave him to his mother. The people were all filled with awe; they praised God and they said, 'A great prophet has arisen among us: God has visited his people.' And before long, all over Judaea and in all the adjoining lands, they were speaking thus of Jesus.

John, who was informed by his own disciples of all these things, summoned two of them and sent them to Jesus with the question, 'Are you he that was coming, or are we to expect another?'

The men presented themselves to Jesus and said: 'John the Baptist sent us to you with the question, Are you he that was coming, or are we to expect another?'

Now this was a day when Jesus cured many people of their diseases and afflictions and of evil spirits, and bestowed the boon of sight on many blind men. So in reply to the messengers he said: 'Go and tell John what you saw and heard. The blind see once more; the lame walk; lepers are cleansed; the deaf hear; dead men are brought back to life; and beggars are proclaiming the Good News. Happy the man who finds no fault in me.'

When John's messengers had gone, Jesus began to talk to the people about John. He said: 'What did you go out into the desert to see? A reed swaying in the wind? No. Then what did you go out to see? A man in fine clothing? But it is in palaces that people fond of luxury and lovely clothes are found. Then why did you go out? To see a prophet. Yes, indeed, someone even greater than a prophet. For he is the man to whom the Scripture points: *Behold I send my Messenger ahead of thee to prepare thy way before thee.*

'I tell you, among men born of woman there is none greater than John, though even the lesser ones in the Kingdom of God are greater than he. And all the people when they heard him, including the tax-collectors, proved the wisdom of God's ways when they accepted baptism by John, whereas the Pharisees and Lawyers frustrated God's designs for them when they refused it.

'To whom then can I compare the men of this generation? Whom are they like? I am reminded of the children that sit in the market-place and call to their play-fellows, "We piped to you, but you did not dance; we sang you dirges, but you did not weep." For John the Baptist came, eating no bread, drinking no wine – and you say he is possessed. Then came the Son of Man, who eats and drinks – and you say, "Look at that glutton and drunkard, a friend of tax-collectors and outcasts." And yet God's ways were proved to have been wise by all His children.'

One of the Pharisees invited Jesus to dine with him. He had gone to this Pharisee's house and taken his place at table when a woman who had a bad name in the town, having learnt that he was dining at the Pharisee's, came up behind him with an alabaster jar of ointment she had brought and stood by his feet weeping. When her tears began to rain down on his feet she dried them with her own hair, kissed them repeatedly and anointed them with the unguent.

His host the Pharisee saw this and said to himself: 'If this man were indeed a prophet, he would know who and what the woman clinging to him is. He would know that she is a sinner.'

Jesus answered his thoughts. 'Simon,' he said, 'may I put something to you?'

'Surely, Master.'

'There was a man who had two people in his debt. One owed him fifty pounds, the other five. As they had no means of paying, he forgave them both. Now which of the two will love him most?'

136

'I imagine,' Simon answered, 'the one whom he forgave the greater debt.'

'You are right,' said Jesus. And turning round to the woman, while still addressing Simon, 'You see this woman? I came into your house and you gave me no water for my feet. She watered my feet with her tears and dried them with her hair. You gave me no kiss. She, from the moment I came in, has not ceased to shower kisses on my feet. You did not anoint my head, even with oil. She anointed my feet with unguent. For which reasons I wish *you* to know that her sins, her many sins, have been forgiven because she loved much; whereas the man who is forgiven little loves but little.'

To the woman he said: 'Your sins have been forgiven.' And while his fellow-guests began to wonder who the man could be who even forgave sins, he said to her: 'Your faith has saved you. Go in peace.'

## 8

SOME time later Jesus made a tour of the country, city by city and village by village, preaching and proclaiming the good tidings of the Kingdom of God. He was accompanied by the Twelve and by some women who had been cured of evil spirits and infirmities – Mary surnamed Magdalene, from whom seven demons had been expelled; Joanna wife of Chuza, Herod's steward; Susanna; and a number of others, who were in a position to minister to his wants out of their own resources.

One day when a big crowd was gathering and the people were coming out to him, as they did from every town, he spoke in allegory. 'The sower,' he said, 'went out to sow his seed. As he sowed, some of the seed fell by the path and was trodden on; and the birds of the sky ate it up. Other seed fell on rock, and when it came up it withered because it found no moisture. Other seed fell in among the thistles, which came up at the same time and smothered it. Other seed again fell into good soil, came up, and yielded a hundredfold.'

As he said this, he cried in a loud voice: 'He that has ears to hear with, let him hear.' And his disciples asked him what this parable might mean.

He replied: 'To you the secrets of the Kingdom of God are revealed. But to the rest – parables, so that *they may see without perceiving and hear without understanding*. However, the meaning of the parable is this. The seed is the Word of God. The people by the path are those that have heard, when in comes the Devil and snatches the Word from their hearts, in order that they may not through their faith be saved. Those on the rock are people who, on hearing it, welcome the Word with joy. But they have no roots, these people who believe for a while, and when trials come, recant. The seed that fell among the thistles stands for people who have heard, but as they go their way, are choked by the cares and riches and pleasures of life and bring nothing to perfection. Whereas that which fell into good soil stands for those who, having heard it, cherish the Word in the true goodness of their hearts and in their constancy bear fruit.

'No one lights a lamp and covers it with a bowl or puts it under a bed; he puts it on its stand, so that people coming in may see the light. For nothing is secret that shall not be revealed; nothing hidden that shall not be known and come into the light. So be careful in what frame of mind you listen. For more shall be given to the man who has; but from the man who has not, even what he thinks he has shall be taken.'

His mother and his brothers came to see him, but they were unable to reach him because of the crowd. However, people told him that they were waiting outside and wished to see him; and he answered them by saying: 'These that hear the Word of God and do it are mother and brothers to me.'

One day he embarked with his disciples and said: 'Let us cross the Lake.' So they put off, and as they sailed he fell asleep.

And now a squall came down upon the Lake and the boat began to fill. They were in danger.

They went and woke him. 'Master, Master!' they said. 'We are lost.'

Roused from his sleep, Jesus rebuked the wind and the high sea. They fell, and it was calm.

'Where is your faith?' he said to his disciples.

They were filled with awe and in their wonder said to one another: 'Who can this be, who gives his orders to the wind and sea and is obeyed?'

They came to land in the Gerasenes' country, which is opposite Galilee, and as he stepped on shore he was confronted by a man from the town who had demons in him. For a long time he had worn no clothes, and he lived in no house, but in the tombs. When he saw Jesus he uttered a cry, threw himself down at his feet and in a loud voice said: 'What is your business with me, Jesus son of God the Highest? I beseech you not to torment me.' This, because Jesus was telling the unclean spirit to come out of the man. For on many occasions it had carried him off; and though they kept him bound in manacles and fetters, he used to break his bonds and be driven by the demon into the wilds.

'What is your name?' Jesus asked him.

'Legion,' he said; for many evil spirits had gone into him. And now they kept beseeching Jesus not to give them orders to depart into the Abyss.

There was a large herd of pigs feeding on the hills, and the demons begged him to let them enter these. He gave them leave, and they came out of the man and entered the pigs, with the result that the herd charged down the cliff into the Lake, where they were drowned. Their herdsmen, when they saw this, fled and brought the news to the town and countryside; and the people went out to see what had happened.

They came to Jesus and found the man from whom the demons had come out sitting at his feet, dressed and in his right mind. They were terrified.

Those who had witnessed it told them how the demoniac had been saved, and the whole population of the Gerasene district, seized by panic, asked him to go away. And Jesus went on board and left them.

The man from whom the demons had come out had begged him to let him stay with him. But Jesus sent him away. 'Go back to your home,' he said, 'and tell people what great things God has done for you.' The man left him and told everyone in the town the wonderful things that Jesus had done for him.

When Jesus got back, the people, who were all awaiting him, received him with open arms. And now there came a man called Jairus, a governor of the synagogue, who threw himself down at Jesus' feet and besought him to come to his house because he had an only daughter, about twelve years of age, who was dying.

As Jesus went, the crowd pressed him hard, and a woman who for twelve years had suffered from a hemorrhage and found no one to cure her, came up from behind and touched the tassel on his cloak.

At once her hemorrhage ceased, and Jesus said: 'Who touched me?'

They all denied having done so, and Peter said: 'Master, you are surrounded by people jostling you.'

But Jesus said: 'Somebody touched me. I knew that power had gone out of me.' And the woman, seeing that she was detected, approached trembling, fell at his feet and, before all the people, gave her reason for touching him and announced her instantaneous cure. Whereupon he said to her: 'Daughter, your faith has saved you. Go in peace.'

Before he had finished speaking, someone from the synagogue official's house came up and said: 'Your daughter is dead. Do not trouble the Master.'

But Jesus heard and said to Jairus: 'Do not be afraid. Only have faith, and she shall be saved.'

When he reached the house he allowed no one to go in with him but Peter, John, and James, and the father and mother of the girl. They were all wailing and beating their breasts for her. But he said: 'Wail no more. She is not dead but asleep.'

They laughed at him, knowing that she was dead. But he seized her hand and cried: 'Little girl, get up!'

Her spirit returned, she rose immediately, and he ordered her some food. Her parents were lost in wonder; but he commanded them to tell no one what had happened.

# 9

HE called the Twelve together, gave them power and authority to deal with every kind of demon and to cure diseases, and sent them out to proclaim the Kingdom of God and to heal the sick.

He said: 'Take nothing for the road, no staff, no knapsack, no bread, no money'; adding that they were not to take a second tunic with them.

'Whatever house you enter, stay there and leave it only when you leave the town.

'When people reject you, leave their town, and as you do so shake the dust off your feet as a demonstration against them.'

So they set forth and toured the country towns, proclaiming the Good Tidings and healing everywhere.

News of all that happened came to the ears of Herod the Tetrarch, and he was perplexed, because some people were saying that John had risen from the dead, while others said that Elijah had appeared, and others that one of the ancient prophets had come back to life.

Herod said: 'John? I beheaded him. But who is this of whom I hear such strange reports?' And he was anxious to see him.

The apostles returned and informed Jesus of all they had done. Taking them with him he withdrew privately to a town called Bethsaida. But the people came to know this and went after him. He made them welcome, spoke to them about the Kingdom of God, and cured those who were in need of healing.

The day was drawing to its close, and the Twelve went up to him and said: 'Dismiss the people, so that they may go to the villages and farms round about to find lodging and provisions; for here we are in a desolate spot.'

'Feed them yourselves,' he replied.

But they said: 'We have no more than five loaves and two fish, unless we go and buy food for all these people.' For the men numbered about five thousand.

He said to his disciples: 'Make them sit down in parties of about fifty each.'

They did as he told them and made them all sit down. He took the five loaves and the two fish, and looking up to Heaven blessed them. Then he broke them in pieces and handed these to the disciples to serve to the people. And they ate and were all of them satisfied. Moreover, twelve hampers were filled with the pieces they left.

On one occasion when he was praying in retirement and his disciples were with him, he put a question to them: 'Who do the people say I am?'

'John the Baptist,' they replied; 'others Elijah; while others say that one of the ancient prophets has come back to life.'

'But you?' he said. 'Who do you say I am?'

It was Peter who answered. 'God's Anointed,' he said.

Jesus admonished them and forbade them to inform anyone of this. He told them: 'The Son of Man must of necessity suffer much, be repudiated by the Elders and Chief Priests and Doctors of the Law, be put to death, and on the third day be recalled to life.'

But to the people in general he said: 'If anyone wishes to walk in my footsteps, let him renounce self, take up his cross day by day and follow me. For the man who chooses to save his life will lose it; while he that loses his life for my sake shall save it. How does a man profit by winning the whole world and losing or forfeiting himself?

'Indeed, if anyone is ashamed of me and my words, the Son of Man will be ashamed of him, when he comes in his glory and that of the Father and the holy Angels. And I tell you in all truth, some of those standing here shall not taste death before seeing the Kingdom of God.'

About a week after he had spoken thus, he took Peter, John, and James, and went up into the mountains to pray. As he prayed the aspect of his face was changed and his clothing had the brilliance of a lightning flash. And behold, two men were talking with him, Moses and Elijah themselves, who appeared in their glory and spoke of that exit from the world which he intended to achieve in Jerusalem.

Peter and his companions, waking from the sleep that had overwhelmed them, saw his glory and the two men who were standing with him. And as these were parting from him, Peter said to Jesus: 'Master, it is a good thing that we are here. Let us make three shelters, one for you, one for Moses, and one for Elijah.' He did not know what he was saying. But as he spoke there came a cloud which enveloped them – the disciples were filled with awe as they entered it. And a voice came out of the cloud, saying: 'This is My son, the Chosen One. Listen to him.'

When the Voice had spoken, Jesus was seen to be alone. They held their peace and told no one at the time of anything that they had seen.

On the following day, when they came down from the

mountains, he was met by a large crowd; and out of the gathering came a man's voice. 'Master,' he cried, 'I beg you to look at my son, who is the only one I have. A spirit seizes him and gives a sudden cry; it rends him till he foams at the mouth; and as the convulsions slowly subside, it leaves him shattered. I begged your disciples to cast it out, but they could not.'

At this, Jesus exclaimed: 'O faithless and perverse generation! How much longer must I be with you and bear with you? Bring your son here.'

The lad was still on his way to Jesus when the demon flung him down and convulsed him. But Jesus rebuked the unclean spirit and cured the lad; then gave him back to his father. And all were filled with awe at the majesty of God.

But while the world was wondering at all he did, 'You,' he said to his disciples, 'should have *these* words ringing in your ears, The Son of Man is going to be delivered into the hands of men.' But they failed to understand this saying. Its meaning was hidden from them in order that they should not grasp it, and they feared to question him about it.

They fell into an argument as to which of them might be the greatest. But Jesus, knowing the thoughts that each was entertaining, took a little child, set it down at his side and said: 'Whoever in my name welcomes this little child welcomes me, and whoever welcomes me welcomes Him that sent me. For he that is least among you all, *he* is great.'

Here, John said to him: 'Master, we saw a man using your name to cast out evil spirits and tried to stop him, since he is not one of us.'

'Do nothing of the kind,' said Jesus. 'Anyone that is not against you is for you.'

As the time drew near for his withdrawal to Heaven, he resolutely set his face towards Jerusalem, despatching couriers ahead of him. These went in advance and entered a Samaritan village to make arrangements for him; but the villagers would not receive him, knowing that he was bound for Jerusalem. His disciples James and John, when they became aware of this, said: 'Lord, would you like us to call down fire from the sky to destroy them?'

But Jesus turned round and rebuked them. And they went to another village.

A man who met them on the road as they were travelling said to Jesus: 'I will follow you, wherever you are going.'

Jesus replied: 'Foxes have holes, and the birds of the sky have nests, but the Son of Man has nowhere to lay his head.'

To another he said: 'Follow me.'

'Give me leave,' this man replied, 'to go and bury my father first.'

But Jesus said: 'Let the dead bury their dead. It is for you to go out and proclaim the Kingdom of God.'

Yet another said: 'I will follow you, Lord. But first give me leave to bid farewell to my people at home.'

'No one,' said Jesus, 'who has put his hand to the plough and looks behind him is fit for the Kingdom of God.'

# 10

AFTER this the Lord appointed others, seventy in number, and despatched them ahead of him in pairs to every town and place that he himself intended to visit. He said to them:

'The harvest is plentiful, but the labourers are few. Ask the Lord of the Harvest to send out labourers to reap it for him.

'Set forth. And know that I am sending you out like lambs among wolves.

'Carry no purse, no knapsack, no sandals. Gossip with no one on the road. On entering a house let your first words be, Peace to this house. And if a man of peace lives there, your blessing will rest upon it. If not, it will come back and rest on you.

'And stay in the house that receives you, eating and drinking what it has to offer – the workman earns his pay. Do not move from house to house.

'When you come to a town where they make you welcome, eat what is put before you, heal their sick and say, "The Kingdom of God has approached you." But when you find the people of a town unfriendly, go out into the streets and say, "See us wipe off the very dust that has clung to our feet in your town. Know, none the less, that the Kingdom of God has been near." I tell you, when the Day comes, Sodom will have less to suffer than that town.

'Alas for you, Chorazin! Alas for you, Bethsaida! For if the miracles that were done in you had been done in Tyre and Sidon, they would long since have repented, sitting in sackcloth and ashes. Yet at the Judgement, Tyre and Sidon will have less to suffer than you. And you, Capernaum! Shall you be raised to Heaven? No; thrust down to Hades.

'He that listens to you listens to me; he that spurns you spurns me; and he that spurns me spurns Him that sent me forth.'

The Seventy came back to him rejoicing. 'Lord,' they said, 'the use of your name brings the very demons under our control.'

'I kept my eyes on Satan,' he replied. 'He fell, like lightning from the sky. Indeed I have given you power to trample on snakes and scorpions and cope with all the forces of the Enemy – they shall hurt you not at all. Yet do not rejoice because the spirits have come under your control. Rejoice because your names have been inscribed in Heaven.'

This was the hour of his exultation in the Holy Spirit. 'Father,' he said, 'I thank thee, Lord of Heaven and earth, for hiding these things from wise and clever men, and revealing them to simple folk. Indeed I thank thee, Father, for having chosen this way.

'All was entrusted to me by my Father. No one but the Father knows the nature of the Son. Nor does anyone know the nature of the Father but the Son and those to whom the Son is willing to reveal him.'

He also said, addressing his disciples privately: 'The eyes that see what you see are privileged. For I tell you, many prophets and kings have wished to see what you see, and have not seen it; and to hear what you hear, and have not heard it.'

On one occasion a lawyer rose and put a searching question to him. 'Master,' he said, 'what must I do to come into eternal life?'

'What is written in the Law?' said Jesus. 'What does your reading tell you?'

He replied: '*Thou shalt love the Lord thy God with all thy heart, with all thy soul, with all thy power, and with all thy thinking* and *Thou shalt love thy neighbour as thyself.*'

'You are right,' said Jesus. 'Do this and you shall live.'

But he, wishing to justify his question, said: 'Who *is* my neighbour?'

Jesus took this up and said: 'A man going down from Jerusalem to Jericho fell into the hands of brigands, who not only robbed but stripped and wounded him, and then made off, leaving him half dead. A priest, who happened to be going down by the same road, saw him and passed by on the other side. In the same way too a Levite, when he reached the spot and saw him, passed by on the other side. But a Samaritan also came upon him as he went along the road, and was filled with compassion directly he saw him. He went up to him, bandaged his wounds, applying oil and wine, put him on his own mount, and took him to an inn, where he attended to his comfort. And in the morning he produced two shillings, gave them to the innkeeper and said: "Take care of him; and on my way back I will repay you any further charges."

'Which of these three, do you think, proved himself a neighbour to the man who fell into the brigands' hands?'

'The one,' he replied, 'who treated him with compassion.'
And Jesus said to him: 'Go and do as he did.'

In the course of their travels, he came to a certain village,
where a woman named Martha made him welcome in her
house. She had a sister called Mary, who did more – she sat
down at the Lord's feet and listened to his words. But Martha
was distracted by her many duties. She stopped in front of
him and said: 'Lord, is it nothing to you that this sister of
mine has been leaving me to serve alone? Come, tell her to
lend me a hand.'

'Martha, Martha,' the Lord replied, 'you fret and fuss
about a number of things; but there is one thing that you lack.
Mary has chosen the good part, and that shall not be taken
from her.'

## 11

HE was staying in a certain place for prayer. When he had
finished, one of his disciples said to him: 'Lord, teach us how
to pray, just as John taught his own disciples.'

He said: 'Let this be your prayer:

> Father,
> Thy Name be hallowed;
> Thy Kingdom come;
> Thy will be done;
> As in Heaven, so on earth;
> Day by day give us the bread of life;
> And forgive us our sins,
> Even as we forgive each debtor what he owes us;
> And do not bring us to ordeal.'

He also said: 'Suppose you have a friend and in the middle
of the night you go to him and say, "My friend, let me have
three loaves. A friend of mine, who is travelling through, has
called on me and I have nothing to offer him." And suppose

he answers from indoors, "Don't put me to the trouble. I locked up long ago – my children are in bed and so am I. I can't get up to give it you."

'You may take it from me that though he won't get up and give it you for friendship's sake, your very importunity will *make* him rouse himself and give you all you want.

'Moreover I say to you, Ask and you shall receive. Seek and you shall find. Knock and the door shall be opened to you. For everyone that asks receives; every seeker finds; and to everyone that knocks the door is opened.

'Would any one of you that is a father hand his son a stone when he asks him for a loaf of bread; or a snake instead of a fish; or a scorpion for an egg? Well then, if you that are by nature evil know how to give your children what is good, how much more shall the Father from his Heaven give the Holy Spirit to those that ask him?'

He was casting out a demon who had made a man dumb. The demon came out and the dumb man spoke. The people were amazed; but there were some of them who said, 'It is through Beelzebub, their Prince, that he casts demons out.' Others, wishing to put him to the proof, asked him for a sign from Heaven.

But he, knowing the nature of their thoughts, said: 'Kingdoms are brought to ruin by internal strife – house falls on house. If Satan also fights against himself, how can his kingdom stand? I say this because you accuse me of casting out demons through Beelzebub. If I do that, through whom do your own people cast them out? You stand condemned by *them*. On the other hand, if I cast out demons by the help of God, it would seem that the Kingdom of God confronts you.

'So long as the Strong One fully armed is guarding his own keep, his property lies safe. But when a Stronger One than he has come up and conquered him, he strips him of the armour he relied on and shares out his goods.

'He that is not with me is against me; and he that does not gather with me casts away.

'When the unclean spirit has come out of a man, it wanders through waterless places, seeking repose; and finding none, it says, "I will go back to the home I left." And if on reaching the house it finds it untenanted, swept and in good order, it goes and fetches seven other spirits worse than itself, and they all go in and settle there, with the result that the man's condition in the end is worse than it was in the beginning.'

He was interrupted here by a woman who called out to him from the crowd: 'Happy the womb that bore you and the breasts you sucked!'

'Yet happier,' he said, 'are those that hear the Word of God and keep it.'

More people still came up to swell the gathering, and he addressed them. 'This,' he began, 'is a wicked generation. It asks for a sign; and Jonah's is the only sign it shall be given. For just as Jonah was a sign to the Ninevites, the Son of Man shall be a sign to this generation. When the Queen of the South is raised on the Judgement Day with the men of this generation, she will condemn them; for she came from the ends of the earth to hear Solomon's wisdom, whereas to-day something greater than Solomon is here. Men of Nineveh, when they rise at the Judgement with this generation, will condemn it; for they repented when Jonah preached to them, whereas to-day something greater than Jonah is here.

'Nobody lights a lamp and puts it in a cellar or under the measuring-bowl, but on its stand, so that people coming in may see the light.

'The lamp of the body is your eye. When your eye is sound, your whole body too is bright. But when it is unsound, your body too is dark. Ask yourself then whether the light within you is not darkness. For if your whole body is full of light and no part of it is dark, it will be wholly bright, as when the lamp is shining full upon you.'

When he had done, a Pharisee invited him to the midday meal at his house, and he went in and took his place at table. The Pharisee was astonished to see that he did not wash before the meal. But the Lord said to him: 'Nowadays you Pharisees clean the outside of the cup and dish while your own hearts are full of greed and wickedness. Foolish people, did not He that made the outside make the heart as well? Besides, you have only to give in charity what is *in* your cups and dishes, and they will all be clean.

'But alas for you Pharisees that pay your tithes of mint, rue, and every kind of herb, and overlook the claims of justice and the love of God. These are the duties that you should have carried out, while not neglecting those.

'Alas for you Pharisees that love the best seats in the synagogue and salutations in the street. Alas for you, who are like the unmarked graves that people tread on without knowing it.'

One of the Lawyers interposed. 'Master,' he said, 'in all this you are insulting us as well as them.'

'Alas,' he said, 'for you Lawyers too, who lay on men burdens they can hardly bear, burdens that you yourselves do not touch with so much as a finger.

'Alas for you that build the tombs of the prophets whom your fathers killed. You thus attest and countenance your fathers' deeds: they killed them and you build their tombs. And that is why God in his Wisdom said: "I will send them prophets and apostles, for them to kill and persecute, so that this generation may be called upon to pay for the blood of all the prophets slain from the foundation of the world, from Abel to Zacharias, who perished between the Altar and the House." Indeed, I tell you, for their blood this generation shall be called upon to pay.

'Alas for you Lawyers who have removed the key to

knowledge; who stand outside the door yourselves, and stop the people that are coming in.'

When he left the house, the Doctors of the Law and the Pharisees gave vent to their animosity and began to catechize him about this and that, setting snares to catch him in some compromising statement.

# 12

MEANWHILE the people had flocked to him in their thousands – they were trampling on each other – and he began to speak, addressing himself to his disciples first:

'Guard yourselves against the yeast of the Pharisees. It is their policy to hide the truth. Yet nothing is hidden that shall not be disclosed, and nothing secret that shall not be known; for whatever you have said in the dark shall be heard in the light, and what you have whispered in secret shall be proclaimed on the housetops.

'And to you that are my friends I say, Do not be frightened of those that kill the body and after that can do no more. I will tell you whom to fear. Fear Him who after killing has the power to cast into hell. Yes, fear Him, I say.

'Is it not true that five sparrows are sold for twopence and one of them is not forgotten in the thoughts of God? But every single hair upon *your* heads is numbered. Cease to fear: you are more valuable than many sparrows.

'And I say to you, Let anybody tell the world that he is mine, and I the Son of Man will tell God's Angels I am his. But he that disowns me to the world shall in the presence of God's Angels be disowned. And whoever says a word against the Son of Man shall be forgiven; but he that blasphemes against the Holy Spirit shall not be forgiven.

'When they hale you before synagogues, authorities and powers, do not give anxious thought to the wording and the

lines of your defence; for when the moment comes, the Holy
Spirit will teach you what you ought to say.'

Here someone in the crowd said to him: 'Master, tell my
brother to share the estate with me.'

'Man,' he replied, 'who appointed me your judge or arbi-
trator?' And to the others, 'Take care,' he said, 'and guard
yourselves against avarice of every kind; for it does not follow, when a man has more than he needs, that his life is made
for him by his possessions.'

Then he gave them a parable: 'There was a rich man whose
land one year produced abundantly. He thought to himself,
"What shall I do? I have no room for my crops." "I know,"
he said. "I will pull down my barns, build bigger ones, and
garner all my grain and goods in them. And I will say to my
soul, Soul, you have plenty of good things saved up for many
a year. Take your ease; eat, drink and be merry." But God said
to him, "You fool; this very night they are coming to reclaim
your soul. And all you have laid by – who will have that?"
Such is the man who lays up treasure for himself instead of
being rich in God.'

And to his disciples he said: 'I bid you therefore not to
fret about your lives and what to eat, nor about your bodies
and what to put on them. For life is more than food, and the
body more than clothing. Consider the ravens. They neither
sow nor reap; they have no storerooms and no barns; and yet
God feeds them. By how much are you more important than
the birds!

'Can any one of you by fretting add a moment to his years?
Then since you cannot alter the least little thing, why fret
about the rest? Consider the lilies and how they grow. They
do no work, they do not spin. But I tell you that not even
Solomon in all his glory was robed like one of these. And if
in the fields God so clothes the grass, which is there to-day
and thrown into the oven to-morrow, will he not all the more
clothe you, slow though you are to trust him?

'Cease then, yourselves, to cast about for food and drink; and be harassed no more. For all these things are what the pagan world pursues; whereas your Father knows you need them. No; pursue his Kingdom, and these things also will be yours. Have no fear, little flock. It has been your Father's pleasure to give you the Kingdom.

'Sell your possessions and give in charity. Make for yourselves purses that do not wear out, a treasure-house that does not fail – in Heaven, where no thief approaches and no moth destroys. For where your treasure is, there will your heart be also.

'Be girt and ready with your lamps alight, like people waiting for their master when the wedding-feast is over, so that when he comes and knocks they may open for him instantly. Happy the servants whom the Lord on his arrival finds awake. Indeed I tell you, he will gird himself, seat them at table, and go round and wait on them. And if it is not till the second or the third watch that he comes, and yet he finds them ready, they are happy men.

'You may be sure that if the owner of the house had known when the burglar was coming he would have stayed awake and would not have let his house be broken into. Be vigilant yourselves, for the Son of Man is coming when you least expect him.'

'Lord,' said Peter, 'do you mean this parable for us, or for all the rest as well?'

'Consider,' said the Lord. 'Who proves himself the wise, the faithful steward, when his master leaves him to direct his household and give out their daily rations? That servant, happy man, whom his master when he comes finds in the faithful discharge of these duties. That surely is the man whom he will make director of his whole estate. But if the servant says to himself "My master is long in coming," and takes to bullying the boys and maids, to gluttony and wine and getting drunk, his Lord will come on a day when he does not expect him, at a time he did not know. And he will tear him to pieces and consign him to the traitors' lot.

'The servant who knew his master's will but did not prepare for him and carry out his wishes receives many strokes of the lash; whereas the one who in his ignorance committed punishable faults receives but few.

'Much is required of him who has been given much; and of the man to whom a great deal is entrusted, something extra shall be asked.

'I came to set the world on fire. And what do I want, if it is already kindled? But I have a baptism to undergo; and what constraint I suffer till that has been achieved!

'Do you suppose that I came here to bring peace on earth? No, I tell you, no – division. From now on there will be five people in one house at odds with one another, three against two and two against three. The father will side against the son, the son against the father; the mother against the daughter, the daughter against the mother; the mother-in-law against her daughter-in-law, and the daughter-in-law against the mother-in-law.'

And addressing himself to the people also, he said: 'When you see clouds coming up in the west you say at once that it will rain, and it does so. And when you see the south wind blow you say it will be very hot, and hot it is. Hypocrites! You can read the face of earth and sky. How is it that you cannot read the signs of the present day? Why can you not do better still and out of your own conscience judge aright? Be warned, and as you go to court with your accuser, bestir yourself before you get there to be quit of him, or he may haul you up before the judge, and the judge hand you over to the bailiff, and the bailiff throw you into prison. I tell you, you shall not come out of it till you have paid the last farthing.'

AT that very moment some people came and told him about the Galileans whose blood Pilate had mingled with that of the beasts they had sacrificed.

He answered them by saying: 'Do you think, because they suffered this fate, that these Galileans had been greater sinners than all other Galileans? No, I tell you. But if you do not repent, you will all perish in much the same way.

'Again, take the eighteen men who were killed when the tower fell on them in Siloam. Do you think they are proved to have been greater transgressors than all the other people of Jerusalem? No, I tell you. But if you have not repented you will all perish in the same way.'

And he told this parable: 'A man who had a fig-tree planted in his vineyard came and looked for fruit on it but found none. He said to the vineyard hand, "Look, for three years I have been coming to this fig-tree in the hope of fruit, and getting none. Cut it down. Why should it clutter up the ground for nothing?" "Sir," said the man, "leave it alone again this year, and I'll hoe it and lay down manure. If it bears next year, well and good. If not, you shall cut it down."'

On a sabbath day when he was teaching in one of the synagogues, a woman appeared who had been possessed by an infirmity for eighteen years. She was bent double and quite unable to lift up her head. When Jesus saw her, he called her to him and said, 'Woman, you are rid of your infirmity,' and laid his hands on her.

She was straightened immediately and praised God. But the governor of the synagogue took the matter up. He was indignant because Jesus had healed on the Sabbath and he said to the congregation: 'There are six days when it is right for us to work. Come and be healed on one of them, and not on the sabbath day.'

'You hypocrites!' the Lord replied to this. 'On the Sabbath, do you not one and all loose your ox or donkey from the manger and take him off to water him? And this woman, this daughter of Abraham, whom Satan bound, yes, eighteen years ago – was it not right for her to have been loosed from those bonds of hers on the sabbath day?'

When he said this, all his antagonists were put to shame, and the people thought with joy of all the glorious things that he was doing.

Next, he said: 'What is the Kingdom of God like? To what shall I compare it? It is like a grain of mustard seed which a man took and sowed in his own garden. And it grew and became a tree and the birds of the sky roosted among its branches.'

Again, he said: ' To what shall I compare the Kingdom of God? It is like the yeast that a woman takes and conceals in three pounds of wheat-meal till the whole is leavened.'

He travelled on, teaching in the towns and villages, and making his way towards Jerusalem.

Someone said to him: 'Lord, are only a few people being saved?'

He said to them: 'Vie with each other to come in by the narrow door; for many, I tell you, will seek to come in.

'And they will not have the power. For when once the Master of the house has risen and has locked the door, and you come up and knock at it and say, "Lord, open for us," he will reply, "I do not know you. Where do you come from?" Then you will say, "We used to eat and drink with you, and you taught in our streets." And he will say, "I tell you that I don't know where you come from. *Away from me, all evil-doers!*"

'There will be weeping in that place, and gnashing of teeth, when you see Abraham, Isaac, and Jacob and all the Prophets in the Kingdom of God, and find yourselves thrown out. Moreover, people will come from the rising and the setting sun and from the north and south, and sit down to banquet in the Kingdom of God. Also remember that some of the last shall be first, and some of the first shall be last.'

It was now that some Pharisees came and said to him: 'You had better leave these parts and go. Herod wants to kill you.'

To which he replied: 'Go and say to that fox, "You may take it that to-day and to-morrow I cast out demons and bring my work of healing to an end; and on the third day my own end is achieved." Yet to you I admit that I am bound to travel on, to-day, to-morrow, and the day after, since it is not right for a prophet to be killed elsewhere than in Jerusalem.

'Jerusalem, Jerusalem, you that slay the prophets and stone those that are sent you, how often have I longed to gather your children to me, as a hen gathers her brood under her wings, and they would not come. And now, *you have your city to yourselves.* And I tell you, you shall not see me till you say, *Blessed be he that cometh in the name of the Lord!*'

# 14

ON a sabbath day, when he had gone into the house of one of the leading Pharisees for a meal and they were watching him closely, a man who suffered from dropsy appeared before him. Whereupon Jesus said to the Lawyers and Pharisees: 'Is it lawful to heal on the Sabbath or not?'

They were silent; and he laid hold of him, cured him and dismissed him.

Then he said to them: 'Which of *you* on the Sabbath, when his donkey or ox falls into a well, will not immediately pull him out?' To which they were unable to reply.

He then gave the guests a parable, having observed the way in which they were selecting the best places for themselves. He said to them: 'When you have been invited by anyone to a wedding, do not sit down in the best place at table, or there may be a more important person than yourself among the guests, and the host, who invited him as well as you, may go to you and say, "Make room for this man"; in which case you to your shame would find yourself in occupation of the last place. No; when you are a guest, go and sit down in the last place, so that when your host reaches you he will say, "Come higher up, my friend." Then you will be held in honour by all your fellow-guests. For in every case the man who exalts himself shall be humbled, and the man who humbles himself shall be exalted.'

To his host he also said: 'When you give a midday or an evening meal, do not ask your friends, your brothers, your relations, or the rich neighbours, lest they invite you in return one day and so repay you. No; when you entertain, invite the poor, the maimed, the lame, the blind, whose inability to pay you back will make you a happy man; for repayment will be yours at the resurrection of the just.'

One of his fellow-guests, when he heard this, said: 'Happy the man who dines in the Kingdom of God!'

But he said to him: 'There was a man who was giving a big dinner-party and had invited many guests. When the time came for the dinner, he sent out his servant to remind the people he had asked, as everything was ready. But they all with one accord began to excuse themselves. The first said, "I have bought a field and I must go and look at it. Please let me be excused." Another said, "I have bought five yoke of oxen and am on my way to try them. Please let me be excused." Yet another said, "I have married and so cannot come."

'The servant came back and told his master this. His master was very angry and said, "Go quickly into the streets and alleys of the town and bring in here the poor, the maimed, the blind, and the lame."

'Reporting to him that these orders had been carried out, "Sir," said the servant, "there is still room for more." Whereupon his master said, "Go out into the highways and lanes and get them to come in, so that my house may be filled."

'And *I* would have you know that not one of those people who were first invited shall taste my banquet.'

Multitudes were travelling with him. One day he turned to them and said: 'Anyone that comes to me and does not hate his father, mother, wife, children, brothers, sisters, and not only them but his own life, can be no disciple of mine. The man who does not shoulder his cross and follow in my steps can be no disciple of mine.

'For suppose that one of you decides to build a tower. Does he not first sit down and calculate the cost, to see whether he has enough to complete the work? Otherwise, when he has laid the foundations and his resources fail before the end, everyone watching will begin to laugh at him and say, "Look at the fellow who began to build and could not finish."

'Or take a king setting out to wage war on another king. Will he not first sit down and consider whether with ten thousand men he can face the one who is coming at him with twice that number? And if he decides that this cannot be done, will he not send out an embassy while the other is still some way off, and sue for peace?

'This then is true of every one of you – if you do not abandon all your possessions you can be no disciples of mine.

'Salt, as I have said, is an excellent thing. But if salt itself deteriorates, what can it be seasoned with? It is of no use either for the land or on the manure-heap. They throw it away.

'He that has ears to hear with, let him hear.'

## 15

ALL the tax-collectors and the outcasts were consorting with him – they came to hear him speak. But the Pharisees and the Doctors of the Law shook their heads at one another. They said: 'The man makes sinners welcome and sits down with them to eat.'

So he gave them this parable: 'What man among you with a hundred sheep, if he loses one of them, does not leave the ninety-nine out in the open and go after the lost one till he finds it? And when he has found it, does he not put it on his shoulders in his joy, and when he gets home gather his friends and neighbours round him and say, "Rejoice with me: I have found my lost sheep"? I tell you it is thus in Heaven – more joy over one sinner that repents than over nine and ninety law-abiding people who have nothing to repent.

'Again, take a woman who has ten silver coins and loses one. Does she not light a lamp and sweep the house and search relentlessly until she finds it? And when she has found it, does she not gather her women friends and neighbours round her and say, "Rejoice with me: I have found the coin I lost"? Such, I assure you, is the jubilation of God's Angels over one sinner that repents.'

He also said: 'A man had two sons. The younger of them said to him, "Father, let me have my share of the estate." So he divided the property between them.

'The younger son realized his whole share and left home after a few days for a distant country, where he squandered his money in extravagant living. But when he had spent it all, there was a serious famine in the country and he faced starvation. So he attached himself to one of the local people; and this man sent him out to look after the pigs on his farm, where no one gave him anything, and he would gladly have gorged himself with the husks that the pigs fed on.

'This brought him to himself and he said, "To think of all my father's paid hands, with more bread than they can eat, while I am dying of starvation here! I will set out and go to my father and say, Father, I have sinned against Heaven and yourself. I am no longer worthy to be called your son. Treat me as one of your hired men." And he set out and went to his father.

'His father saw him when he was still a long way off, and was filled with pity. He ran and fell on his neck and kissed him tenderly. "Father," said the young man, "I have sinned against Heaven and yourself. I am no longer worthy to be called your son. Treat me as one of your hired men."

'But the father said to his servants: "Quick! Bring out a robe, the best we have, and put it on him. Give him a ring for his hand and sandals for his feet. And bring the fatted calf and kill it. Let us eat and make merry; for this son of mine was dead and has come back to life, he was lost and he is found."

'So they began to make merry; and the elder son, who had been in the fields, heard music and dancing as he approached the house on his way back. He called one of the boys to him and asked him what this meant; and the boy said: "Your brother has come, and your father has killed the fatted calf because he has him safe and sound."

'The elder son was angry and did not care to go in. But his father came out and began to plead with him. Whereupon he said to his father: "Listen! All these years I have slaved for you and never disobeyed you once. Yet you never gave *me* a kid so that I could enjoy myself with my friends. But here comes that son of yours, when he and his harlots have got through your estate, and for him you kill the fatted calf!"

'"My boy," said his father, "you are always with me, and all I have is yours. But we *had* to make merry and rejoice, because your brother here was dead and came to life, he was lost and he is found."'

# 16

To the disciples he also said: 'A rich man was informed that an agent he employed was squandering his means. He summoned him and said, "What is this I hear of you? Send in your agency accounts. You cannot be my agent any longer."

'The agent said to himself, "What shall I do, now that my master is depriving me of my employment? I am not strong enough to dig; I am ashamed to beg. Ah, I know how to make them welcome me to their houses when I have lost the agency!" And he called to him every one of his employer's tenants and said to the first, "What rent do you have to pay my employer?" "A hundred measures of oil," said the man. "Take your lease," he said, "sit down quickly and write fifty." To another he said, "And you, what is your rent?" "A hundred measures of wheat." "Take your lease and write eighty."'

The Lord praised this dishonest agent because he had acted shrewdly: 'For the children of this world are shrewder than the children of light in their dealings with their own kind. And my advice to *you* is to make friends for yourselves from out of this dishonest world, so that when it comes to an end they may welcome you to the tents of eternity.

'Honesty in little things means honesty in great; dishonesty in little things dishonesty in great. If then you have not been honest in your dealings with the dishonest world, who is going to trust you with the true riches? If you have not been honest in handling another's wealth, who is going to give you the wealth that is your own?

'No servant can be the slave of two masters. Either he will hate the one and love the other, or he will cling to one and despise the other. You cannot be a slave to God and Mammon too.'

The Pharisees, who were very fond of money, had been listening to all this and sneering at Jesus. He said to them: 'You like the world to look at you and say, "What upright men!" But God, abominating what the world esteems, looks into your hearts.

'The Law and the Prophets were enough till John appeared. But ever since, the Kingdom of God has been proclaimed and everyone is storming his way into it. Nevertheless it is an easier thing for heaven and earth to pass away than for one comma of the Law to be deleted. Every man that divorces his wife and marries another woman commits adultery. So does the man who marries a woman who has been divorced.

'There was a rich man who used to dress in purple and fine linen, passing his days in splendid ease, while at his gate there lay a beggar called Lazarus, covered with ulcers, longing to satisfy himself with the scraps that fell from the rich man's table, and forced to put up even with the dogs who used to come and lick his sores.

'The beggar died and was borne away by the Angels to Abraham's arms. The rich man also died and was buried. And raising his eyes from Hades in the torment of his lot, he saw Abraham far away with Lazarus in his arms and called to him, "Father Abraham, have pity on me and send Lazarus to wet the tip of his finger and cool my tongue, for I am tortured in these flames."

'"My child," said Abraham, "remember that in life you had your fill of your good things, and Lazarus had his fill of bad; but now it is his turn for comfort here, your turn for pain. In addition to this, a great gulf has been established between us and you, to prevent all intercourse between our place and yours."

'"Father," he said, "I beg you then to send him to my father's house, where I have five brothers, to tell them the whole truth, so that they may not also come to this place of torment."

'"They have Moses and the Prophets," said Abraham. "Let them listen to them."

'"No, Father Abraham," he replied. "But they *will* repent if someone comes to them from the grave."

'"If they do not listen now," said Abraham, "to Moses and the Prophets, they will not be convinced, even though someone should come back to life."'

# 17

HE said to his disciples: 'It is impossible that corruption should not be, but alas for the man who causes it! It would pay him better to be thrown into the sea with a millstone tied round his neck than to corrupt a single one of these little ones.

'Look to yourselves. If your brother does wrong, rebuke him; and if he repents, forgive him. And if he does you wrong seven times in a day and seven times comes back to you and says, "I am sorry," you shall forgive him.'

On one occasion the apostles said to the Lord: 'Give us more faith.'

The Lord said: 'If you have faith like a grain of mustard seed, you could say to this mulberry-tree, "Be rooted up and planted in the sea," and it would obey you.

'If one of you has a slave working for him at the plough or with the sheep, does he say to the man when he is back from the fields, "Come and have some food at once"? Does he not rather say, "Get something ready for my supper, then tuck up your clothes and wait on me at table. After that you can have your own meal"? He surely does not thank his slave for having done the work he was given?

'It is the same with you. When you have done all the work you were given, you should say, "We are unprofitable servants: we have done our duty."'

On the journey to Jerusalem he passed between Samaria and Galilee, and as he came to one of the villages he was faced by ten lepers, who kept their distance and called across to him, 'Jesus! Master! Have pity on us.'

Directly he saw them he said, 'Go and show yourselves to the priests,' with the result that as they went they were cleansed. And one of them, seeing that he was cured, turned back with a great cry of praise to God, prostrated himself at Jesus' feet and thanked him. This man was a Samaritan.

Jesus asked: 'Were not all ten cleansed? Where are the other nine? Can it be true that none of them except this foreigner have come back to give glory to God?' And to the man he said, 'Rise and go. Your faith has saved you.'

He was asked by the Pharisees when the Kingdom of God was coming, and he answered them by saying: 'Watch as you may, you will not *see* it come. People will not be saying, "Here it is!" or "There!" And the reason why is this – the Kingdom of God is within you.'

And he said to the disciples: 'A time will come when you will long for one glimpse of the Son of Man and will not see him. People will say to you, "See, he is there!" or "There he is!" But do not move or go off in pursuit. For, like the lightning when it flashes out and lights the heavens from horizon to horizon, so the Son of Man will come. But first it is his destiny to suffer much and be rejected by this generation.

'And when he comes, things will happen as they did in Noah's time. They were eating, they were drinking, they were marrying and giving in marriage, up to the very day when Noah entered the ark – and the Flood came and destroyed them all.

'So too, what happened in the time of Lot will be repeated. They were eating and drinking, buying and selling, planting and building, but on the day when Lot left Sodom, the Lord rained fire and brimstone from the sky and destroyed them all. So will it be on the day when the Son of Man is brought into the light.

'On that day let no one who is on his roof, with his possessions in the house, come down to save them. Nor let the man who is in the fields turn back. Remember Lot's wife. He that is anxious to preserve his life will lose it, but he that loses it shall keep it.

'I tell you, on that night there will be two in one bed; one will be taken, the other left. There will be two women grinding at the same mill; one will be taken, the other left.'

At this point they asked him: 'Where, Lord, will it happen?' And he said to them: 'Where the corpse is, there the vultures will foregather.'

# 18

HE also gave them a parable to make it clear that they must pray continually and never slacken. He said: 'There was a judge in a certain town who had no fear of God and no respect for man. In the same town there was a widow who came to him repeatedly and begged him to protect her from an enemy of hers by giving judgement against him. For some time he refused; but presently he said to himself, "I have no fear of God and no respect for man. Yet since this widow is making such a nuisance of herself, I will decide in her favour, or she may end by boring me to death with her appeals."'

The Lord went on to say: 'Contrast the thoughts of this dishonest judge with those of God. Will He not vindicate his own elect, who call upon him day and night, and whom he listens to with *no* impatience? I tell you that he will indeed give judgement for them, and with speed. Nevertheless, when the Son of Man comes, will he find the necessary faith on earth?'

He gave this parable also, in reference to certain people who felt secure in their own righteousness and despised all others.

'Two men, one a Pharisee and the other a tax-collector, went up into the Temple to pray. The Pharisee took his stand and silently prayed thus: "I thank thee, God, that I am not like all the rest of mankind – extortioners, law-breakers, adulterers – nor indeed like this tax-collector here. I fast twice a week; I pay tithes on all my income." Meanwhile the tax-collector, who stood some way off and did not even like to raise his eyes to Heaven, was beating his breast and saying, "God, have mercy on the sinner that I am."

'I tell you that if either of the two went home approved by God, it was the tax-collector. For in every case the man who exalts himself shall be humbled, but the man who humbles himself shall be exalted.'

People even brought him their babies to touch. The disciples when they saw this scolded them. But Jesus called them to him and said: 'Let the little children come to me. Do not forbid them; for the Kingdom of God belongs to such. Believe me, the man who does not accept the Kingdom of God like a little child shall certainly not enter it.'

A man of high standing came to him with a question. 'Good Master,' he said, 'what must I do to come into eternal life?'

'Why do you call me good?' said Jesus. 'No one but God is good. You know the commandments – *Thou shalt not commit adultery; Thou shalt not murder; Thou shalt not steal; Thou shalt not perjure thyself; Honour thy father and thy mother.*'

He replied: 'I have kept all these from boyhood.'

Whereupon Jesus said: 'There is still one thing left for you to do. Sell all you have and distribute to the poor – you will have treasure in Heaven. Then come and follow me.'

But when he heard this he was filled with gloom, for he was very rich. Jesus, seeing what he felt, said: 'How difficult it is for men of wealth to enter the Kingdom of God! It is indeed an easier thing for a camel to pass through the eye of a needle than for a rich man to enter the Kingdom of God.'

'Then who can be saved?' said the people who heard this.

'What is impossible for men,' he said, 'is possible for God.'

Peter now said: 'Did not *we* give up our possessions and follow you?'

Jesus said to them: 'Hear the truth. There is no one that has given up his house, wife, brothers, parents, or children for the sake of the Kingdom of God, who shall not get back many times as much, now in the present, and in the coming age eternal life.'

And he took the Twelve aside and said to them: 'Listen. We are going up to Jerusalem, and everything that was foretold for the Son of Man through the Prophets is going to be fulfilled. For he will be handed over to the pagans, and will be mocked, reviled and spat on. And when they have scourged him they will put him to death; and on the third day he will live again.'

But they took in nothing of all this. The significance of the saying was hidden from them. Nor did it sink into their minds.

As he drew near to Jericho, there was a blind man sitting by the road begging. Hearing a crowd of travellers on the road, he asked what was happening, and they told him that Jesus of Nazareth was passing by.

He called out: 'Jesus, son of David, have pity on me!'

Those in front told him to hold his tongue, but this only made him cry out all the more, 'Son of David, have pity on me!'

Jesus stopped, ordered him to be brought to him, and when he came up asked him: 'What do you wish me to do for you?'

'To make me see again, Lord,' said the blind man.

'See,' commanded Jesus. 'Your faith has saved you.'

His sight came back immediately, and he followed him, glorifying God. And all the people when they saw what had been done gave praise to God.

HE entered Jericho, and as he was passing through, it occurred to a man called Zacchaeus, a commissioner of taxes and a rich man, that he would like to see how Jesus looked. But being short he could not see him for the crowd. So he ran ahead and climbed a sycamore to get a view of him, knowing that Jesus was going to take that way across the town. Jesus, when he reached the place, looked up at him and said: 'Come down, Zacchaeus, quickly. You must be my host to-day.'

Zacchaeus came down quickly and took him home with him rejoicing. Whereupon they all shook their heads. 'The man who is putting him up is an outcast,' they said.

But Zacchaeus took his stand and said to Jesus: 'Bear witness, Lord, that I am giving half my fortune to the poor and making fourfold restitution to anyone I have defrauded.'

And Jesus said to him: 'To-day salvation has come to this household, its master having proved himself a child of Abraham. What did the Son of Man come for but to seek and find the lost?'

While these words were ringing in their ears, he went on to give them a parable, his reason being that he was near Jerusalem and they imagined that the Kingdom of God would very shortly burst upon the world. He said: 'A nobleman was going to a distant country to have himself made king and then return. He summoned ten of his retainers and gave them each a pound, telling them to trade with it till he came back. Now the people of his country hated him, and sent an embassy after him to say they did not wish to have him as their king. But he *was* made king, and on his return he ordered the servants to whom he had given the money to be summoned, so that he might learn what business they had done.

'The first presented himself and said, "My lord, your pound has made ten more." "Well done!" he said. "You are a good servant. Having shown that you can be trusted in small things, take command of ten cities."

'The second came and said, "Your pound has made five pounds, my lord." And to him he said, "You too shall take command – over five cities."

'But the next came up and said: "See, my lord; here is that pound of yours. I kept it safe in a handkerchief. I was afraid of you because you are a hard man: you take what you have not laid by, and harvest what you have not sown."

'To him he said: "Out of your own mouth I condemn you, wicked servant that you are. You knew that I am a hard man, taking what I have not laid by, and harvesting what I have not sown. Then why did you not put my money in the bank, and on my return I should have withdrawn it with interest?" And to his attendants he said, "Take the pound from him and give it to the man with ten."'

Here someone said to Jesus: 'Lord, he *has* ten pounds!'

'My answer to that is, More shall be given to everyone who has, but from the man who has not, even what he has shall be taken. And the king said: "As for those enemies of mine that did not wish me to reign over them, bring them here and slay them in my presence."'

When he had finished this parable he took the road and led the way up to Jerusalem.

As they approached Bethphage and Bethany, near the hill called the Mount of Olives, he sent two of the disciples on an errand. 'Go to the village over there,' he said, 'and as you enter it you will find a tethered colt, which nobody has ridden yet. Untie it and bring it. And if anyone asks you why you are untying it, you will say, "The Lord needs it."'

His messengers went off and found things just as he had told them. As they were untying the colt its owners said to them, 'Why are you untying that colt?' And they said, 'The Lord needs it.'

They brought the colt to Jesus, threw their cloaks on its

back and mounted Jesus on it. People, as he moved on, spread their cloaks before him on the road; and when in his approach to the city he had reached the spot where the road comes down from the Mount of Olives, the whole crowd of disciples began in their joy to sing a loud song of praise to God for all the wonders they had witnessed. They sang: '*Blessed be the King that cometh in the name of the Lord!* In Heaven peace, and glory in the Heights!'

Some of the Pharisees called to him from the crowd: 'Master, check your disciples.'

'I tell you,' he answered, 'if these keep silence, the very stones will cry out.'

As he drew near, he saw the city and wept over it, saying: 'Ah, if only you too to-day had found the road to peace! But as things are, you were not allowed to see it. Indeed a time is coming when your enemies will fix a palisade around you, and will encircle you and hem you in on every side, and cast you down, you and your people in you, leaving not one stone standing on another – because you did not recognize the moment when the Lord approached you.'

He went into the Temple and began to drive out the people who were trading there. He said to them: 'The Scriptures say *My House shall be the House of Prayer;* but you have turned it into a robbers' den.' And he spent every day in the Temple teaching.

Meanwhile the Chief Priests and the Doctors of the Law were bent on destroying him, and so were the leading citizens. But they could not hit upon a way; for the people, to a man, were hanging on his words.

# 20

ON one of these days, when he was teaching the people in the Temple and proclaiming his gospel, the Chief Priests and Doctors of the Law together with the Elders came up and interrupted him with a question. They said: 'Tell us by what authority you are doing these things? And who gave you that authority?'

He replied: 'I will ask *you* for a statement. Tell me; was John's baptism sanctioned by Heaven or by man?'

They considered this and said to themselves: 'If we say by Heaven, he will ask us, "Why did you not have faith in him?" But if we say by man, the people will all stone us, for they are persuaded that John was a prophet.'

In the end they answered that they did not know. To which Jesus replied: 'Then I too will not tell you by what authority I am acting.'

Next, he gave the people this parable: 'A man planted a vineyard, let it to some farmers and went abroad for a long time. In due season he sent a servant to the farmers to receive his share of the produce of the vineyard; but the farmers thrashed him and sent him off empty-handed. He proceeded to send them another servant; but him too they sent off empty-handed, after showing their contempt by thrashing him. Still persisting, he sent them a third, whom they also threw out after wounding him. Then the owner of the vineyard said, "What shall I do? I will send them my son, my beloved son. Maybe they will respect him." But when the farmers saw him they put their heads together. "This is the heir," they said. "Let us kill him, and make his inheritance ours." And they threw him out of the vineyard and killed him.

'Now what will the owner of the vineyard do to them? He will come and destroy these farmers and give the vineyard to others.'

'Heaven forbid!' they said when they heard this.

But Jesus fixed his eyes on them and said: 'Then what is the meaning of this Scripture, *The stone that the builders rejected has become the headstone of the corner?* Any man who falls upon that stone will be shattered, but the man on whom it falls will be reduced to dust.'

The Doctors of the Law and the Chief Priests would have liked to get their hands on him then and there, for they knew well enough that his parable had been aimed at them. But the crowd alarmed them.

So they bode their time. And presently they sent him some men they had suborned to pose as conscientious people and pounce on something he might say that would enable them to hand him over to the jurisdiction and authority of the Procurator. These men put a question to him. 'Master,' they said, 'we know that you say and teach what is right, favouring no one, but teaching the way of God in all sincerity. Are we justified or not in paying the capitation-tax to Caesar?'

But he saw through the cunning of their scheme and said: 'Let me see a shilling. Whose portrait and inscription does it bear?'

'Caesar's,' they replied.

'Well then,' he said, 'pay Caesar what is due to Caesar, and God what is due to God.'

With the people there, they could not cavil at this. They marvelled at his answer and were silent.

The next to come to him were some of the Sadducees, who do not believe in the resurrection. They set him a problem. 'Master,' they said, 'Moses laid it down for us that if a man's brother dies, leaving a widow and no children, he should marry the widow and so provide his brother with descendants. Now there were seven brothers, the first of whom married and died childless. The second married his widow; so did the third. And in the same way all seven died and left no children. Last of all the widow herself died. Whose wife then will she be in the resurrection, since she was married to all seven of them?'

Jesus replied: 'The children of this age marry and are given in marriage, but those who are judged worthy to attain that other time, and resurrection from among the dead, neither marry nor are given in marriage. Indeed they can no longer die. For they are equal to the Angels, and being children of the resurrection, are children of God. Moses himself revealed the fact that the dead are awakened, in the chapter on the Bush, where he spoke of the Lord as *the God of Abraham and God of Isaac and God of Jacob*. He is not a God of the dead, but of the living; for to Him all people live.'

Some of the Doctors of the Law now said, 'Master, you spoke well'; for they dared not ask him any further questions.

He went on to say to them: 'How can people maintain that the Messiah is a son of David? For David himself says in the Book of Psalms, *The Lord said to my Lord, Sit on my right hand till I make thy enemies thy footstool*. Thus David himself calls him *Lord*. So how can he be David's son?'

And in the hearing of all the people he said to the disciples: 'Guard yourselves against the Doctors of the Law, who like to walk about in robes; who love to be saluted in the streets and get the best seats in the synagogue and the best places at banquets; who devour the livelihood of widows and seek to justify themselves by making lengthy prayers. Their sentence shall be all the more severe.'

# 21

LOOKING up, he saw the people throwing their gifts into the offertory chests. These were the rich; but he also saw a poverty-stricken widow putting in a couple of mites, and he said: 'I tell you in all truth that this widow, poor as she is has put in more than all the rest. For all of these have more than they need, and they contributed from that; whereas she, who has less than she needs, threw in all she had to live on.'

There was some talk about the temple-buildings and the beautiful marbles and votive offerings that had gone to their adornment. He said: 'All this that you admire – a time is coming when not a block of stone here will be left standing on another. All shall be cast down.'

They questioned him. 'Master,' they said, 'when will this be? And what portent will there be when it is going to happen?'

He said: 'Take care not to be led astray. For many will appear and use my name, saying "I am he," and "The time is at hand." Do not follow their lead. And when you hear of wars and revolutions, do not be perturbed. These things must happen; but the end is not at once.'

Then he said to them: 'Nation will rise against nation, and kingdom against kingdom. There will be great earthquakes, and plagues and famines in one land or another; there will be sights of terror and mighty portents from the sky.

'But before all this, they will lay their hands on you and persecute you; they will drag you to their synagogues and prisons to hale you before kings and governors on my account. That is your opportunity; then you can declare your faith. And remember this. Prepare no speeches in your own defence, for I will endow you with such eloquence and wisdom as all your enemies will not be able to withstand or to refute.

'And you will be betrayed, even by parents, brothers, relatives and friends; and some of you they will send to their death. You are going to be hated by all men because you use my name. Yet not a hair of your head shall perish – by your endurance you shall win your life.

'When you see armies closing round Jerusalem, know that her desolation is at hand. Then, let those in Judaea take refuge in the hills; let people in the city leave it, and people in the country not go in. For those are the days of vengeance and fulfilment of all that the Scriptures have foretold.

'Alas, in those days, for a woman with a child in her womb or at her breast! For great calamity will come upon the land, and wrath upon this people. They will fall at the sword's edge, and be led captive into every pagan land. And pagan feet will tread Jerusalem till pagan days are done.

'There will be portents too, in sun and moon and stars; and on earth, nations confounded by the surge and thunder of the sea, men fainting in their panic as they wait for what is coming to the peopled world; for the mighty ones of heaven will be shaken. *Then* they shall see the Son of Man coming in a cloud with power and great glory. But straighten your backs and lift up your heads when all these things begin, for your deliverance will be at hand.'

And he gave them a parable: 'Look at the fig-tree, look at any tree. You can see for yourselves when they have begun to put out leaves that summer is near. In the same way, when you see all this befall you may be sure that the Kingdom of God is near. Indeed I tell you, this generation shall not pass away till all has taken place. Heaven and earth shall pass away, but my words shall not.

'But look to yourselves, lest at any time your faculties be numbed by debauch, by drunkenness or by the cares of life, and the Day catch you unawares like a fowler's noose. For wherever he lives on the face of the earth, that Day will dawn on each and every man.

'See therefore that you keep awake, praying at all times for the power to survive all these disasters that are on their way, and to take your place before the Son of Man.'

During the daytime he was in the Temple, teaching; but every evening he left the city for the hill called the Mount of Olives, and there he spent the nights. And all the people rose betimes, to join him in the Temple and hear him speak.

THE Feast of Unleavened Bread, which is called the Passover, was drawing near, and the Chief Priests and Doctors of the Law, being frightened of the people, were casting about for a way to destroy him.

Satan now entered Judas, surnamed Iscariot, who was enrolled among the Twelve. He went off to the Chief Priests and Commanders of the Temple force, and to them he unfolded a scheme he had for getting Jesus into their hands. They were glad, and agreed to give him money. So he undertook the task and watched for a moment when he could arrest him for them without the interference of a crowd.

The Day of Unleavened Bread arrived. This was when they had to kill the Paschal Lamb, and he despatched Peter and John with instructions to go and make arrangements for their celebration of the Passover.

'Where do you wish us to make ready?' they asked him.

'Listen,' he said. 'As you go into the city, a man carrying a jug of water will meet you. Follow him into the house he enters and tell the owner of the house that the Master wishes to know which is the room where he will be received and can eat the Passover with his disciples. He will then show you a large upper room furnished with couches. Make ready there.'

They went off, found everything as he had told them, and made arrangements for the Passover.

When the time came for the evening meal, he took his place at table and the apostles sat down with him. He said: 'With all my heart I had desired to eat this Passover with you before I suffer. For I tell you, I shall eat no Passover till the day of the perfect Passover in the Kingdom of God.'

He was handed a cup, gave thanks to God, and said: 'Take this and share it among yourselves. For I tell you that from this moment I shall not enjoy the fruit of the vine till the Kingdom of God has come.'

And he took a loaf, gave thanks to God, broke it and gave it to them. 'This,' he said, 'is my body, which is offered up for you. Do this in remembrance of me.'

And after they had eaten their supper, he dealt in the same way with the cup by saying: 'This cup is the new Covenant in my blood, which is being shed for you.

'But see, the hand of the man who betrays me is on the table with mine. For the Son of Man goes hence, as is decreed; but alas for him through whom he is betrayed!'

Hereupon they began to ask one another which of them could be the one who was about to do this thing. They even fell to wrangling as to which could be regarded as the greatest. But he said to them: 'The kings of the pagans lord it over them, and their rulers claim the title *Benefactor*. With you it is not so; far from it. With you, the senior must take the junior role, and your leader act the servant's part. For who is senior, the diner or the man who serves? Surely the diner. Yet it is I that play the servant's part among you.

'However, you are the men who have endured with me in my ordeals. And for my part, as my Father made me King, so I endow you with the royal right to eat and drink at my table in my Kingdom and to sit on thrones judging the twelve tribes of Israel.

'Simon, Simon, do you realize that Satan has made good his claim to put you all on trial? But I prayed for you, Simon, I prayed that your faith might not for ever fail you. And you – once you have retraced your steps, strengthen your brothers.'

'Lord,' he replied, 'with you I am prepared to go even to prison and to death.'

'And I say to you, Peter,' said Jesus, 'that the cock will not crow to-day before you deny all knowledge of me thrice.'

He also said to them: 'When I sent you forth without purse, knapsack or sandals, did you lack anything?'

'Nothing,' they said.

'But now,' he said, 'if you have a purse take it, and a knapsack too; and if you have no purse sell your cloak and buy a sword. For I tell you that the Scripture which says *They numbered him among the criminals* is due to be fulfilled in me. Indeed for me the course is run.'

They said: 'See, Lord; there are two swords here.'

'Enough, enough!' he said.

Leaving the house he went as usual to the Mount of Olives and the disciples followed him. When he reached the place, he said to them: 'Pray that you may not be brought to ordeal.' Then he withdrew about a stone's throw from them, sank to his knees, and prayed.

'Father,' he said, 'if thou art willing, take this cup away from me. Nevertheless, thy will be done, not mine.'

There now appeared to him an Angel from Heaven, who gave him strength; and being in agony, he prayed with even greater vehemence. The sweat upon him was like drops of blood streaming to the ground.

He rose from prayer and joining the disciples found them in their grief asleep. 'Why do you sleep?' he said. 'Rise, and pray that you may not be brought to ordeal.'

He was still speaking when a force appeared and at their head the man called Judas, one of the Twelve, who went up to him to kiss him.

'Judas,' said Jesus, 'are you betraying the Son of Man with a kiss?'

Those about him, when they saw what was afoot, said: 'Master, shall we use the sword?' And one of them struck the High Priest's slave, shearing off his right ear.

'No more of this!' said Jesus. And he took hold of the ear and healed him.

Then Jesus said to the Chief Priests and Temple officers and Elders who had come out to take him: 'I see you have come out with swords and sticks as though I were a brigand. When

I was with you in the Temple day after day, you did not raise a hand against me. But this is your hour. Night takes command.'

Arresting him, they led him off and brought him to the High Priest's palace. Peter followed at a distance, and when they had lit a fire in the middle of the courtyard and sat down together, he sat down among them. But one of the maid-servants, who saw him sitting in the firelight, stared at him and said, 'Here is another who was with him.'

Peter denied it. He said: 'Woman, I do not know him.'

Presently someone else noticed him and said: 'You too are one of *them*.'

'Sir,' said Peter, 'I am not.'

About an hour passed by, and then another man spoke up with confidence. 'It is a fact,' he said, 'that this man too was with him. For quite apart from other things, he is a Galilean.'

Peter said: 'Sir, I do not know what you are talking about.' And at once, before he had finished, a cock crew. The Lord swung round and looked at Peter intently. And Peter, remembering how he had said to him, 'Before the cock crows to-day you will disown me thrice,' went out and wept bitterly.

And now the men who were holding Jesus mocked and mishandled him. They blindfolded him, and then asked him to prophesy and tell them which of them had struck him. And they heaped insults upon him.

When day broke, the Elders of the people, the Chief Priests and Doctors of the Law met and took him before their Council. 'If you are the Christ,' they said, 'tell us.'

'If I tell you,' he replied, 'you will certainly not believe me; and if I question you, you will certainly not answer. Yet from this moment the Son of Man shall be seated at the right hand of the Power of God.'

'So you are the Son of God?' they all said.

'It is you that say I am,' he answered.

And they said: 'What further evidence do we need? We have heard it ourselves from his own lips.'

# 23

THE Council rose and without dispersing took him off to Pilate and proceeded to charge him. 'We caught this man,' they said, 'teaching our people sedition, telling them not to pay taxes to Caesar, and saying that he was the Christ, that is, a King.'

Pilate interrogated him. 'Are *you*,' he said, 'the King of the Jews?'

To which he replied: 'The words are yours.'

Pilate then said to the Chief Priests and the crowd: 'I do not find this person guilty.'

This made them even more insistent. 'He is stirring up the people,' they said, 'teaching everywhere in Judaea. He started in Galilee and now he has come here.'

When he heard this, Pilate asked whether the man was a Galilean, and having ascertained that he came from a country under Herod's jurisdiction, he sent him over to Herod, who at the time was also in Jerusalem.

Herod was delighted when he saw Jesus. For some time he had been wanting to see him, because of what he had heard about him. And now he hoped to see some marvel at his hands. He examined him at length; but Jesus answered none of his questions. And the Chief Priests and Doctors of the Law stood there, relentlessly denouncing him.

In the end, Herod with his soldiers round him dismissed him as of no account. He made a mockery of him by dressing him in a splendid robe, and sent him back to Pilate. And before the day was over, Herod and Pilate, who had been at enmity, were reconciled.

Pilate now called together the Chief Priests, the leading men and the people, and said: 'You accused this man before me of fomenting rebellion. Accordingly I examined him in your presence and did not find him guilty of anything you charged him with. Nor did Herod; for he sent him back to us, and as you see, no capital charge has been brought home to him. Therefore I propose, after due correction, to release him.'

'Away with him!' they shouted as one man. 'And let us have Barabbas.'*

Pilate again addressed them – he was anxious to let Jesus go. But they kept shouting back: 'Crucify him, crucify him.'

For the third time Pilate spoke to them, and said: 'But what crime has he committed? I found him guilty of no capital offence. So, after due correction, I propose to let him go.'

But they kept insisting at the top of their voices that he should be crucified; and their voices won the day. Pilate passed sentence: it should be as they wished. He let them have the man they had been asking for, who was in prison for rioting and murder, and he surrendered Jesus to their will.

As they were taking him off, they fastened on a man called Simon, a Cyrenaean, who was coming in from the country, laid the cross on his shoulders and made him carry it behind Jesus.

He was followed by a large crowd of townsfolk and of women who beat their breasts and wailed for him. Jesus turned round to the women and said: 'Daughters of Jerusalem, do not weep for me; but weep for yourselves and for your children. For I tell you that a time is coming when people will say, "Happy the barren women and the wombs that have not borne and the breasts that never suckled." Then they will begin to say, *Fall down on us, you mountains, and cover us, you hills*. For if they do this when the wood is green, what will happen when the wood is dry?'

Two other malefactors were taken out for execution with him. And when they reached the place called The Skull, they crucified him and the malefactors there, one on his right, the

* There had been a disturbance in the city, involving murder, and as a result this man had been thrown into prison.

other on his left. Jesus said: 'Father, forgive them, for they do not know what they are doing.'

They parcelled out his clothing and cast lots for the shares. And the people stood there looking on. There too were their rulers, scoffing at him. They said, 'He saved others: let him save himself if he is the Anointed One of God, the Elect.' Even the soldiers made a jest at his expense when they went up and offered him some vinegar. 'If you are the King of the Jews,' they said, 'save yourself.' There was also a placard over his head, with the words *This man is King of the Jews*.

He was taunted by one of the two malefactors crucified, who said: 'Are you not the Christ? Save yourself and us.'

But the other intervened and rebuked him. 'Have you, condemned to die like him, no fear of God? *We* were justly sentenced: we deserved what we have got. But he did nothing wrong.' And he said, 'Jesus, remember me when you come into your kingdom.'

Jesus said to him: 'I tell you in all truth, to-day you will be with me in Paradise.'

It was now about the sixth hour, and there was darkness over the whole country, which lasted till the ninth – the sun had been eclipsed. And the Curtain of the Temple was torn in two.

Jesus cried out in a loud voice: 'Father, to thy hands I entrust my spirit.' And with that he breathed his last.

The centurion, when he saw what had happened, glorified God by saying, 'This was indeed a righteous man.' And all the people who had flocked there to see the spectacle went home smiting their breasts when they had seen it. But all the men who knew him, and the women who had followed him from Galilee, stood watching some way off.

And now a man called Joseph, from the Jewish town of Arimathaea, a member of the Council and a good and upright man who had not approved of what they planned and did but was in search of the Kingdom of God, approached

Pilate and asked him for the body of Jesus. He took it down, wrapped it in linen, and laid him in a rock-hewn sepulchre where nobody had lain before. This was on the Eve, with the Sabbath approaching. The women who came from Galilee with Jesus had followed Joseph, and they now observed the tomb and the laying down of his body. Then they returned and prepared spices and ointments.

# 24

THEY rested on the sabbath day, keeping the commandment. But on the first day of the week, in the dim light of dawn, they came to the tomb with the spices they had prepared, and found that the stone had been rolled away from it. They went in, but they looked in vain for the body of the Lord Jesus. And while they were asking themselves what could have happened, two men in glistening clothes appeared beside them. The women were overcome with fear and lowered their eyes. But they said to them: 'Why do you seek the living among the dead? He is not here but has come back to life. Remember how he told you, when he was still in Galilee, that the Son of Man must be betrayed to sinful men, be crucified, and on the third day rise.'

They called to mind his sayings, and returning from the tomb reported everything to the Eleven and to all the rest. The women concerned were Mary Magdalene, Joanna, and Mary the mother of James; and the others with them also told the apostles. But all these reports struck the apostles as nonsense. They did not believe the women. However, Peter got up, ran to the tomb, and peering in saw nothing but the linen wrappings. And he came away amazed.

Now on that very day two of them were walking to a village called Emmaus, about seven miles from Jerusalem.

They were talking to each other of all these events, and were engrossed in their discussion, when Jesus himself came up with them and walked beside them. But a spell was on their eyes – they did not recognize him.

He asked them what they were so earnestly discussing on a walk.

Disconcerted, they came to a halt; and one of them, whose name was Cleopas, replied: 'Are you the only stranger in Jerusalem who has not heard what has just happened there ?'

'What are you referring to?' he asked them; and they both explained.

'To what they did to Jesus the Nazarene, who had proved himself a prophet, powerful in word and deed, before God and all the people. – How the Chief Priests and our leading men had him condemned to death and crucified. – And we had been hoping it was he that would set Israel free! – But now all that is in the past, and the third day is passing too. – Yet there is this: some of our womenfolk astounded us. They had been to the tomb at dawn, and not finding his body, came and reported among other things that they had had a vision, they had seen Angels who told them he was alive. Some of our party went to the tomb and found everything as the women had described it. – But they did *not* see him.'

'Foolish men!' said Jesus. 'So slow to put your trust in *all* that the Prophets said. Was it not fated that the Christ should suffer thus, and then should come into his glory?' And beginning with Moses and with all the Prophets, he expounded to them every passage in the Scriptures that concerned himself.

They drew near to the village they were making for and Jesus gave them to understand that he was going on. But they pressed him, saying, 'Stay with us. Evening is falling and the day is nearly done.' So he agreed to stay with them and went in.

He took his place at table with them and presently picked

up the loaf and said a blessing. And as he broke and gave it to them, their eyes were opened, they knew him, and he vanished from their sight.

They said to each other: 'Did not our hearts burn in our breasts as he talked to us on the road, as he opened our eyes to the Scriptures?' And without a moment's delay they set out and returned to Jerusalem, where they found the Eleven and their followers assembled, and learnt from them that the Lord had indeed come back to life and appeared to Simon. And in their turn they gave an account of what had happened on the road and how they had recognized him as he broke the bread.

They were telling their story, when he himself stood in their midst and said: 'Peace be with you.' Amazed and terrified, they thought they were looking at a ghost. But he said: 'Why are you alarmed? And why these questions rising in your hearts? Look at my hands and feet to see that I am I. Touch me and look. A ghost has not the flesh and bones that I have, as you see.' And with that he showed them his hands and feet.

And when for very joy they could not yet believe, and still wondered, he said: 'Have you anything here to eat?' And they handed him a portion of cooked fish, which he took and ate in their presence.

And he said to them: 'It was this that I taught you while I was still with you, namely that all that was written about me in the Law of Moses and the Prophets and Psalms must be fulfilled.' Then he opened their minds to an understanding of the Scriptures, and said to them: 'Thus it is written – Christ to suffer, and to rise from the dead on the third day; and in his name repentance, for the forgiveness of sins, to be preached to all the nations, beginning at Jerusalem. You are the witnesses for what has happened; while I for my part endow you with my Father's promised gift. But stay in the city till you have been invested from on high with power.'

He took them out with him as far as Bethany, where he lifted up his hands and blessed them. And it was as he blessed them that he parted from them [and was carried up to Heaven]. They worshipped him, and greatly rejoicing went back to Jerusalem, and were in the Temple every day, praising God.

THE GOSPEL AS RECORDED BY

# JOHN

IN the beginning the Word was.
And the Word was with God,
And the Word was God.

He was with God in the beginning.
All things came to be through him,
And without him not one came to be.

What came to be in him was Life;
And Life was the Light of mankind.

And the Light is shining in the Dark:
The Dark did not conquer it.

Came a man sent forth from God:
His name was John.
He came to testify, to speak for the Light,
That all men might have faith through him.

This man was not the Light,
But he was to speak for the Light.


The Light, the true Light
That illumines all mankind,
Was on its way into the world –


Was *in* the world, which came to be through him,
And the world did not know him –
Came to his own,
And his own did not take him to themselves.


Yet he gave to as many as took him
The power to be Children of God;
Gave it to those with faith in his Name,
Who were not begotten of blood,
Nor the will of the flesh,
Nor a man's will,
But of God.


And the Word became flesh
And pitched his tent among us,
Full of grace and truth.


We saw his glory,
Glory such as comes
From father to only son.


John tells us what he is.
He cried aloud:
'This is he of whom I said,
He that comes after me precedes me,
Because, before me, he was.'

Indeed from his full hands
We have all of us received –
Yes, grace upon grace.

For the Law was given through Moses:
Grace and truth came through Jesus Christ.

God, no one has seen ever.
The Only Son, who *is* in the bosom of the Father,
*He* made Him known.

And this is how John testified when the Jews sent Priests and Levites from Jerusalem to ask him what he claimed to be. He told the truth, he kept nothing back. 'I,' he confessed, 'am not the Christ.'

'Well then,' they said, 'are you Elijah?'

'I am not,' he answered.

'Are you the Prophet?'

'No.'

So now they said: 'Who are you? We must have something to report to those that sent us. What can you tell us of yourself?'

He replied in the words of the Prophet Isaiah: '*I am the voice of one crying in the wilderness, Make straight the way of the Lord.*'

These envoys were of the Pharisaic party. They questioned him further. 'Why then do you baptize,' they said, 'if you are not the Christ, nor Elijah, nor the Prophet?'

'I', answered John, 'baptize in water. In your midst stands one whom you do not know – he that comes after me, whose sandal-strap I am not worthy to undo.' This took place in Bethany beyond the Jordan, where John was baptizing.

The next day he saw Jesus coming towards him and said: 'Behold, the Lamb of God, who takes away the sin of the world. This is he of whom I said, "After me there comes a

man who takes precedence of me; for before me, he was."
And I did not know him! Yet it was in order that he might
be revealed to Israel that I came baptizing in water.'

And John gave proof. He said: 'I saw the Spirit descend
like a dove from heaven – it rested on him. And I did not
know him! But He that sent me to baptize in water said to
me, "He on whom you see the Spirit descend and rest is the
one that will baptize in the Holy Spirit." And I saw. Since
when, I have been testifying that this is the Elect of God.'

Again, on the following day, John was standing there with
two of his disciples when Jesus passed by. John looked at him
intently and said, 'Behold, the Lamb of God.' And his two
disciples, hearing what he said, went in pursuit of Jesus.

Jesus turned, saw them following him, and said: 'What are
you seeking?'

'Rabbi,'* they replied, 'where are you lodging?'

'Come and see,' he said. So they went and saw where he was
lodging; and they stayed that day with him. It was about the
tenth hour.

Andrew, Simon Peter's brother, was one of the two that
heard John's words and went after Jesus. In the morning he
sought out his brother Simon and said to him, 'We have found
the Messiah.'†

He brought Simon to Jesus. And Jesus, looking at him
closely, said: 'You are Simon son of John. You shall be called
Cephas.'‡

The next day he decided to travel to Galilee; and he found
Philip, a man from Bethsaida and a fellow-townsman of
Andrew and Peter. Jesus said to him: 'Follow me.'

Philip found Nathanael and said to him: 'We have found
the man of whom Moses wrote in the Law, and the Prophets
wrote – Jesus son of Joseph, the man from Nazareth.'

Nathanael said: 'Can any good come out of Nazareth?'

* This means Master.                † This means the Christ.
‡ This means Rock.

'Come and see,' said Philip.

Jesus saw Nathanael approaching and said of him: 'Indeed an Israelite in whom there is no guile.'

'How do you come to know me?' said Nathanael.

Jesus replied: 'Before Philip called you, I saw you under the fig-tree.'

'Rabbi,' Nathanael said, 'you are the Son of God, you are the King of Israel.'

Jesus answered: 'Is it because I told you I had seen you underneath the fig-tree that you have faith? You shall see greater things than these.' And he also said to him: 'I tell you in all truth that all of you shall see Heaven opened and *the Angels of God ascending and descending* on the Son of Man.'

## 2

THREE days later there was a wedding at Cana in Galilee. Jesus' mother was there, and Jesus and his disciples were also among the wedding guests.

The wine ran short, and Jesus' mother told him that they had no more.

He said to her: 'Lady, why bring your troubles to me? My time has not yet come.' Whereupon his mother said to the servants, 'Do whatever he tells you.'

Now the Jews rinse their hands in water before meals, and for this purpose six twenty-gallon stone jars were standing there.

Jesus said to the servants: 'Fill those jars with water.' And they filled them to the brim.

Then he said to them: 'Draw now, and serve the Master of the Feast.' And they served him.

The master tasted the water, which by now was wine, and not knowing where it came from (though the servants who

had drawn it knew) he called to the bridegroom and said:
'It is the usual practice to begin by serving vintage wine, and
when the guests are drunk, to serve a poorer kind. *You* have
kept the vintage wine till now.'

Thus at Cana in Galilee Jesus wrought the first of his
miracles. It bore the mark of his glory and his disciples' faith
in him was fixed.

After this he and his mother and his brothers went down to
Capernaum and stayed there for a few days.

The Jewish Passover drew near, and Jesus went up to Jerusalem. Finding people in the temple-precincts selling oxen,
sheep and doves, and the money-changers sitting at their
tables, he made a scourge of cords and drove them out of the
sacred buildings, men, sheep, oxen and all. He poured out the
money-changers' cash and upset their tables. And to the dove-
sellers he said: 'Away with all this! Do not make my Father's
house a place of business.' His disciples were reminded of the
Scripture, *Zeal for thy house will eat me up.*

The Jews took up the matter and said to him: 'What sign
can you show us to justify your action?'

Jesus replied: 'Pull down the Temple and in three days I
will raise it up.'

'This Temple,' said the Jews, 'took forty-six years to build.
Could *you* in three days put it up again?'

But he was speaking of the temple of his body. And later,
when he had risen from the dead, his disciples remembering
that he used to say this were convinced by the Scripture and
by Jesus' prophecy.

During his stay in Jerusalem for the Passover and the
Festival days, many people, witnessing the miracles he did,
began to put their trust in him. But for his part Jesus was not
going to trust himself to *them*, knowing all men as he did, and
needing no one to demonstrate to him what human nature is.
He knew without being shown.

# 3

THERE was a man called Nicodemus, one of the Pharisees and a member of the Jewish Council. This man came to him by night and said: 'Rabbi, we know that you are a teacher who has come from God; for no one can do such miracles as yours if God is not with him.'

Jesus replied: 'Hear the truth, Nicodemus. Unless a man is born again he cannot set eyes on the Kingdom of God.'

'How can anyone be born when he is old?' said Nicodemus. 'Surely he cannot go back into his mother's womb and so be born?'

Jesus said: 'I tell you in all truth, unless a man is born of water and Spirit he cannot come into the Kingdom of God. What is born of the flesh is flesh, and what is born of the Spirit is spirit. Do not be astonished at my telling you that men must be born again. Think of the wind – it blows where it will and you hear its voice, but whence it comes and where it goes you do not know. Such is everyone that is born of the Spirit.'

'How can these things be?' said Nicodemus.

Jesus said: 'You are Israel's teacher. Yet you know nothing of all this? I assure you that we speak of what we know, we testify what we have seen. Yet you reject our testimony. If you do not believe when I have told you earthly things, how are you going to believe when I tell you heavenly things? And no one has gone up to Heaven but he that came down from Heaven. Moreover, as Moses lifted up the serpent in the wilderness, so must the Son of Man be lifted up in order that all that have faith in him may win eternal life.'

Indeed, God so loved the world that he gave the Son, the Only Son, in order that all who have faith in him should not perish but should win eternal life. For God did not send the Son into the world to judge it, but to save it through him. The man that has faith in him is not under judgement; but he that rejects him has been judged already, because he had no faith in the Name of the Only Son of God.

And how is this judgement reached? Upon these grounds, that when the Light came into the world men loved the Darkness better and showed this by their evil lives. For all that live ignoble lives detest the Light and will not come to it lest their actions be exposed; whereas the man who lives the truth comes to the Light so that the world may see that all he does is done in God.

After his stay in Jerusalem, Jesus and his disciples went to Judaea, where he remained with them for some time and baptized. Meanwhile John, who had not yet been thrown into prison, was also baptizing, at Aenon near Salim, where there was plenty of water. People still went to him and were baptized.

In consequence, this cleansing rite became a matter of contention between the Jews and John's disciples, who went to John and said: 'Rabbi, are you aware that the man who was with you on the far side of the Jordan, and whom you vouched for, is baptizing and that everyone is going to him?'

John replied: 'No man endows himself – if he has gifts they must have come from Heaven. You yourself heard me say that I was not the Christ, but had been sent before him. None but the Bridegroom has the Bride. And yet his friend, the man who stands and hears him speak, is rendered truly happy by the Bridegroom's voice. And so *my* cup of happiness is filled. He must wax, and I must wane.'

He that comes from Above stands above all. He that is sprung from earth is earthly and speaks to us from earth. But he that comes from Heaven has seen and heard, and what he saw and heard he tells us. No one believes.

But those that do believe are thereby vouching for the truth of God. For he whom God sent forth tells us the thoughts of God – and God bestows the Spirit on him with no grudging hand.

The Father loves the Son and has entrusted him with all. He wins eternal life who has faith in the Son, but he that disobeys the Son shall not set eyes on life; the wrath of God is with him.

# 4

NOW when Jesus learnt that the Pharisees had heard that he was making and baptizing more disciples than John,[*] he forsook Judaea and went back to Galilee. His journey, since he had to cross Samaria, brought him to the Samaritan town of Sychar. This was near the piece of land that Jacob gave to his son Joseph, and Jacob's Spring was there.

It was midday and Jesus, tired by walking, had sat down at the Spring just as he was, when a Samaritan woman came there to draw water; and Jesus, whose disciples had gone off to the town to buy provisions, asked her to give him a drink.

Jews and Samaritans are not on friendly terms. So the woman said: 'What makes you ask *me* for a drink? You are a Jew and I a Samaritan woman.'

Jesus replied: 'If you had known the generosity of God, and who it is that asks you for a drink, you would have asked *him* and he would have given you living water.'

'You have no bucket, sir,' said the woman, 'and the well is deep. Where do you get your living water? Are you greater than our father Jacob, who gave us the well and drank from it himself together with his sons and cattle?'

Jesus replied: 'Everyone that drinks this water will be thirsty again; but he that drinks the water I give him will thirst no more. The water I give him will become in him a spring of water mounting to eternal life.'

'Sir,' said the woman, 'give me this water, so that I may not be thirsty and come here to draw.'

[*] Though it was not Jesus himself but his disciples that baptized.

Jesus said: 'Go now, fetch your husband and come back.'
'I have no husband,' she replied.

'You are right,' said Jesus, 'when you say you have no husband. You have had five, and the man you live with now is not your husband. You spoke the truth.'

'Sir,' said the woman, 'I perceive that you are a seer. Now our fathers worshipped on the mountain here; but you Jews say that the place where one should worship is in Jerusalem.'

Jesus said: 'Believe me, woman, a time is coming when you will worship the Father neither on this mountain nor in Jerusalem. You Samaritans worship what you do not know. We worship what we know – Salvation is to come from us. But a time is near, in fact has come, when those that really worship will be worshipping the Father in spirit and in truth – indeed the Father is already seeking such to worship him. God *is* Spirit, and his worshippers are bound to worship in spirit and in truth.'

The woman said: 'I know that the Messiah* is coming. When he is here, he will tell us everything.'

'I am he,' said Jesus. 'He is talking to you.'

At this point his disciples returned. They were astonished to find him in conversation with a woman, but no one asked her what she wanted, or asked Jesus why he was talking with her; and the woman left her water-pot, went to the town and said to the people: 'Come and see a man who told me everything I had done. Can he be the Messiah?' So they left the town and made their way to him.

Meanwhile the disciples had been begging him to eat. But he said: 'I have food to eat that you do not know of.' Whereupon the disciples said to one another: 'Has anyone brought him something to eat?'

But Jesus said: 'I find my food in doing the will of Him that sent me and finishing the task He gave me. You have a saying, have you not, "Four months to harvest time"? Well,

* Whom we call Christ.

my saying is, Use your eyes, look at the fields and see them already whitening for the harvest. The reaper is drawing his wages, he is gathering a crop into eternal life, so that Sower and reaper may rejoice together. For in this case what the proverb says is true – one man sows, another reaps. I sent you to reap a field in which you had not laboured. Others had laboured: you have come in for the fruits of their toil.'

When the woman told them how he had revealed her past, many of the Samaritans in Sychar believed in Jesus on the strength of her story, and when they had found him, begged him to stay with them. He stayed there for two days; and as a result still more of them were convinced by what he told them himself. They said to the woman: 'We no longer believe because of your story. *Now* we have heard for ourselves and know that this man is indeed the Saviour of the world.'

After these two days he left for Galilee. His own experience there had shown that a prophet is not honoured in his own country. But the Galileans had witnessed all he did at Jerusalem during the Festival, which they too had attended. And so when he arrived they welcomed him. Thus he came once more to Cana in Galilee, where he had turned the water into wine.

Now one of the noblemen at court had a son lying sick at Capernaum. Hearing that Jesus had moved from Judaea into Galilee, this man sought him out and begged him to come down from Cana and cure his son, who was at the point of death.

Jesus said: 'Will nothing but the sight of miracles and portents make you believe?'

'Sir,' said the nobleman, 'come down before my child is dead.'

'You can go back,' said Jesus. 'Your son is living.' And the man set out, convinced that he had heard the truth from Jesus.

As he was travelling down he was met by his servants with the news that his boy was living; and he asked them when he had got better.

'The fever left him yesterday,' they said, 'at noon.' Whereupon the father realized that this had happened at the very time when Jesus said to him, 'Your son is living.' And he and his whole family believed.

Thus once again Jesus wrought a miracle after leaving Judaea for Galilee.

# 5

THERE followed the Jewish Festival, and Jesus travelled up to Jerusalem.

By the sheep-gate in that city there is a pool with five arcades, which in Aramaic is called Bethzatha. A number of disabled people, blind, lame, and withered, used to lie in these arcades; and there was a man there who had suffered from his trouble for thirty-eight years.

Jesus, seeing him lying there and knowing that he had been ill for a long time, said to him: 'Have you the will to become well again?'

'Sir,' said the sick man, 'I have no one to put me in the pool when the water is ruffled, and while I am on the way someone else gets in before me.'

Jesus said: 'Rise, pick up your stretcher and walk.' And immediately the man was cured, picked up his stretcher and walked.

It was a sabbath day, and the Jews said to the man who had been cured: 'This is the Sabbath and you ought not to be carrying your stretcher.'

He replied: 'It was the man who cured me. He *told* me to pick it up and walk.'

They asked him who this person was that had told him to do so; but the man who had been cured did not know. The place was crowded and Jesus had disappeared.

Later, Jesus came upon him in the Temple and said: 'See now, you have been cured. Sin no more, lest something worse befall you.'

The man went off and informed the Jews that it was Jesus who had cured him. And that was why the Jews began to take action against Jesus – he was doing this kind of thing on the sabbath day. But his answer to them was: 'My Father has not ceased to work: I go on working too.' Which made them more determined than ever to put him to death. For not only was he breaking the Sabbath, but he talked of God as his own Father, putting himself on a level with Him.

In answer Jesus said to them: 'Hear the truth. The Son can do nothing of his own accord – only what he sees the Father doing. As the Father does, so does the Son. For the Father loves the Son and shows him all He does himself. Moreover, to make you marvel, He will show him greater deeds than these that you have seen. For as the Father raises the dead and gives them life, so does the Son give life to whom he will. Again, the Father judges no one, but has left all judgement to the Son, so that all may honour the Son as they honour the Father.

'He that does not hold the Son in honour pays no honour to the Father who sent him. Truly I tell you, he that hears my words and has faith in Him that sent me has eternal life, and is not brought to judgement but has passed from death to life.

'Indeed, indeed, I tell you that the time is coming, and has come, when the dead will hear a call from the Son of God and those that hear the call will live. For the Father, being as He is the source of Life, has made the Son the source of Life, and because he is Son of Man has given him authority to judge mankind.

'Do not marvel at this. For a time is coming when all people in the grave will hear his voice and will rise from it – those whose lives were good, to the resurrection that is Life; and those whose lives were evil, to the resurrection of the Judgement Day.

'I can do nothing of my own accord. I judge as I am told, and my judgement is just because I follow, not my own will, but the will of Him that sent me.

'If I bear witness as to what I am, my witness is not valid. There is another who bears witness for me, and I know that what He says of me is true.

'You sent to John and he bore witness to the truth. Now I myself rely on no credentials from mankind. But in order that you may be saved I state these facts. He was the Lamp that burns and gives its light; and you were glad enough for a time to enjoy the light he gave.

'John vouched for me, but I have better guarantees than his. The work that the Father gave me to accomplish, the very work I am doing now, declares that it was He who sent me here. Moreover, though you have never heard His voice nor seen His form, the Father who sent me has himself borne witness as to what I am. And yet the words He spoke have found no lodging in your hearts, since you reject His own Ambassador.

'You search the Scriptures, thinking to find eternal life in them. But those very Scriptures are my witnesses. And yet you will not come to me in order to possess yourselves of life.

'I take no praise from men. But then I know you – I know that the love of God finds no place in your hearts. I came here in my Father's name and you reject me. Yet if another comes in no name but his own you will accept him. How can such as you believe, content as you are with praise from one another, and not seeking the approval that comes from the Only God?

'Do not imagine that I shall accuse you in the Father's

Court. You *have* your accuser – in Moses, on whom you have based your hopes. For if you believed Moses you would believe me, because it was of me that he wrote; and if you do not believe what he wrote, how are you going to believe what I say?'

# 6

JESUS now crossed the Sea of Galilee.* But he was pursued by multitudes who had been witnessing his miraculous cures. So he went up into the hills, and sat down there with his disciples. This was a little while before the Passover, the Jewish Festival.

When Jesus looked up and saw that a great crowd was approaching him, he said to Philip: 'Where are we to buy bread so that these people may have something to eat?' He said this to test Philip, knowing well enough himself what he was going to do.

Philip replied: 'We could spend ten pounds on bread, and they would not have a mouthful each.' And one of his disciples, Andrew, Simon Peter's brother, said to Jesus: 'There is a small boy here with five barley loaves and two dried fish. But what is that among so many?'

Jesus said: 'Make the people settle down.'

There was plenty of grass there, and the men, about five thousand of them, settled down. Jesus took the loaves, and after saying a blessing distributed them among his guests. He did the same with the fish, giving them as much as they wanted. And when they had had their fill he said to his disciples: 'Collect the pieces left, so that nothing may be wasted.' And they collected them, filling twelve hampers with pieces from the five barley loaves left over by the men who had eaten.

* That is, the Sea of Tiberias.

When the people saw what a miracle he had done they began to say: 'This is indeed the Prophet whom the world awaited.' And Jesus, realizing that they were about to come and seize him so that they might make him king, withdrew once more into the hills, this time alone.

Late in the afternoon his disciples went down to the sea, embarked, and set out for Capernaum on the other side. But night overtook them before Jesus had rejoined them. There was a gale too and the sea was rising.

They had rowed about three or four miles when they saw Jesus walking on the sea and approaching the ship. They were terrified. But he said: 'It is I. Do not be afraid.' And just as they made ready to take him on board, the ship came to land at the spot they had made for.

Some of the crowd stayed on the far side of the Sea till the next morning. They had observed that only one dinghy was there and that Jesus did not board the ship with his disciples, who went off alone. So when some small boats from Tiberias came to shore near the place where they had eaten the bread after the Lord had blessed it, these people, seeing that neither Jesus nor his disciples were there, got into the boats and made for Capernaum in pursuit of Jesus. And when they had found him on the other side they said: 'Rabbi, when did you get here?'

Jesus replied: 'Hear the truth. You seek me out, not because you have seen miracles, but because you had your fill of bread. I would have you work, not for the food that perishes, but for the food that keeps, the staple of eternal life, the food that the Son of Man will give you. For the Father, God himself, has set his seal on him.'

'And how,' they asked, 'are we to set about the work God wishes us to do?'

Jesus replied: 'The work God asks of you is a life of faith in him that He has sent.'

'If that is so,' they said, 'what sign can you produce which we could see and so believe you? What marvel can you show? Our fathers ate manna in the wilderness. The Scriptures tell us so: *He gave them bread from heaven to eat.*'

Jesus said: 'Hear the truth. It was not Moses who gave you that bread from heaven; but it *is* my Father who offers you the bread from Heaven, the true bread. For the Bread of God is the bread that comes down from Heaven and gives life to the world.'

'Lord,' they said, 'give us that bread every day.'

Jesus said to them: 'I am the Bread of Life. He that comes to me shall not be hungry, and he that has faith in me shall never thirst. But as I said, you have seen but you do not believe.

'All that the Father gives me shall come to me; and anyone who comes to me, I will surely not reject. For I have come down from Heaven, not to do my own will, but the will of Him that sent me; and it is His will that of all he gave me I should lose none, but raise them all on the Last Day. Indeed it is my Father's will that everyone who sees the Son and has faith in him shall have eternal life. And it is I that will raise him up on the Last Day.'

When he said he was the Bread that had come down from Heaven there were muttered protests from the Jews. They said: 'Is this not Jesus son of Joseph, whose father and mother we know? How can he say now that he came down from Heaven?'

Jesus spoke. 'Cease to mutter to each other,' he said. 'No man can come to me but he that is drawn by the Father who sent me – and him I will raise up on the Last Day. In the Prophets' Books we read the words *All men shall be taught by God.* Everyone that has heard the Father's words and learnt them comes to me. Not that anyone has seen the Father but he who was and is with God. He *has* seen the Father.

'Hear the truth once more. He that has faith has eternal life. I am the Bread of Life. Your fathers ate the manna in the wilderness, and died. But here is the Bread that comes down from Heaven – eat it and you shall not die. I am the Bread, the Living Bread that came down from Heaven. If anyone eats this Bread he shall live for ever. Know too that the Bread which I will give, to bring the world to Life, is my flesh.'

At this the Jews fell out with one another. 'How can he give us his flesh to eat?' they said.

'Hear the truth,' said Jesus. 'If you do not eat the flesh of the Son of Man and drink his blood you have no Life in you. He that feeds upon my flesh and blood has eternal life, and I will raise him up on the Last Day. For my flesh is true food and my blood is true drink. He that feeds upon my flesh and blood dwells in me and I in him. As the Living Father sent me and I live through Him, so he that feeds on me shall live through me.

'Such is the Bread that came down from Heaven. Your fathers ate a different kind, and died. He that eats this Bread shall live for ever.'

He said these things in synagogue, when preaching at Capernaum; and many of his disciples after listening to him said: 'This doctrine goes against the grain. How can anyone accept it?'

But Jesus, knowing that this was the subject of their muttered questionings, said: 'This shocks you? Then what would you say if you saw the Son of Man ascend to where he came from? It is the spirit that gives life: the flesh is of no use whatever. The words I used to you *are* spirit and *are* life. But there are some of you that have no faith.'

Jesus said this because he had known from early days which were the unbelievers and who it was that would betray him. Indeed he made it clear that this was why he had warned them that nobody could come to him without a warrant from the Father.

In the end, many of his disciples fell away and no longer

went about with him. Jesus then said to the Twelve: 'Surely you also do not propose to leave me?'

Simon Peter answered: 'Lord, to whom are we to go? You have the secret of eternal life. We have had faith, and now we know that you are the Holy One of God.'

Jesus replied: 'Did I not pick you out myself, the twelve of you? Even so, one of you is a devil.' He meant Judas son of Simon of Kerioth who, though one of the Twelve, was going to hand him over to his enemies.

# 7

AFTER this, Jesus went about in Galilee, not wishing to travel in Judaea because the Jews were determined to kill him. But the Jewish Feast of Tabernacles was drawing near, and his brothers suggested to him that he should leave Galilee and go to Judaea so that the disciples he had there might also see the miracles he did. They pointed out that no one who seeks public recognition keeps his doings secret. 'Show yourself to the world,' they said, 'if you really do these things.' In fact, even his brothers did not believe in him.

Jesus replied: 'My day has not yet come; whereas for you one day is as good as another. The world has no excuse for hating you; but me it hates because I demonstrate the evil of its ways. Go up to the Festival yourselves. I am not going up to this Festival because my time has not yet run its course.' And having said this he himself stayed behind in Galilee.

Nevertheless, when his brothers had left for the Festival he too went up, not openly but so to speak by stealth. At the Festival the Jews began to look for him. 'Where is the man?' they said. And among the common people there was much whispering about him, some saying 'He is a good man,' but others 'No; he is leading folk astray.' Yet nobody spoke openly about him for fear of the Jews.

However, half-way through the Festival, Jesus went up into the Temple and began to teach. The Jews were amazed and said: 'How did he get his learning? He has never been properly taught.'

In answer to them Jesus said: 'My teaching is not mine; it comes from Him that sent me here. Anyone who tries to do His will can readily find out whether my teaching comes from God or whether what I say is of my own devising. The man who teaches on his own authority is seeking glory for himself. But he that seeks glory for the Author of his teaching, he is the true teacher.

'And what is more, he is no law-breaker. Moses gave you the Law, did he not? And yet there is not one of you that keeps it. Why do you want to kill me?'

Someone in the crowd exclaimed: 'You are possessed! Who wants to kill you?'

But Jesus went on with his defence: 'I did one piece of work which has set you all wondering. Moses instructed you in circumcision (not that he was the first: it began with our ancestors), and so you circumcise even on the sabbath day. But if a man is circumcised on the Sabbath so as to comply with Moses' law, why are you angry with me because on a sabbath day I made a man's whole body sound? Do not judge offhand. Let your judgements be justified.'

By now some of the people of Jerusalem were saying: 'Is not this the man they want to kill? Yet there he is, speaking in public, and they do not say a word to him. Is it possible that our rulers really know him to be the Messiah? No; for this man's past is known, whereas when the Messiah is here no one will know where he came from.'

Jesus, teaching in the Temple, cried: 'You know where I came from just as well as you know me. And what if I did not come here in my own right? None can dispute the right of

Him that sent me. You do not know Him. I do. For I come from Him and it was He that sent me here.'

For this they would gladly have arrested him. Yet because his hour had not yet come nobody touched him.

Of the common people, however, many believed in him and said: 'Is it likely that the Christ when he comes will do more miracles than this man did?'

When the Pharisees learnt that such talk about him was rife among the people, they and the Chief Priests sent Temple police to arrest him. Whereupon Jesus said: 'I am with you only for a little while, then I go my way to Him that sent me. You will seek me and you shall not find; and where I am, there you cannot come.'

The Jews said to one another: 'Where is he proposing to go, when he says we shall not find him? Does he think of going to our countrymen abroad among the Greeks, and teaching the Greeks themselves? What did he mean by saying, "You will seek me and you shall not find; and where I am, there you cannot come?"'

On the last day of the Festival, the great day, Jesus stood up and cried: 'If any one is thirsty let him come to me and drink. He that has faith in me shall, as the Scripture says, have rivers of living water streaming from within him.' But he was speaking of the Spirit, which those that had faith in him were later to receive. For the Spirit was not yet in being, as Jesus had not yet been glorified.

Some of the people after listening to these words of his began to say, 'He really is the Prophet,' and some, 'He is the Christ.' But others said: 'Can the Messiah come from Galilee? Did not the Scriptures say that the Messiah would come from David's House and David's town of Bethlehem?'

Thus the people disagreed about him; and some were inclined to arrest him, though nobody in fact laid hands on him.

Now when the Temple police reported to the Chief Priests

and Pharisees and were asked why they had not brought him with them, they replied: 'No man ever spoke like that.'

'Have you too been taken in?' said the Pharisees. 'Did a single one of our leading men believe in him, or a single Pharisee? But this unlettered rabble is bewitched.'

Nicodemus, who had approached Jesus earlier though he himself was a Pharisee, now said to them: 'Surely our laws do not condemn a man without giving him a hearing and finding out what he is really doing?'

'Are you by any chance a Galilean too?' they said. 'Think again, and you will see that here is no Galilean prophet coming to the fore.'

# 8

[THEY scattered to their several homes, but Jesus went to the Mount of Olives. At dawn he appeared once more in the Temple. All the people came to him and he sat down and taught them.

The Doctors of the Law and the Pharisees now brought in a woman who had been caught in the act of adultery and made her stand in the centre. They said to him: 'Master, this woman was caught in the very act of adultery. Moses laid it down for us in the Law that such women should be stoned. What have *you* to say about her?'

They said this to put him to the proof, hoping to have a charge to bring against him. But Jesus stooped down and wrote with his finger on the ground, pretending not to hear them.

However, when they persisted in their questions he looked up and said: 'Let him among you that has never sinned cast the first stone at her.' Then he bent down again and wrote on the ground. And one by one the Jews went out, the eldest first; and he was left alone with the woman, who was still standing in the centre.

Jesus raised his head. 'Woman,' he said, 'where are they? Did no one pass sentence on you?'

'No one, sir.'

'I pass no sentence on you either. Go now, and sin no more.']

Once more Jesus addressed them. 'I am the Light of the world,' he said. 'He that follows me will not be walking in the dark but shall have the light of life.'

To this the Pharisees replied: 'You are testifying for yourself. Such evidence has no validity.'

'What if I am?' said Jesus. 'My evidence is sound because I know where I came from and where I am going. Which you do not. You judge superficially. I judge no one. And even if I do judge, my judgement is sound because I am not alone but I and He that sent me judge together.

'In your law it is laid down that when two witnesses agree you get the truth. I *have* two witnesses for what I am, myself and the Father who sent me.'

'Where is your Father?' said the Pharisees.

Jesus replied: 'You know neither me nor my Father. If you knew me you would know my Father also.'

He made these pronouncements in the Treasury, when he was preaching in the Temple. Yet nobody arrested him, since his hour had not yet come.

Again, he said to them: 'I go my way. And you will seek me and will die in your sin. Where I am going you cannot come.' Which drew the comment from the Jews: 'Does he mean to kill himself when he says that he is going where we cannot come?'

He also said to them: 'You are from below: I am from above. You are of this world: I am not. That was why I said you would die in your sins. Indeed, if you do not believe that I am He, you *shall* die in your sins.'

'Who are you then?' they said.

'So we go back to our starting-point!' said Jesus. 'Should I be talking to you at all if I had not much to say about you, much to judge? Nevertheless, He that sent me is the true judge; and what I tell the world is what I heard from Him.'

They did not understand that he was speaking of the Father. So Jesus said to them: 'When you have lifted up the Son of Man, then you will realize that I am He, and that I do nothing of my own accord, but in saying these things am saying what the Father taught me. He that sent me is with me. He has not left me to myself, for I am busy all the time in pleasing Him.'

These words of his gave many people faith in Jesus, and he now said to the Jews who had believed him: 'If you are faithful to my word you are real disciples of mine, and you shall learn the truth and the truth will make you free.'

'We are sprung from Abraham,' some of them replied. 'We have never been anyone's slaves. What do you mean by saying that we shall be freed?'

'Hear the truth,' said Jesus. 'Every man that lives in sin is a slave of sin. But slaves do not stay in a household for ever – it is the son that stays for ever. So, if the Son sets you free, you will indeed be free men.

'I know that you are sprung from Abraham. And yet you want to kill me because my words find no room in your hearts. I tell you what I have seen in my Father's house. So you have heard your Father's wishes. Act accordingly.'

'*Our* father is Abraham,' they replied.

'If you are children of Abraham,' said Jesus, 'act as Abraham acted. As it is, you are trying to kill me, a man who has taught you the truth he had from God. That was not Abraham's way. You have another father who dictates your actions.'

'We,' they retorted, 'are not illegitimate children. We have one Father, who is God.'

Jesus said: 'If God were your Father you would love me. For I came, and I am here, from God. Not that I was the author of my coming – it was He that sent me forth.

'Why do you not understand my language? Because you cannot comprehend my thought. You are children of your father, the Devil, and are glad to carry out your father's wishes. He was a murderer from the beginning, who never dealt in truth because no truth is in him. When he tells a lie he is faithful to himself; for he *is* a liar and the father of the lie. But when I speak the truth you do not believe me. Which of you can convict me of sin?

'If I am telling the truth why do you not believe me? A child of God hears the thoughts of God. It is because you are not His children that you do not hear.'

'How right we were!' replied the Jews. 'You are a Samaritan and possessed.'

'I am not possessed,' said Jesus. 'No; I honour my Father – and you insult me. However, I am not seeking glory for myself. There is One who seeks it for me and who is the Judge. I tell you in all truth, he that cherishes my word shall never come in sight of death.'

'Now we *know* you are possessed,' said the Jews. 'Abraham died and so did the Prophets, yet you say that the man who cherishes your word shall never know the taste of death. Are you greater than our father Abraham, who died; and the Prophets, who are also dead? Who do you claim to be?'

Jesus answered: 'If I honour myself my honour is a thing of naught. My honour is bestowed upon me by my Father, whom you call your God though you have never known Him. But I know Him, and were I to say that I do not I should be a liar like you. I do know Him and cherish his word. Abraham your father exulted in the thought that he would see my day. And he saw it and rejoiced.'

'You are not yet fifty,' said the Jews; 'and Abraham saw you?'

Jesus said: 'Hear the truth. Before Abraham came to be, I *am*.'

Whereupon they picked up stones to cast at him. But Jesus made his way out of the Temple unobserved.

# 9

As he passed along he saw a man who had been blind from birth. His disciples put a question to him. 'Rabbi,' they said, 'when this man was born blind, was it he or his parents that had sinned?'

Jesus replied: 'Neither he nor his parents had sinned. What was desired was that through this man the way in which God works should be made manifest. He sent me here to do His work, and I must do it while the daylight lasts. There comes the night, when nobody can work. While I am in the world, I am the light of the world.'

With that, he spat on the ground, made clay with the spittle and smeared it on the man's eyes. Then he said: 'Go now and wash yourself in the Pool of Siloam.'*

The man went and washed himself, and when he came away he could see. His neighbours and those who had known him by sight as a mendicant said: 'Isn't this the man who sits and begs?' Some said it was. Others said no, though they saw a likeness. Meanwhile the man himself kept saying it was he.

So they said to him: 'If that is true, how were your eyes opened?' And he replied: 'The man called Jesus made clay, smeared it on my eyes and told me to go to Siloam and wash. I went and washed myself, and I could see.'

'Where is this man?' they asked.

'I do not know,' he said.

They took the man who had been blind to the Pharisees. And as the day when Jesus made clay and opened his eyes had been a Sabbath, he was asked once more, this time by the Pharisees, to explain how he had gained his sight. And he told them: 'He put clay on my eyes; I washed; and I can see.'

Some of the Pharisees now said: 'This man Jesus does not come from God: he breaks the Sabbath.' But others said:

* So called because the water was brought through a conduit.

'How could a sinful man achieve such miracles?' They were divided in opinion.

So they questioned the blind man again. 'What do *you* say about him? It was your eyes that he opened.'

'I say he is a prophet.'

But the Jews would not believe that he had been blind and gained his sight till they had summoned and examined his parents.

They said to them: 'Do you identify this man as your son whom you declare to have been blind from birth? If so, explain the fact that he can see.'

The man's parents replied: 'We know that this is our son. We know that he was born blind. But how he is now able to see, we do not know. Nor do we ourselves know who opened his eyes. He is of age. He will tell you his own story.'

They said this because they were afraid of the Jews, who had agreed to excommunicate anyone who acknowledged Jesus as the Messiah. It was the thought of this that made them say: 'He is of age. You had better question *him*.'

So the Jews recalled the man who had been blind, swore him in, and said: 'We have satisfied ourselves that the man you told us about is a sinner.'

'Whether he is a sinner I do not know,' he answered. 'But I do know this – I was a blind man and I see.'

'What did he do to you? How did he open your eyes?'

'I have already told you and you would not listen. Why do you want to hear the story again? Do you wish to join the ranks of his disciples?'

They became abusive. 'It is you that are a disciple of that fellow. We are disciples of Moses. We know that God spoke to Moses. But as for him, we do not even know where he came from.'

'What a remarkable thing!' he said. 'You don't know where he came from – and he opened my eyes. We know that God does not listen to sinners, but he does listen to the man that worships him and does his will. No one, from the beginning of time, has ever been known to open the eyes of one born blind. If this man had not come from God he could do nothing at all.'

'Are you that were born, every bit of you, in sin presuming to teach *us*?' they said, and threw him out.

When Jesus heard that they had thrown him out, he found the man and said: 'Are you prepared to believe in the Son of Man?'

'Sir,' said he, 'tell me who he is, so that I may believe in him.'

Jesus said: 'You have seen him. He is talking to you.'

'Lord, I believe,' said the man, and worshipped him.

Jesus said: 'I came into this world so that people might be set asunder, so that those who cannot see should see, and those who can see should become blind.'

When the Pharisees who were with him heard this they said: 'We surely are not numbered with the blind?'

'If you were blind,' said Jesus, 'you would be guiltless. But as it is, you say that you can see. Your guilt endures.

# 10

'HEAR the truth. He that does not come into the sheepfold by the gate, but climbs in by some other way, is a thief and a brigand. But he that comes in by the gate is a shepherd, and for him the keeper opens. And the sheep recognize his voice. He calls his own sheep, each by name, and leads them out. When he has driven all his own sheep out he walks in front of them, and they follow him because they know his voice. But they will not follow strangers. They run away from them because they do not know their voices.'

Jesus had given them an allegory, but they did not

understand what he was telling them. So once more Jesus said to them:

'Hear the truth. I am the Sheep-gate. All who came before me were thieves and brigands. But the sheep did not listen to them. I am the Gate.

'Anyone that has come in through me will be safe. He shall pass in and out and will find pasturage. A thief comes in, only to steal, slaughter and destroy. I came to give them Life, and something more.

'I am the shepherd, the Shepherd Beautiful, who lays down his life for the sheep. The hired man, not being a shepherd nor regarding the sheep as his own, deserts them when he sees the wolf coming. He runs away and the wolf pounces on the sheep and scatters them. For the man is a hireling and the flock does not concern him.

'I am the Shepherd Beautiful. As the Father knows me and I know him, so I know my own and my own know me. And I lay down my life for the sheep.

'Moreover I have other sheep, not of this fold. It is ordained that I shall lead them also. They will recognize my voice; and there shall be one flock, one Shepherd.

'Why does the Father love me? Because I lay down my life so that I may take it up again. No one took it from me, but I lay it down of my own accord. I have authority to lay it down; I have authority to take it up again. Such were my Father's orders.'

These words of his set the Jews once more at variance. Many of them said: 'He has a demon and is mad. Why do you listen to him?' Others said: 'These are not the thoughts of one possessed. And can a demon open blind men's eyes?'

The Feast of Reconsecration in Jerusalem came round. It was winter; and in the temple-precincts Jesus was walking to and fro in Solomon's Arcade. Seizing this opportunity, the Jews surrounded him and said: 'How long do you propose to keep us on tenterhooks? If you are the Christ, tell us in so many words.'

Jesus replied: 'I told you – and you have no faith. These things that I do in the name of my Father bear witness as to what I am. But you do not believe because you are not numbered with my sheep. My sheep recognize my voice and I know them, and they follow me. I give them life eternal. They will not perish in eternity, and nobody shall snatch them from my hand. My Father, who gave them to me, is all-powerful and no one can steal from His hand. I and the Father are one.'

Once more the Jews fetched stones to cast at him. Whereupon Jesus said: 'I have done in your presence many wonderful things with the Father's seal upon them. For which of these do you propose to stone me?'

The Jews replied: 'We are not stoning you for any marvel, but for blasphemy, and because you that are man are claiming to be God.'

Jesus answered: 'Does not your Law contain the words *I said you are gods?* If the writer gave the name of gods to men inspired by God – and this Scripture cannot be dismissed – are you accusing me, whom the Father sanctified and sent into the world, of blasphemy because I said I am a son of God? If I fail to do my Father's work do not believe in me. But if I do it, even though you do not believe in me, believe in the work, so that you may see and comprehend that the Father is in me and I in the Father.'

This led them once more to attempt his arrest. But he slipped through their hands and went back beyond the Jordan to the place where John first practised baptism. And there he stayed and many came to him. 'John may have done no miracle,' they used to say, 'but everything he said about this man was true.' And many people put their trust in him there.

## 11

A MAN lay sick – Lazarus of Bethany, the village of Mary and her sister Martha. Mary was the woman who anointed the Lord with unguent and dried his feet with her hair, and the sick man Lazarus was her brother. So the sisters sent a message to Jesus saying, 'Lord, do you know that your friend is ill?'

When Jesus received the message he said: 'Beyond the illness of this man I see, not death, but the glory of God and glory coming to the Son of God.'

Accordingly, though he loved Martha and her sister and Lazarus, Jesus after hearing of his sickness stayed where he was for two days. Then he said to the disciples: 'Let us go back to Judaea.'

'Rabbi,' they said, 'the Jews have just been trying to stone you. Are you going back *there*?'

Jesus replied: 'Are there not twelve hours in the day? If anyone walks by day he does not stumble, because he sees the light of this world. But if anyone walks by night he stumbles, because the Light is not in him.'

This was his answer. And presently he said: 'Lazarus, our friend, has fallen asleep. But I intend to go and wake him.'

The disciples said: 'Lord, if he has fallen asleep he will recover.'

Jesus had been speaking of his death, whereas they thought he had meant the rest that we call sleep.

So now Jesus told them in plain terms. 'Lazarus has died,' he said. 'And for your sakes and the sake of your faith I am glad I was not there. But come, let us go to him.'

Whereupon Thomas, the one who was called the Twin, said to his fellow-disciples: 'Let us also go, so that we may die with him.'

Lazarus had already been four days in the tomb when Jesus arrived; and as Bethany was only about two miles from

Jerusalem, many of the Jews had come out to Martha and Mary to condole with them on their brother's death. Martha was told that Jesus was approaching, and it was she that went out to meet him, leaving Mary sitting in the house.

Martha said to Jesus: 'Lord, had you been here my brother would not have died. Yet even now I know that whatever you may ask of God, God will give you.'

'Your brother will come back to life,' said Jesus.

Martha replied: 'I know that he will rise at the resurrection on the Last Day.'

'I am the Resurrection and the Life,' said Jesus. 'He that has faith in me, even though he dies, shall live. And all that live and have faith in me shall never die. Do you believe this?'

'Yes, Lord,' she said. 'I do believe that you are the Christ, the Son of God, whom the world awaited.'

With that she left him and went home, where she beckoned her sister Mary and whispered in her ear: 'The Master is near-by and wishes to see you.'

When she heard this Mary got up quickly and made her way to Jesus, who had not yet reached the village but was still in the place where Martha had met him. And the Jewish visitors who had been condoling with Mary, when they saw her hastily get up and leave, followed her out under the impression that she was going to the tomb to wail.

Mary reached the place where Jesus was, and when she saw him, fell at his feet and said: 'Lord, had you been here my brother would not have died.'

When Jesus saw how she and the Jews who had come with her were wailing he gave way to such distress of spirit as made his body tremble.

'Where have you laid him?' he asked. And they said, 'Lord, come and see.'

Jesus wept. And the Jews said, 'See how he loved him!' some of them adding, 'He opened the blind man's eyes; could he not also have prevented Lazarus' death?'

Jesus was once more shaken by emotion as he reached the tomb. This was a cave with a stone across the entrance.

'Remove the stone,' said Jesus.

But Martha, the dead man's sister, said: 'Lord, there must be a stench by now. He has been dead four days.'

Jesus replied: 'Did I not tell you that if you had faith you should see the glory of God?'

So they removed the stone. And Jesus raised his eyes to Heaven and said: 'Father, I thank thee for having heard me. I myself knew that thou dost always hear me; but I act for the sake of these people standing round me, so that they may believe that thou didst send me here.'

Then he cried in a loud voice: 'Lazarus, come out.' And the dead man came out, wrapped hand and foot in grave-clothes, with a napkin over his face.

'Undo him and let him go home,' said Jesus.

As a result of this many of the Jews, those who had visited Mary and witnessed what he did, had faith in him. But some of them went to the Pharisees and reported Jesus' actions.

Accordingly the Chief Priests and the Pharisees called a meeting of the Council. 'What are we doing?' they said. 'This man is working many miracles. If we just let him be, the whole people will believe in him and the Romans will come and uproot our worship and our race itself.'

But one of them called Caiaphas, who was High Priest in that year, said: 'Have you no sense at all? Do you not realize that it is to your advantage that one man should die for the people rather than that the whole nation should perish?'

These words, it must be noted, were put into his mouth. As High Priest in that fateful year he was prophesying that Jesus would die for the nation, and not for the nation only, but to gather in one fold the scattered family of God.

From that day then it was their policy that he should die. So Jesus no longer walked openly among the Jews but withdrew to the edge of the desert, to a place called Ephraim, where he stayed with the disciples.

The Jewish Passover drew near and many country people went up to Jerusalem before the Feast to purify themselves. These began to look for Jesus. As they stood about in the Temple they said to one another: 'What do you think? Surely he won't come to the Festival?' Meanwhile the Chief Priests and the Pharisees had issued orders that anyone who knew where he was should inform them, so that they could arrest him.

# 12

SIX days before the Festival, Jesus went to Bethany, the home of Lazarus whom he had raised from the dead; and there they gave a dinner in his honour. Martha served and Lazarus took his place at table with Jesus and the other guests. Mary, bringing a pound of true and very costly spikenard ointment, anointed Jesus' feet and dried them with her hair. The house was filled with the scent of the ointment, and Judas of Kerioth, one of his disciples and his future betrayer, said: 'Why was this ointment not sold? We could have given three hundred shillings to the poor.'

He said this, not because he cared about the poor, but because he was a thief and being in charge of the money-box used to help himself to people's offerings.

But Jesus said to him: 'Let her be, so that she may keep it for the day of my burial. The poor you have among you always; but me you have not always.'

The Jewish populace had discovered that Jesus was in Bethany and they came out, not only for his sake, but to see Lazarus whom he had raised from the dead. And since, because of Lazarus, many of them were falling away and believing in Jesus, the Chief Priests now decided to kill Lazarus too.

On the following day a great crowd who had come in for

the Festival, hearing that Jesus was on his way into Jerusalem, plucked branches off the palms and went out to meet him. They were shouting, '*Hosanna! Blessed be he that cometh in the name of the Lord! Blessed be the King of Israel!*' And another Scripture was fulfilled. It said, *Fear not, Daughter of Sion; behold, thy King is coming, mounted on the foal of an ass* – and Jesus found a donkey colt and mounted it. At the time, his disciples did not understand. But when Jesus had been glorified they realized that these Scriptures had referred to him, and remembered how he had been welcomed in this very way.

Thus the people who were with him when he called Lazarus from the tomb and raised him from the dead expressed their faith in Jesus; while the other crowd, which came to meet him, had the same motive – they had heard that he had wrought this miracle. 'You see, we are defeated,' said the Pharisees to one another. 'The whole world is running after him.'

There were some Greeks also who had come up with the others to worship at the Festival. These approached Philip, the man from Bethsaida in Galilee, with a petition: 'Sir, we should like to meet Jesus.' Philip went and told Andrew; and Andrew went to Jesus with Philip and they told him.

In reply to them Jesus said: 'The hour has come for the Son of Man to be glorified. Truly I tell you, if the wheat-grain does not fall into the soil and die, it stays as it was, a single grain; but if it dies it yields abundantly. He that loves his life loses it; and he that hates his life in this world shall keep it in eternity.

'If a man is to serve *me*, let it be me that he follows. And where I am, there my servant shall be also. Anyone that serves me will be honoured by the Father.

'Now, my soul is troubled. And what am I to say? "Father, save me from this hour"? No; it was for this end that I have lived till now. Father, show the glory of thy Power.'

There came a voice from heaven: 'I have shown My glory. I will show it yet again.'

Bystanders who heard this said that it had thundered; others that an Angel had been talking to him.

Then Jesus spoke. 'This Voice came, not for my sake, but for yours. The day of judgement for the world is here; the Prince of this world shall be cast out now. And I, when I am lifted from the earth, will draw the whole creation to myself.' He indicated in these words the manner of his coming death.

The people replied: 'We have learnt from the Law that the Christ endures for ever. What do you mean by saying that the Son of Man is destined to be "lifted up"? Who is this Son of Man?'

Jesus said: 'For yet a little while the Light is in your midst. Walk while you have the Light, lest darkness overtake you. For the man who walks in the dark does not know where he is going. Put your trust in the Light while you have it, and so become Children of Light.'

Having spoken thus, Jesus withdrew from them into privacy. In spite of all the miracles he had done in their presence, they did not believe in him. For the words of the Prophet had to be fulfilled. *Lord*, said Isaiah, *who has believed our tidings? To whom was the Lord's hand revealed?* And the reason for their unbelief lay in another saying of Isaiah's, *He has blinded their eyes and darkened their hearts, lest they should see with their eyes and perceive with their heart and repent, and I should heal them.* Isaiah said these things because he saw his glory. It was of Jesus that he spoke.

Yet many even of their leading men believed in him; but because of the Pharisees they would not admit it, being afraid of excommunication. They loved their good name in the world more than their good name with God.

But Jesus cried aloud: 'He that believes in me believes, not in me, but in Him that sent me; and he that has his eyes on me is seeing Him that sent me. I have come into the world as Light so that all who have faith in me should not be left in the darkness. Yet if anyone listens to my words and does not abide by them, I do not condemn him; for I did not come to judge the world but to save it. The man who spurns me and rejects my words has his judge waiting for him – the very words that I have spoken will condemn him on the Last Day. For I was not the author of the words I spoke; the Father who sent me gave me His own instruction as to what to say and how to speak. And I know that His instruction means eternal life. Thus it is true of all I say, that I speak as the Father told me.'

# 13

IT was the Eve of the Passover, and Jesus knew that the hour had come for him to leave this world and go to the Father. He had loved those friends of his who were in the world and now he showed how utterly he loved them.

They were at supper and the Devil had already prompted Judas son of Simon of Kerioth to betray him, when Jesus, who knew that the Father had put all things in his hands and that he had come from and was going to God, rose from table, laid his clothes aside, and wrapped a towel round his waist. Then he filled the jug with water and began to wash the disciples' feet and dry them with the towel he had on. In due course he came to Simon Peter, who said: 'Lord, do you mean to wash my feet?'

Jesus replied: 'What I am doing you do not at the moment know, but shortly you will understand.'

'Never,' said Peter, 'shall you wash my feet.'

Jesus answered: 'If I do not wash you, you have no part in me.'

'Lord,' said Simon Peter, 'not only my feet, but my hands and head also.'

Jesus said: 'One who has bathed himself does not need to be washed, save only his feet – his whole body is cleansed.

And all of you *are* cleansed. No; not all.' He spoke with knowledge of his betrayer, which was why he said that they were not all of them pure.

When he had washed their feet he put on his clothes and resumed his place at table. Then he said: 'Understand what I have done for you. You address me as Master and Lord. And rightly – that is what I am. If I then, your Lord and Master, washed your feet, it is your duty to wash one another's feet. I have set you this example so that you may do what I did for you. But remember also that a servant is not greater than his master, nor an apostle greater than he that sent him. If you understand these truths it will be your happiness to act accordingly. I am not speaking of you all – I know the kind of men whom I picked out. But the Scripture says, *The man who eats my bread has lifted up his heel against me*, and it had to be fulfilled. I warn you now, before it happens, so that when it happens you may believe that I am He. And be assured that the man who receives an apostle of mine receives me, and the man who receives me receives Him that made me His Apostle.'

After saying this Jesus was profoundly moved and made a declaration: 'Hear the truth. One of you is going to betray me.' And the disciples looked at one another, wondering whom he meant.

One of them was reclining side by side with Jesus. Jesus loved him; and when Simon Peter made a sign to him to find out who it was, this disciple, without moving from his place, leant back on Jesus' breast and said: 'Lord, who is it?'

Jesus replied: 'It is the man to whom I give the morsel I shall dip.'

Then he dipped the morsel and gave it to Judas son of Simon of Kerioth. And no sooner had he taken it than Satan entered Judas.

Jesus said to him: 'The quicker you act the better.'

None of those at supper understood what he meant by

saying this to him. Some of them thought that as Judas was their treasurer Jesus was telling him to buy what they needed for the Feast or to give something to the poor.

Judas left the house directly he had had the morsel. And it was night.

When he had gone, Jesus said: 'Now is the Son of Man glorified and God is glorified in him. If God is glorified in him, God will also give him glory of his own.

'And He will give it *now*. My children, you and I have but a short time together. You will miss me. I said to the Jews, "Where I am going, you cannot come." I say it now to you.

'I give you a commandment that is new, Love one another, love one another as I loved you. It is by the love you show for one another that all men will know you for disciples of mine.'

Simon Peter said: 'Lord, where are you going?'

Jesus answered: 'Where I am going you cannot follow me now. But you shall follow later.'

'Lord,' said Peter, 'why can I not follow you at once? I will lay down my life for you.'

'Lay down your life for me?' said Jesus. 'Truly I tell you, the cock will not crow till you have disowned me thrice.

# 14

'LET not your heart be troubled. Have faith in God; have faith in me. There are many resting-places in my Father's dwelling. Were this not so, should I have told you that I am on my way to prepare a place for you? And having gone to prepare a place for you, I shall come back and take you to myself, so that where I am, you may be also. As for my destination, you know the way.'

'Lord,' said Thomas, 'we do *not* know your destination. How can we know the way?'

Jesus said to him: 'I am the Way and the Truth and the Life; no one comes to the Father but through me. If you had learnt to know me you would know my Father also. Now, you begin to know Him and indeed have seen Him.'

'Lord,' said Philip, 'show us the Father and we shall be satisfied.'

Jesus said: 'So you have not come to know me, Philip, in all the time we have been together? He that has seen me has seen the Father. How can you say "Show us the Father"? Do you not believe that I am in the Father and the Father in me? The knowledge I give you springs, not from me, but from the Father dwelling and accomplishing his work in me. Believe what I say – that I am in the Father and the Father is in me. Or else believe because of the work itself.

'Indeed I tell you, he that has faith in me shall himself do the things that I do, and greater wonders still, since I am journeying to the Father. Whatever you ask in my name, that I will do, in order that the Father may be glorified in the Son. Ask for anything in my name and I will do it.

'If you love me you will keep my commandments. And I will ask the Father, and He will give you another to serve as Advocate and be with you to the end of time, the Spirit of Truth, which the world cannot take to itself because it neither sees nor knows it. But you begin to know it because it lodges with you and will be within you.

'I will not leave you orphaned. I will come to you. Yet a little while and the world sees me no more, but you see me because I have Life and you too shall have Life. In that hour you will know the truth that I am in my Father, and you in me, and I in you.

'He that takes hold of my commandments and keeps them, he is the one that loves me. And he that loves me shall be loved by my Father, and I will love him and show myself to him.'

'Lord,' said Judas (not Judas of Kerioth), 'what is behind

your words when you speak of showing yourself to us and not to the world?'

Jesus replied: 'If anyone loves me he will cherish my word; my Father will love him and we will come to him and make him our abode. He that does not love me neglects my words. Yet the word you hear is not my own but that of the Father who sent me.

'I have said these things to you while still with you. But the Advocate, the Holy Spirit, whom the Father will send in my name, will teach you everything and recall to your minds all that I have said to you.

'I leave you peace: my peace I give to you. Nor do I give to you as the world gives. Let not your heart be troubled; have no coward fears. You heard me say "I am going, and I will come to you." If you loved me you would have been glad that I am going to the Father, because the Father is greater than I.

'And now I have told you before the event so that when it happens you may believe. I shall not talk of many more things with you, for the Prince of this world is on his way. And yet he has no concern in me – none. But the world must be taught that I love the Father, and that as the Father bade me so I act. Up now and let us go.

## 15

'I AM the Vine, the true Vine, and my Father is the Vine-dresser. Every branch in me that bears no fruit He cuts away; and every fruitful branch He cleanses so that it may yield more fruit. You are cleansed already by the teaching I have given you. Remain in me, and I in you. Just as the branch alone can bear no fruit but must stay in the vine, so you can bear no fruit unless you stay in me.

'I am the Vine; you are the branches. It is the one who stays in me, with me in him, that bears abundant fruit; because, cut off from me, you can do nothing at all. He that does not stay in me is cast out of the vineyard, like the branch, and withers. Such branches are collected, thrown into the fire and burnt.

'If you remain in me and if my thoughts remain in you, you may ask for whatever you will, and for you it shall be done.

'Herein lay glory for my Father, that you should bear abundant fruit and be my disciples. As the Father loved me, so I loved you. Stay in my love. You *will* stay in my love if you do as I bid, just as I stay in my Father's love by having done what he commanded me.

'I have said these things to you so that my joy may be yours and your joy may be complete. This is my commandment, Love one another as I loved you. No one can show greater love than by laying down his life for his friends. *You* are my friends if you do as I bid you. I no longer call you servants because a servant does not know what his master is doing. But I have called you friends because I have passed on to you everything I heard from my Father.

'It was not you that picked me out, but I that picked out you. And in appointing you I meant you to go and bear fruit; I meant your fruit to last; I meant that the Father should grant you whatever you ask of him in my name.

'Such are my commandments: love one another.

'If the world hates you remember that it hated me before you. If you were of the world, the world would love its own. But you are not of the world. I picked you out of it, and that is why it hates you. Bear in mind the saying I gave you, "The servant is not greater than his master." If they persecuted me, they will persecute you also. If they cherished my word, they will cherish yours as well. But no, they will treat you shamefully on my account, because they know not

Him that sent me. If I had not come and spoken to them, they would be innocent of sin; but now they have no excuse for their sin. He that hates me hates my Father also. If they had not seen me do my miracles – miracles that no one else has done – they would be innocent. But as it is, they have seen both me and my Father, and hated both of us. There is a Scripture, *They hated me for nothing;* it is in their Law and it had to be fulfilled. But when the Advocate has come, whom I will send you from the Father – the Spirit of Truth which issues from the Father – he will bear witness as to what I am. And you are also witnesses, you that have been with me from the beginning.

# 16

'I HAVE told you all this so that you should not be shaken in your faith. They will expel you from their synagogues. There will even come a time when anyone who kills you will think that he is serving God. And they will treat you so because they did not learn to know the Father or myself. But I warn you of these trials now so that when they come you should remember that I told you. I did not warn you of them in the early days, because I was with you. But now I am going back to Him that sent me.

'And not one of you asks where I am going – you are too full of sorrow at my news. But it is good for you that I should go away. That is the truth. For if I do not go the Advocate will not come to you. But if I make this journey I will send him to you. And when he has come he will overthrow the world's ideas of sin and righteousness and judgement. He will convict it of sin, in that it has no faith in me; he will show it righteousness, because I go to the Father and you see me no more; and he will teach it what judgement is, since the Prince of this world is condemned.

'I have much more to tell you, but you could not bear it now. But when he comes, the Spirit of Truth, he will lead you into truth entire. For what he tells you will not be his own, but all that he has heard. And he will tell you of the things to come. He will enhance my glory; for he will be enriched from what is mine and pass it on to you. Everything the Father has is mine. That is why I say that he receives from what is mine and hands it on to you.

'A little while and you behold me no longer; and again a little while and you shall see me.'

Some of his disciples asked each other what he meant by saying, 'A little while and you do not behold me; and again a little while and you shall see me'; and also by saying that he was going to the Father. 'What is this little while of which he spoke?' they said. 'We do not understand him.'

Jesus, realizing that they were anxious to question him, said: 'Are you discussing what I meant by saying, "A little while and you do not behold me; and again a little while and you shall see me"? I tell you in all truth that *you* will weep and wail, but the world will rejoice. You will grieve, but your grief shall be turned into joy. A woman in childbirth grieves because her hour has come; but when the child is born she forgets her suffering, for joy that a man has been born into the world. So for the moment you also have your grief. But I will see you again; there will be joy in your hearts, joy that nobody can take from you. And when that day has come you will ask nothing of *me*. I tell you in all truth that if you ask the Father for anything He will give it you in my name. Hitherto you have not asked for anything in my name. Ask and you shall receive, to make your joy complete.

'I have spoken to you in the language of metaphor. A time is coming when I shall speak to you in metaphor no longer, but shall tell you plainly what the Father is. When that time has come you will make your prayers in my name. Which does not mean that I shall approach the Father on your behalf

– the Father needs no prompting in the love He bears for you because you have loved me and believed that I came from Him.

'I came out from the Father and I went into the world. In due course I leave the world and travel to the Father.'

His disciples said: 'This is indeed plain speaking; there is no metaphor here. Now we see that you know everything – there is no need for a man to put his questions into words. By this token we believe that you have come from God.'

Jesus replied: 'At the moment you believe. But indeed a time is coming, and has come, when you will scatter each to his own home and leave me alone. No; I am not alone, for the Father is with me.

'I have told you these things so that in me you may find peace. In the world you will find suffering. But all is well – I have conquered the world.'

# 17

WHEN Jesus had said this he raised his eyes to Heaven and prayed:

'Father, the hour has come. Glorify your son so that your son may glorify you, and with that power over all mankind that you bestowed on him may give eternal life to all whom you have granted him. And this is Life Eternal, to know you, the one true God, and your Apostle Jesus Christ.

'I glorified you on earth by finishing the task you had given me. Now, Father, invest me at your side with the glory that I had beside you when the world had not yet come to be.

'I made your Being manifest to the men you gave me from the world. They were yours, and to me you gave them. They have kept your Word.

'Now, they have come to know that you are indeed the

source of all I have from you; for I have given them the knowledge you bestowed on me. They embraced it, and they recognized the truth that I came forth from you, and they believed that it was you that sent me forth.

'I pray for them. I am not praying for the world but for those you gave me, because they are yours and all I have is yours and all you have is mine.

'In them I have been glorified. And now I am no longer in the world, but they are in it and I go to you. Holy Father, keep them in your Being, which you shared with me, so that they may be one, as we are. While I was with them I kept them in your Being, which you shared with me; and I watched over them, and none of them perished but the son of perdition – the Scripture had to be fulfilled. But now I am coming to you; and before I leave the world I make this prayer so that my joy may be possessed in full by them.

'I have taught them your Word and the world has hated them; for like myself they do not belong to the world. I do not ask that you should take them out of the world, but that you should protect them from the Evil One. They belong to the world no more than I do.

'Consecrate them in the truth – your Word *is* truth. I sent them into the world as you sent me into the world. In their behalf I consecrate myself, to the end that they too may be consecrated in the truth.

'But I am not thinking of them only but also of those that are brought by their teaching to have faith in me, when I pray that all of them may be one; that like you, Father, in me and me in you, they also may be one in us; so that the world may believe that it was you that sent me forth.

'I myself have given them the glory you gave me, to the end that they may be one, as you and I are one, I in them and you in me; that they may be brought to perfect unity, so that the world may know that it was you that sent me forth and loved them as you loved me.

'Father, for those that you have given me it is my wish that where I am they may be there with me, to see the glory you have given me, loving me as you did before the foundation of the world.

'Father, good Father; yet the world did not know you. But I knew you, and these men knew that you had sent me forth; and I revealed to them and will reveal your Being, so that the love you had for me may be in them and I be in them also.'

# 18

WHEN he had finished his prayer Jesus took his disciples out of the city to a place beyond the watercourse of Kedron, where there was a garden which he entered with them. Judas, who was going to arrest him, also knew the place since Jesus went there frequently with his disciples. So taking a party of soldiers as well as some police from the Chief Priests and Pharisees, he came to the place with torches, lanterns and weapons. And Jesus, who knew all that was impending for him, came out and said to them: 'Whom are you seeking?'

'Jesus of Nazareth,' they replied.

'I am he,' said Jesus. And although Judas, who was to hand him over, was himself standing there with them, these men, when Jesus said that it was he, fell back and cast themselves on the ground.

Once more Jesus asked them whom they were seeking, and they said, 'Jesus of Nazareth.'

'I told you I am he,' Jesus answered. 'If I am the man you want, let these others go.'

Had he not said *Not one of those you gave me did I lose*? And now he sought to make this saying true.

Simon Peter, who had a sword with him, now drew it and

struck the High Priest's slave, shearing off his right ear. The slave's name was Malchus.

But Jesus said to Peter: 'Put the sword in its scabbard. Am I not to drink the cup that the Father has given me?'

Then the soldiers and their captain and the officers of the Jewish police arrested Jesus, bound him, and brought him first to Annas, since he was the father-in-law of Caiaphas, who was High Priest in that year. It was Caiaphas who had pointed out to the Jews that it was to their advantage that one man should die for the people.

Simon Peter followed Jesus, and so did another disciple. Now this disciple was known to the High Priest and went with Jesus into the courtyard of his palace. But Peter stayed outside, standing by the door. So this other disciple, whom the High Priest knew, went out again and after a word with the maidservant at the door brought Peter in.

Presently this girl, the doorkeeper, said to Peter, 'Surely you are not another of that man's disciples?' And he said, 'I am not.' The servants and Temple police had made a charcoal fire, as it was cold, and stood there warming themselves; and Peter too was standing there with them and warming himself.

The High Priest questioned Jesus about his disciples and his teaching.

Jesus replied: 'I have spoken openly to the world. I always taught in synagogue and in the Temple, where all the Jews foregather, and I never spoke in secret. Why do you ask *me*? Ask those who heard me to tell you what I said to them. These people here know what I said.' Whereupon one of the Temple police who was standing by Jesus said, 'Is that the way to answer the High Priest?' and gave him a slap in the face.

Jesus replied: 'If I said anything wrong, bring a charge against me. But if I was in order, why do you strike me?' And Annas sent Jesus, bound as he was, to Caiaphas the High Priest.

Simon Peter meanwhile was standing outside and warming himself. Somebody said to him, 'Surely you are not another of his disciples?' And he said, 'No, I am not.' Whereupon one of the High Priest's slaves, who was related to the man whose ear Peter had cut off, said, 'Didn't I see you with him in the garden?' And once more Peter said no. And at that moment the cock crew.

From Caiaphas they took Jesus to the Residence. It was early morning, and the Jews refrained from entering the Residence, so that they might not be defiled but could eat the Passover. Accordingly Pilate came outside to them and said: 'What charge do you bring against this man?'

They said: 'If he were not a criminal we should not have handed him over to you.'

'Take him yourselves,' said Pilate, 'and judge him by your own laws.'

But the Jews replied: 'We are not allowed to execute anyone.' Jesus himself had indicated the manner of his coming death and his prophecy had to be fulfilled.

So Pilate went back into the Residence, summoned Jesus, and said: 'Are *you* the King of the Jews?'

Jesus replied: 'Is this your own suggestion? Or have others told you this about me?'

'Am I a Jew?' said Pilate. 'Your own people and the Chief Priests have handed you over to me. What have you done?'

Jesus answered: 'My kingdom is not of this world. If it were, my own men-at-arms would be fighting to save me from the clutches of the Jews. But as it is, my kingdom is not here.'

'So you are a king after all?' said Pilate.

Jesus replied: 'It is you that say I am a king. I was born and I came into the world for the one purpose of bearing witness to the truth. Every child of truth listens to my voice.'

'What *is* truth?' said Pilate.

And with that he went out again to the Jews and said: 'I

find him guilty of no crime. And you have a custom that requires me to release one man for you at the Passover. Do you wish me to let you have the King of the Jews?'

'Not him but Barabbas,' they shouted back. And Barabbas was a brigand.

# 19

PILATE now took Jesus and had him scourged. The soldiers plaited a garland of thorns, placed it on his head and clothed him in a purple robe. Then they went up to him and said, 'Hail, King of the Jews!' And they struck him on the face.

Presently Pilate went out again and said: 'See now, I am bringing him out to you. I wish to make it clear that I find him guilty of no crime.'

Jesus came outside wearing the garland of thorns and the purple robe; and Pilate said to them, 'Behold, the man!'

But when the Chief Priests and their satellites set eyes on him they shouted, 'Crucify him, crucify!'

'Take him and crucify him yourselves,' said Pilate. 'I do not find him guilty.'

'We have a law of our own,' the Jews retorted. 'And by that he ought to die, for he claimed to be the Son of God.'

Their use of this expression added to Pilate's fears. He went back into the Residence and said to Jesus: 'What *is* your history?' But Jesus gave him no reply.

'Do you refuse to talk to me?' said Pilate. 'Are you not aware that I have authority to set you free and authority to crucify you?'

Jesus replied: 'You would have no authority whatever over me if Heaven had not empowered you. Which makes the man who put me in your hands all the more guilty.'

This decided Pilate. His aim was now to set him free. But the Jews kept up a steady roar: 'If you let him go you are no friend of Caesar's. Any would-be king is disloyal to Caesar.' And in the end Pilate, who had not been deaf to what their words implied, led Jesus out and sat down in an official chair on what was known as the Pavement, in Aramaic *Gabbatha*. The day was the Eve in Passover Week. The time was the sixth hour.

'Behold, your King!' said Pilate to the Jews.

'Away with him!' they yelled. 'Away with him! Crucify him!'

'Your King?' said Pilate. 'Am I to crucify your King?'

The Chief Priests said: 'We have no king but Caesar.' And so at last he gave him up to them for crucifixion.

Thus they took Jesus from him. And carrying his own cross, he passed out of the city to what was called the Place of the Skull, in Aramaic *Golgotha*, where they crucified him, and with him two others, one on either side with Jesus in the centre.

Pilate had prepared a notice of the charge and fixed it on the cross. The wording was *Jesus of Nazareth, the King of the Jews*. This notice was read by many of the Jews, as the place where they crucified Jesus was near the city and the charge was written in Aramaic, Latin, and Greek. So the Chief Priests of the Jews asked Pilate to delete the title *King of the Jews*, and replace it with the words *He said he was King of the Jews*.

Pilate said: 'What I have written stands.'

The soldiers, when they crucified Jesus, took his clothes and arranged them in four portions, one for each of them. They also took his coat; but this was seamless, being woven in one piece from top to bottom. So they said: 'Rather than cut it up let us cast lots to see who shall have it.' The Scripture had to be fulfilled. It says *They shared my clothes among them: for my clothing they cast lots*. And that is what the soldiers did.

Meanwhile there stood by Jesus' cross his mother and his mother's sister; Mary, wife of Clopas; and Mary Magdalene. Jesus, seeing his mother and the disciple whom he loved standing beside her, said to his mother: 'Woman, this is your son.' Then he said to the disciple: 'This is your mother.' And from that day the disciple made a place for her in his own home.

Shortly after this, Jesus, knowing that all had now been done, said, 'I am thirsty,' so that the Scripture might be fulfilled. A vessel full of vinegar was standing there. So they put a sponge soaked in this vinegar on a javelin and lifted it up to his mouth. Jesus after taking the vinegar said: 'The task is done.' And he let his head fall forward and gave up his life.

It was the Eve, and the Jews, not wishing to leave the bodies on the cross during the Sabbath, which on this occasion was a day of great importance, asked Pilate to give orders for the breaking of their legs, and for their removal. Accordingly the soldiers came and broke the legs of the first man and of the other who was crucified with him. But when they came to Jesus and saw that he was dead already they did not break his legs; but one of them pierced his side with a spear, and forthwith blood and water came out.

This is vouched for by the man who saw it, and his evidence may be relied on. Also, to assure you, the writer knows that he is telling the truth. For these things took place to *make* the Scripture true, *Not a bone of his shall be broken*. And is there not another Scripture, *They shall look on him they pierced*?

Later, Joseph of Arimathaea, being a disciple of Jesus though a secret one for fear of the Jews, asked Pilate for permission to remove his body and Pilate gave him leave. So he came and took it from the cross. Nicodemus, the man who had approached Jesus by night in the first instance, came also, with about a hundred pounds of mingled myrrh and aloes. They took Jesus's body and wrapped it with the spices in strips of linen, as the Jews do when burying their dead. There was a garden in the place where he was crucified, and in the garden a new tomb in which no one had hitherto been laid. Here then, because it was the Jewish Eve and the tomb was near at hand, they laid Jesus.

## 20

ON the first day of the week, very early, while it was still dark, Mary Magdalene came to the tomb and saw that the stone had been removed from the entrance. So she ran to tell Simon Peter, as well as the other disciple whom Jesus loved. She said: 'They have taken the Lord out of the tomb and we do not know where they have laid him.'

Peter and the other disciple set out and were coming to the tomb when with one accord they both began to run. But the other disciple shot ahead, outstripping Peter, and was the first to reach it. He peered in and saw the linen wrappings on the ground, but he did not go inside. Simon Peter, who had followed, now arrived and went inside the tomb. He saw that the wrappings were lying on the ground and that the napkin which had covered his head was not lying with them but had been separately folded up in a place of its own. In the end the other disciple, who had been the first to reach the tomb, also went in, and saw, and believed. They had indeed failed hitherto to understand the Scripture where it is ordained that he should die and then come back to life.

The disciples returned to their lodgings. But Mary stayed by the tomb and stood weeping outside it. In the midst of her tears she peered inside and saw two Angels in white sitting where the body of Jesus had lain, one at the head and one at the feet.

These said to her: 'Lady, why do you weep?'

'They have taken my Lord away,' she replied, 'and I do not know where they have laid him.'

As she said this she turned and saw Jesus standing there, but did not recognize him.

Jesus said: 'Lady, why do you weep? Whom are you looking for?'

She thought it was the gardener and said: 'Sir, if it was you that carried him off, tell me where you have put him and I will take him away.'

'Mary!' said Jesus. And she, facing him once more, said in Aramaic, 'Rabbouni!' which means Master.

Jesus said: 'Do not be alarmed, for I have not yet gone up to the Father. But go to my brothers and give them this message: I am going up to my Father and your Father and my God and your God.'

Mary Magdalene went to the disciples with the news that she had seen the Lord, who had given her this message. And so, in the evening of the same day, the first day of the week, when for fear of the Jews the doors of the disciples' quarters had been shut, Jesus came. And he stood in their midst and said: 'Peace be with you.' With that he showed them his hands and his side. And the disciples were filled with joy at the sight of the Lord.

Once more Jesus said: 'Peace be with you. As the Father sent me forth, so I send you.' And after saying this he breathed on them and said: 'Receive the Holy Spirit. Sins you forgive in any man are forgiven; sins you do not forgive are not forgiven.'

Now Thomas, one of the Twelve, who was called the Twin, had not been with them when Jesus came. The others told him they had seen the Lord. But he said: 'Unless I see in his hands the imprint of the nails, and put my finger in the place, and put my hand in his side, I will not believe.'

Eight days later his disciples were once more in their quarters and Thomas was with them. Jesus came when the doors were shut and stood in their midst and said: 'Peace be with you.' Then he said to Thomas: 'Come here and feel my hands with your finger. And put your hand in my side. Do not be an unbeliever, but believe.'

And Thomas said: 'My Lord and my God.'

Jesus said to him: 'You have believed because you have seen me. Happy those that never saw me and have yet believed.'

Now it is true that Jesus, in the disciples' presence, wrought many other miracles, which are not recorded in this book. But this record has been made so that you may believe that Jesus is the Christ, the Son of God, and that, believing, you may have life eternal in his Being.

# 21

AFTER this, Jesus showed himself once more to the disciples. It was by the Sea of Tiberias and this is how it happened.

There were gathered together Simon Peter, Thomas who was called the Twin, Nathanael from Cana in Galilee, Zebedee's sons, and two more of his disciples. Simon Peter said to them: 'I am going off to fish.' And they said they would go with him. So they left the town and got into the boat.

That night they caught nothing, but as dawn was breaking, there stood Jesus on the beach – not that they knew that it was he.

Jesus called to them: 'Have you lads caught anything to eat?' And when they answered 'No,' he said, 'Make a cast on the starboard side and you will find them.'

So they cast their net; and they caught so many fish that their strength failed them, they could not lift it out.

It was then that the disciple whom Jesus loved said to Peter: 'It is the Lord.' And Simon Peter, when he heard it was the Lord, took his long coat (he had been stripped), tucked it up, and threw himself into the water. But the other disciples came in the dinghy, as they were only seventy yards or so from land, towing the net full of fish behind them.

When they stepped on shore they saw a charcoal-fire on the beach, with a fish on top of it. Also a loaf of bread.

Jesus said: 'Bring some of the fish you have just caught.' So

Peter went aboard the dinghy and hauled the net on shore, full of big fish, a hundred and fifty-three of them. But for all those fish the net did not break.

'Come and have breakfast,' said Jesus. And none of the disciples dared to question him and say, 'Who are you?' They knew it was the Lord.

Jesus came and took the bread and gave it to them. And so with the fish.

This was the third time that Jesus had appeared to the disciples after rising from the dead.

When they had breakfasted Jesus said to Simon Peter: 'Simon son of John, do you love me more than all these things?'

'Yes, Lord. You know I love you.'

'Feed my lambs,' said Jesus.

And once more he said: 'Simon son of John, do you love me?'

'Yes, Lord, you know I love you.'

'Be a shepherd to my sheep,' said Jesus.

And for the third time he said: 'Simon son of John, do you love me?'

Peter was grieved when for the third time he asked whether he loved him. 'Lord,' he said, 'you know all things. You can see that I love you.'

'Feed my flock,' said Jesus. 'Truly, truly, I tell you that when you were young you girt yourself and walked where you wished; but when you are old you shall stretch out your hands and another man will gird you and carry you where you do not wish to go.' He indicated thus the death by which Peter was to glorify God. And he ended by saying to him: 'Follow me.'

But Peter, turning round, saw that they were followed by the disciple whom Jesus loved, the same that had leant back on his breast at the supper and said, 'Lord, who is your betrayer?'

When Peter saw him he said to Jesus: 'And what of this man, Lord?'

Jesus replied: 'If it is my will that he should stay till I come, what is that to you? For yourself, follow me.'

As a result, word went round among the brethren that this disciple was not going to die. But Jesus did not say he was not going to die. He said to Peter: 'If it is my will that he should stay till I come, what is that to you?'

This same disciple is our authority for these events – the maker of this book. And we know that what he vouches for is true. But there are many other things that Jesus did. If each and all of them were written down I do not think the world itself could hold the volumes they would fill.

*Some other Penguin and Pelican books are described on the following pages*

# BEYOND THE GOSPELS

Roderic Dunkerley's book *Beyond the Gospels* gives the answer to the question often asked – What information is there about Jesus Christ elsewhere than in the Gospels? There are two aspects of this study – what confirmatory evidence is there that he lived and taught as in the Gospels, and what extra facts are there regarding him in addition to those found there? Pagan and Jewish writers are called in witness, and archaeological evidence is examined, including that from the catacombs. Uncanonical stories and sayings are culled from many sources, even Moslem books. The sum of the matter is that there is valuable external evidence of the historicity of Jesus, and also quite an amount of interesting additional information, some part at least of which may be considered authentic and of real worth. John Allegro's Pelican book on *The Dead Sea Scrolls* gives a wonderful account of the discovery of the scrolls at the remains of an Essene community on the shores of the Dead Sea and an exciting account of their assembly and interpretation, to give us an idea of the mental and religious climate of the Holy Land at the time when Christ lived and they throw an amazingly clear light on the texts from which our Bible was translated.

# CHRISTIAN LIVES

Walter Hilton is probably the most influential of the English fourteenth-century mystics. He was a Canon Regular of S. Augustine, and belonged to the community of Thurgarton Priory, near Southwell, where he probably died in 1395. His work, which is in two parts, deals with the vital matters of man's spiritual development and destiny. Today there is a widespread interest in the lives and writings of great men and women of prayer, and it is this vital need for self-discipline and the substitution of holiness for indifference and mediocrity, which provides for the modern reader the supremely relevant theme of *The Ladder of Perfection*. After the Bible itself probably the best-known and best-loved book in Christendom is *The Imitation of Christ*, Thomas à Kempis's guide towards Christian perfection, which for over five hundred years has continued to exercise a widespread influence over Christians of every age and race. Unfortunately most English translators have tended to misrepresent this book – so that many would-be readers have passed it by, and missed the advantage of Thomas's profound wisdom, his clarity of thought and vision, his wide knowledge of the Scriptures and Fathers, and his clear understanding of human nature and its needs which have been brought out in Leo Sherley-Price's new translation.

# THE FAITH OF THE BIBLE

The idea of Canon Fison's book is twofold. It aims at showing Christians that the basis of the claim of the Christian Church to be one, holy, catholic, and apostolic is to be found in the Bible and that the church can only fulfil her proper function in so far as she is loyal to her Bible title-deeds. This means that her faith must not be narrower than that of the Bible. There is room for wide diversity of outlook within a common loyalty to God. He also wants to make clear to Christians and non-Christians alike the secret of the triumphant faith of the ancient people of God. Its object therefore is not primarily to record ancient history or to analyse ancient documents, but rather to communicate an ancient secret in terms comprehensible to modern man. It is written in the conviction that Christians have still much to learn from Jews and Jews from Christians; and that a rediscovery of the secret of the Judaeo-Christian biblical faith in all its breadth and depth is the greatest need of our time, with which Canon Fison is very familiar from his great experience of mission work in the Middle East and his work at Oxford, Rochester, and Truro. His knowledge of modern Jewish and Arab communities has given greater interest to his studies.

# COMMUNISM AND CHRISTIANITY

Communism has been called a religion, and in so far
as it has a creed which is wholeheartedly believed the
name is not unjustified. What the Apostles' Creed is
for Christianity, the Communist Manifesto is to its
followers, a call to belief and action. Both creeds
claim to give an answer to the chief problems which
agitate man – his individual and social life, his origin
and destiny. The aim of *Communism and Christianity*
by Father Martin D'Arcy, S.J. is to compare their
answers, to examine their validity, and to see how
far they are at variance and where, if at any place,
they come together. The writings of Marx are first
studied in their historical setting and in relation to
the place of the individual in society. An account is
then given of the development of Communism.
Communism has always claimed to be a revolutionary system dependent upon a few simple and fundamental ideas. These ideas are examined and then
contrasted with the principal tenets of Christian
philosophy, which has had a formative influence on
the culture of the West. The last part of the book
deals with this Christian philosophy of man against
the background of the Communist view of human
life. The Christian view is exposed not so much in
its strictly religious teaching as in its cultural value
and its claim to truth.